A ROOTS resource

PRAYER & PRAYER ACTIVITIES

For worship with adults, children and all ages
Years A, B & C

Edited by Gill Ambrose, Maureen Baldwin,
Jean Harrison and Pam Macnaughton

CANTERBURY
PRESS
Norwich

© ROOTS for Churches Ltd 2013

First published in 2013 by the Canterbury Press Norwich
Editorial office
3rd Floor, Invicta House,
108–114 Golden Lane,
London EC1Y 0TG.

Canterbury Press is an imprint of Hymns Ancient & Modern Ltd
(a registered charity)
13A Hellesdon Park Road, Norwich,
Norfolk, NR6 5DR, UK

www.canterburypress.co.uk

British Library Cataloguing in Publication data

A catalogue record for this book is available
from the British Library

978 1 84825 263 9

Typeset by Regent Typesetting
Printed and bound in Great Britain by
CPI Group (UK) Ltd, Croydon

Contents

Year C

For Common Worship Variation pages, please see CD-ROM.

List of Contributors

Angus Adams
Paul Allinson
Janet Alun
Tom Ambrose
Clare Amos
Jean Armin
Louise Armitage
Andrew Atkins
Judy Bainbridge
Anna Baker
Maureen Baldwin
Imelda Barnard
Wendy Baskett
John Baxter–Brown
Michael Begg
Jan Berry
Santou Beuklian
Adam Biddlestone
Rachel Bird
Ann Blackett
Alison Booker
Dave Bookless
Mike Bossingham
Barbara Brent
Kay Brewer
Paul Brewerton
Sarah Brewerton
Nicola Briggs
Stella Bristow
Alun Brookfield
John Brown
Stephen Brown
Susan Brown
Arnold Browne
Elizabeth Bruce Whitehorn
Kevin Buchanan
Karen Bulley
John Burniston
Helen Burns
Scott Burton
Steve Butler
Andy Campbell
Roderick Campbell
David Campton
Roger Catley
Vanessa Cato
Nigel Chapman
Jane Chevous
Ken Chippindale
Lynne Chitty
Gill Christie
Janet Clark
Sandra Clark
Lisa Clarke
Christopher Clinch
Dudley Coates
David Cockerell
Margaret Collins
Claire Connor
Anesia Nascimento Cook
David Coote
Janet Corlett
Mary Cotes

Diane Cox
Gill Crippen
Andrew and Julie Cunningham
Cathy Curran
Luke Curran
Gill Dallow
Alison Davis
Anne Dawtry
Jan Dean
Janet Delaney
Dana Delap
Stephen Dixon
Sam Donaghue
Sandra Doore
Bridget Down
Mark Drane
Elizabeth Duffy
Susan Durber
Linda Dye
Sarah Earnshaw
Catherine Edmunds
Ian Ellis
Jenny Ellis
Jeremy Fagan
Claire Farley
Gray Featherstone
Christine Ferguson
Fiona Fidgin
Matt Finch
Rebecca Froley
Ken Fuller
Penny Fuller
Lynda Gallimore
Maura Garside
Helen Garton
Alec Gilmore
Eileen Goddard
Elaine Goddard
Jan Godfrey
Jan Godfrey
David Goodbourn
Victoria Goodman
Isabel Goshawk
Edward Green
Philip Greig
Karen Hall
Robert Halshaw
Jacynth Hamill
Julian Hamilton
Roddy Hamilton
Vittoria Hancock
Nick Harding
Petra Hardy
Sarah Hargreaves
John Harley
Anne Harrison
John Hartley
Maureen Hassett
Mary Hawes
Brian Haymes
Catherine Haynes
Martin Hazell
Yvonne Hendrie

Heather Henry
Nicholas Henshall
Elizabeth Hewitt
Penny Hewlett
David Hinchcliffe
Maggie Hindley
Maggie Hindley
Elizabeth Hopkinson
Alan Howard
Alison Hughes
Rosalind Hughes
Alison Hulse
Beverley Humphries
Lesley Husselbee
Jacqui Hyde
Judy Jarvis
David Jenkins
Liz Jenkins
John Johansen-Berg
Heather Johnston
Rosemary Johnston
Helen Jones
Linda Jones
Sue Jones
Pete Kelsall
Steve Kersys
John Kewley
Sue Kirby
Alan Kirkland
Andrew Kleissner
Ronni Lamont
George Lane
Jonathan Leach
Janet Lees
Adrian Legg
Susan Levis
Nicky Lord
Andrew Lunn
N□irin Lynch
Marjorie Macaskill
Clare MacLaren
Pam Macnaughton
Michael Malleson
Steve Mallon
Sue Mannion
Frances Martin
Jayne Maycock
Clare McBeath
Joel McBeath
Deborah McVey
Hannah Middleton
Sandra Millar
Richenda Milton-Thompson
Khera Missen
Khera Missen Elliott
Sheila Mitchell
Mark Montgomery
David Moore
Mirella Moxon
Veronica Murphy
Elaine Murray
Jo Musson
Linda Neilands

Katie Nelson
Philip Nevard
Alison Newell
Peter Nicholls
Chris Nickolay
Candace Nolan-Grant
Terry Oakley
Kathleen O'Brien
Anne O'Connor
Rona Orme
Simon Oxley
Liz Pacey
Terry Palmer
Marjory Parker
Rachel Parkinson
John Parr
Martyn Payne
Morven Petticrew
Sandra Pollerman
Rachel Poolman
Andrew Pratt
Richard Prescott
Tim Presswood
Anne Priest
Peter Privett
John Proctor
John Reaney
John Reaney
Richard Reddie
Rachel Rice

Andrew Roberts
David Rose
Judith Sadler
Lindsey Sanderson
Anne Sardeson
Pat Saunders
Stuart Scott
Peter Sharrock
Ingrid Shelley
Kay Shotter
Philip Skelton
Angela Smith
Owen Smith
Peter Stanton
Kenneth Steven
Simon Stewart
Suzi Stock
Suzi Stocks
John Sutcliffe
Susan Swires
Simon Taylor
Stephen Taylor
Neal Terry
Richard Tetlow
Bev Thomas
Bruce Thompson
Stephen Thornton
Jane Tibbs
Duncan Tuck
Carl Turner

Val Turner
Brenda Vance
Barry Vendy
Fred Vincent
Mark Wakelin
Stella Wallace-Tween
Jenny Warbrick
Ellie Watson
Peter West
Peter West
Cathy Westby
Janet Whitcombe
Ruth Whitehead
Caroline Wickens
Stuart Wild
Jacqui Wilkinson
Marilyn Wilkinson
Jo Williams
Jacqui Williamson
Becky Wills
Ellie Wilson
Robert Windsor
Sue Witts
Judith Wood
Simon Woodman
Timothy Woods
Tony Wright
John Young
Michaela Youngson

Introduction

We are delighted to offer this prayer handbook, a compilation of the best prayers written over the last ten years by writers drawn from across the UK and from a wide range of traditions. We have been privileged to collaborate with this fantastic team of people who work in many churches and groups and who have generously shared their expertise and creative inspiration.

The ROOTS resources are based on the *Revised Common Lectionary*, which offers a selection of readings for each week of the year on a three-year cycle. On each of the following pages you will find prayers for one week, together with a list of readings and a quotation from the Gospel. The prayers relate primarily to this reading for the week, except where indicated.

In addition to prayers for each week of the year you will find a selection of prayers for use at major festivals, celebrations and commemorations.

On the CD

You will find the text of all the prayers on the CD so that you can include or adapt them for your own presentations or service sheets. Also included are prayers for weeks of the year where the *Church of England Common Worship Lectionary* varies completely from the *Revised Common Lectionary*.

The ROOTS weekly resources

All the prayers in this collection are taken from the ROOTS weekly resources. ROOTS is an ecumenical publication, founded by churches and church publishers to offer a wide range of worship and learning resources to use across all ages, and in different denominations, contexts, styles and traditions. The writers are experienced practitioners working in churches throughout the UK in urban and rural settings, and from many denominations.

Varieties of prayer

Each week the ROOTS resources offer a range of prayers to support diverse needs and circumstances. Offering a variety of ways into prayer ensures that all feel welcome and included. This collection offers prayers to say and prayers that need action; prayers for the quiet of our hearts and prayers to proclaim together. There is generally a call to worship, a prayer of intercession, a prayer for all ages and a prayer activity. We encourage you to use this variety and be confident that all the prayers have been tried and tested in a range of communities and contexts. Each church offers its own provision and we hope this collection will add variety to supplement your existing tradition and so help you to provide prayer that is accessible to all people, whatever their age or wherever you gather.

Gill Ambrose, Adult & All Age Editor
Maureen Baldwin, Children & Young People Editor

The ROOTS team
Rosemary Nixon, Managing Director
Kate Mennell, Production Editor
Harriet Jenkins, Administrator

Compilers of this prayer resource
Lynne Chitty and Sally Whitehead

Illustrator
Martina Farrow

Introduction

Year A

Year A   ADVENT 1

Isaiah 2.1–5; Psalm 122; Romans 13.11–14;
Matthew 24.36–44 *Keep awake, therefore, for you do not know on what day your Lord is coming.*

Call to worship *based on Isaiah 2.1–5*

This call is read by the two halves of the congregation responding to each other:
In the place where swords become ploughshares,
we meet you, our God.
In the place where spears become pruning-hooks,
we meet you, our God.
In the place where conflict turns to peace,
we meet you, our God.
In the place where prejudice turns to love,
we meet you, our God.
In the place where darkness is filled up with light,
we meet you, our God.
In the place where longing turns to expectation,
we meet you, our God.

A prayer of confession

You ask us, patient God,
to be awake and ready,
but we are sleepy and habit-bound people who prefer
to do what we've always done.
Yet we long for you,
thirsty for the light of your goodness.
Forgive our unwillingness to welcome you,
our fear of seeing the shabbiness of our lives in the
light of your holiness
and our readiness to blame others for our own
shortcomings.
Wake us up, gently or urgently, according to our
need, to see your face, and to rise and serve you,
in the name of the baby born in Bethlehem.
Amen.

A prayer for all ages for Advent Sunday

Light a candle in our world, O God,
Thumbs-up symbol and wiggle thumb
let it brighten our faces
Hands at side of faces and wiggle fingers
that we may tell this world
Hands moving away from mouth
the time is arriving
Point to watch on wrist
when you will put on flesh
Mime putting on a coat
and walk among us.
Draw a circle in front of you with both index fingers
Amen.

A prayer for children

Dear God,
In Advent time we are waiting.
We are waiting for the weeks to pass.
We are waiting to play our parts in the school play.
We are waiting to celebrate with our families and
friends.

We are waiting to share presents with each other.
But most of all we are waiting for you.
Help us not to forget that we are waiting to celebrate
Jesus' birth.
Amen.

A prayer activity

*Give everyone a candle. Explain that the wilderness
is a place on the edge, where people are far from
community. Many people are involuntary wilderness
dwellers. Ask the group to think of where the
wilderness places are and who finds themselves
there. As people light their candles, ask them to say:
'I pray for...' to which all respond:*
For ...., God, be a candle in the wilderness.

A prayer of intercession

In the places in this world where there is greatest
need:
Let there be light.
Where there is war, destitution, hunger, thirst and little
medical care:
Let there be light.
Where there is anger at injustice and inequality;
where there is hopelessness about the future;
where there is violence on the streets and in homes:
Let there be light.
Where there is loneliness;
at home, in prisons, in hospitals:
Let there be light.
Where there is meaninglessness;
where people long to live the life of the Spirit but don't
know how to begin;
where there is disillusion and despair:
Let there be light.
In the life of our church,
in the hearts of our people,
in our own eyes as we meet with others:
Let there be light.
And let it blaze and grow until the whole world is filled
with peace:
Let there be light.
Amen.

A responsive prayer

If you want to hear the good news of Christmas,
come on out into the wilderness.
See the man dressed in camel's hair,
**hear him calling, 'Repent, for the Kingdom of God
has come near!'**
If you want to be transformed at Christmas,
taste his recipe of honesty and truthfulness,
bear fruit worthy of repentance
and be touched by the tenderness of God.
Amen.

Year A ADVENT 2

Isaiah 11.1–10; Psalm 72.1–7, 18–19; Romans 15.4–13; **Matthew 3.1–12** *Prepare the way of the Lord, make his paths straight.*

Call to worship

Let us quieten ourselves and become aware of
where we are, how we are,
whom we seek, whom we expect,
whom we long to please.
Prepare the way of the Lord.
We listen for the sound of his footsteps,
his touch on our arm,
his smile and his greeting.
Prepare the way of the Lord.
He chose us – you and me,
invited us to come,
called us here in person.
Prepare the way of the Lord.
Because we are his friends and followers,
his co-workers in the world,
he needs us to be fit and ready,
reared on God's love, filled with the Spirit.
On your marks. Get set. Go!
Prepare the way of the Lord.

A prayer of adoration

The kingdom of heaven is nearby.
Great and glorious God, above and beyond us all,
yet intimately close, may your wisdom and
understanding, counsel, mercy and right judgement
fill the Church, the world, and the universe that you
have made.
We bow before you, longing for your kingdom of
justice and joy to come in all its fullness.
May your creation be healed of division, enmity, and
fragmentation:
the wolf living with the lamb;
the leopard lying down with the kid;
the haves sharing freely with the have nots, and all
dwelling together in perfect harmony and wholeness,
that every knee should bow and every tongue
confess Christ Jesus as Lord and Saviour, and the
earth be filled with the glory of God as the waters
cover the sea.
Amen.

A prayer of confession

We will not hide from you,
God and Father of our Lord Jesus Christ.
We come to you just as we are.
We see that what we are is not all you made us to
be; and we ask you to help us to be honest about our
weaknesses.
Forgive the faults we are aware of, and those we hide
even from ourselves.
Each day let us bring more of ourselves into the
searching light of your beauty so that we may be
changed, and shine, to reflect your own glory back to
you.
Amen.

A prayer of praise

God of steadfastness and encouragement,
how much you care for us,
watching and waiting and forbearing
and choosing just the right moment to come into our
world and into our lives.
You come with wisdom and understanding,
with justice for the poor,
bringing peace between predator and prey.
You come like sweet rain
releasing the scent of spring.
You come as the baby in the manger.
May you find the path before you straight.
May you find us steadfast.
May the earth be full of the knowledge of the earth
as the waters cover the sea.
Amen.

A prayer activity

READY – We light a red candle. In the stillness, God,
we bring to you all the things that we need to get
ready this week and in this Advent season.
STEADY – We light an orange candle and bring to
you all we will do, that it may be done well and with
love.
GO – We light a green candle and pray that we may
leave this place and tell others about your love in all
that we say and do.
Amen.

A prayer of intercession

**Judge your people with righteousness, O God,
and your poor with justice.**
We pray for the poorest people of the world, and their
children.
We pray for the rich nations, that they may know what
is just and act on it.
**May the mountains yield prosperity for the
people, and the hills righteousness.**
We pray for a more equal sharing of wealth in our
own nation, so that it may be a safe and healthy and
prosperous place for all its people.
**Defend the cause of the poor of the people,
give deliverance to the needy, and crush the
oppressor.**
We give thanks for those who act as advocates for
the voiceless, and for those who enable the voiceless
to speak for themselves.
**Live while the sun endures, throughout all
generations.**
Teach us to live for future generations, that they may
inherit an earth that is inhabitable, fruitful, prosperous,
and peaceful.
Amen.

A sending out prayer

Go, and prepare a way for the Lord.
**We hear the voice crying out and we will make a
straight path for him.**
Amen.

Year A ADVENT 3

Isaiah 35.1–10; Psalm 146.5–10, or Luke 1.46b–55; James 5.7–10; **Matthew 11.2–11** *See, I am sending my messenger ahead of you, who will prepare your way before you.*

Call to worship

God of all trust, we gather trusting that you are with us now and always.
May we identify in ourselves the doubts and fears that suggest you are not,
and receive your power and love, through our worship and our friendship together in Christ.

A prayer of thanksgiving

For after the lighting of the Advent candles
Lord God, light of light eternal,
Thank you for bringing the light of life and hope into our darkness.
We cannot live without you, the light of life.
We cannot see where we are going without you, our guiding light.
We cannot understand clearly without your enlightening Spirit.
We cannot thrive and grow without the warm sunlight of your encouragement and help.
We cannot be made whole without the searching light of your truth,
revealing our hidden darkness and chaos and inviting us to change.
Thank you for sending the Lord Jesus,
star of the morning, dayspring, sun of righteousness, light of the world,
to hold God's torch for all who are lost.
Amen.

A prayer of confession

Great and good God,
We are feeble witnesses to you. Our lives are fearful.
We are prisoners of our limitations,
avoiding the paths you want us to walk in.
We are touchy and grudge-bearing;
but you come to set prisoners free.
Open our eyes to you,
open our ears to your messages,
our hearts to forgive and be forgiven;
and strengthen us to speak of you with joy.
Amen.

A prayer activity

Give each person a tealight. Pile up some cardboard boxes on the floor and ask the group to gather around them. Invite everyone to write on the boxes things that are roadblocks in their life journey. Encourage them to say a prayer as they light the candle and place it on a level and safe place on a box. Play some suitable music while they are doing this.

An all-age prayer for the shepherds

We thank you, God, for the shepherds,
the first people to tell others about baby Jesus.
We offer you our lives to be filled with the same eagerness and sense of wonder, the same spirit of praise that they had on Christmas night, in every moment of our weekday lives.
Amen.

A prayer of intercession

This day we pray for all who journey:
children at the beginning of life's journey,
adults with family and social responsibilities,
men and women whose decisions affect the lives of others.
Jesus, our guide through life,
hear our prayer.

We pray for those whose journeying is intolerably difficult,
those denied the warmth and security of love and home,
those who struggle with internal and external pressures beyond their capacity,
those who are intimidated by the complexity of life.
Jesus, our willing guide,
hear our prayer.

We pray for those for whom this approaching Christmas is a nightmare,
those who have no resources to share,
those who, like Christ, have no place to call their own,
those who struggle with faith.
Jesus, our loving guide,
hear our prayer.

Into your care and keeping
we commit those near and dear to us;
in sickness or in health, in wealth or in poverty,
in love or alone.
Come close, O Spirit of God, and journey with them.
We ask this in Jesus' name.
Amen.

A sending out prayer

Dear God,
Today we think about John the Baptist, the shepherds and all the people who bring stories and messages to others.
Help us to tell the stories we learn about you as we get ever nearer to Christmas Day.
Amen.

Year A   ADVENT 4

Isaiah 7.10–16; Psalm 80.1–7, 17–19; Romans 1.1–7; **Matthew 1.18–25** *Look, the virgin shall conceive and bear a son, and they shall name him Emmanuel.*

A prayer of approach

May we thrill to the messages of the angels,
and let us also, for dear Christ's sake,
be bringers of good news to others.
May we so listen to your words that we are made
brilliant at sharing them with others,
O Light of the World.
Amen.

A prayer of thanksgiving for all ages

We light a candle for the angel,
God of goodness and light,
and thank you for the messages of encouragement
you have given us in our lives;
for moments of illumination and for answers to prayer
and for the people.
O God, we thank you for the many human angels in
our lives:
for the people who have listened to us patiently;
heard our despair or uncertainty; and who
sometimes, by hardly saying anything, have made the
way ahead seem possible, giving us hope and peace
and blessing.
May they, too, be blessed.
May your name be blessed. God with us, Emmanuel.
Amen.

A prayer for inward renewal

O holy God, we are all Mary and Joseph,
astonished and puzzled by your extraordinary ways.
You choose through our humanity to share your
divinity.
May each of us nurture the Christ you plant in us.
Out of our sometimes unpromising and erring ways,
may you make something beautiful,
a life worthy of our King, our Saviour, Jesus Christ.
Amen.

A prayer for parents

As we prepare to celebrate Christ's holy birth,
we remember all parents, praying that as with the
Holy Family so may it be that all children may know
love and stability.
Help parents to walk in the way of truth.
May they cultivate patience and understanding,
for Jesus' sake.
Amen.

A prayer activity

Set out tealights in a suitable place. In a time of quiet, read the prayer below and introduce the response, 'be our light'. Afterwards invite the group to light a candle as a reminder of the hope we have in Jesus:

In times of doubt, living Lord,
be our light.
When we find it hard to live as you would like,
living Lord,
be our light.
When we struggle to see you at work in the world,
living Lord,
be our light.
When things happen that shake our faith, living Lord,
be our light. Amen.

A prayer of intercession

How good you have been to us, O God. From the
time of our birth, through childhood and school years,
into work, training or education; through relationships
until we find love, and then, for some of us, the
miracle of birth in our own lives:
how good you have been to us.
So we pray for all who will find this Christmas a
difficult time. For men and women who are seeking
meaning and purpose in life. For those who have
choices and those who have none:
hear our prayers, Lord.
We pray for your Church, the community of your
people here; and for the Church of Jesus Christ in
this land and around the world:
hear our prayers, Lord.
May the opportunity of this Christmastime be grasped
with open hands and warm hearts:
hear our prayers, Lord.
For all who are lonely and afraid:
hear our prayers, Lord.
For all who are sick and awaiting results of tests:
hear our prayers, Lord.
For all who are nearing the end of their journey in this
dimension:
hear our prayers, Lord.
For all who mourn:
hear our prayers, Lord.
So take us sensitively into Christmas, and may the
mystery, the promise and the hope of the Christ child
be born in each of us and in all your people.
Amen.

A prayer of reflection

God of all people and all places,
when the shelves are full but our purses are almost
empty;
when the shops are crowded, but we feel alone;
when the festive music is lively, but we feel so tired;
help us to think of Joseph, turned away from a
crowded inn,
of Mary, tired after a long journey,
of Jesus, born into poverty,
but born for us and all who find life hard, especially
at Christmas.
Amen.

Year A CHRISTMAS 1

Isaiah 63.7–9; Psalm 148; Hebrews 2.10–18;
Matthew 2.13–23 *This was to fulfil what had been spoken by the Lord through the prophet.*

Call to worship

The party's over! The presents have been opened and the wrapping paper cleared away; the special food has been eaten; visitors have returned home. Joseph and Mary didn't get much time to relax with the new baby. Very soon, they had to pack up and take the baby far from home to Egypt, because his life was in danger.
Today, so soon after the joy of Christmas Day, we accompany them on that journey and make ourselves ready to get up and go, to take action for God in whatever ways we are called.

A gathering prayer

Hope of the world,
come to us as the baby born in Bethlehem.
Come and open our hearts and minds;
open our lives to the child within each one of us;
open our lives to the presence of children in our community.
Hope of the world,
help us to put aside our privilege and power and renew our spirit of wonder and awe.
Release us to rest in the presence of love;
restore to each other the other's lost infancy.
Hope of the world,
Come to us as the baby born in Bethlehem.

A prayer celebrating diversity

Lord God, thank you for the richness of your world: millions of colours and countless varieties of species;
for people of different races and cultures,
each person with a face that is theirs alone and fingerprints that uniquely belong to them.
We live in a land that has grown suspicious of strangers, fearing the foreigner as a potential terrorist.
As we celebrate the coming from different lands of those who followed a star that led them to Jesus, so teach us to value difference and rejoice in diversity.
Make us proud of what we are
and humbly accepting of what others have to offer us.
Amen.

A prayer for refugees

Lord, you bid us feed the hungry, aid the oppressed, shelter the homeless.
You tell us to seek God's justice for your world.
We pray for all those in fear of their lives within their own countries.
We give thanks for the work of Amnesty International and all agencies combating oppression, but chiefly on this day when we recall our Lord's flight into a less hostile land,
we remember all those whose desperation has driven them to our shores.

May our doors be wide and our hearts be generous to all who face persecution in their home countries, knowing that we too are strangers and pilgrims on the road to heaven.
Amen.

A prayer of intercession

We pray for your Church.
And we pray for those of other faiths;
that in the community of belief we may respect each other with love.
Lord, hear our prayer.
We pray for the nations of the world:
that in the rich diversity of culture and creed,
a new sense of our common humanity and inter-dependence will lead us forward.
Lord, hear our prayer.
For our sick and our sad, for those afraid of the future.
Lord, hear our prayer.
For our young and bold, with all of life before them.
Lord, hear our prayer.
And for ourselves, that your rich blessing will continue.
Lord, hear our prayer.
Amen.

A prayer activity

Ask the group to get comfortable for this guided meditation. Dim the lighting if possible. Ask them to relax and close their eyes. After a few minutes read the following:
Imagine you are in a place you love. This is a place where you feel safe and warm, a place of which you have happy memories. Picture it vividly. Think about how it looks, how it smells, how it feels. Then imagine that Jesus is with you in this safe place. Tell him about something that is worrying you. Let him listen. Think how he might respond. Then gently come back to the room you are in.

A prayer for all ages

Loving God,
as we think of Mary and Joseph travelling,
we ask you to keep us safe on our journeys.
When we enjoy our travels,
we remember how frightening it must have been for them.
As we think of Jesus being kept safe, we think of the children in the world who aren't safe.
Jesus, we thank you for our fun,
but think of others too.
Amen.

Year A   CHRISTMAS 2

Jeremiah 31.7–14, or Sirach 24.1–12; Psalm
147.12–20, or Wisdom of Solomon 10.15–21;
Ephesians 1.3–14; **John 1.(1–9), 10–18** *The true
light which enlightens everyone, was coming into
the world.*

Call to worship

In wonder and gratitude and silence we enfold
ourselves in your presence. *(Silence)*
Jesus said, 'I am the light of the world.'
**The darkness and the light
are the same to you, O God.**
We remember that you create day and night.
**The darkness and the light
are the same to you, O God.**
In a world where many feel that they live in darkness
we remember that
**the darkness and the light
are the same to you, O God.**
We thank you for the darkness that nurtures us.
**The darkness and the light
are the same to you, O God.**
We come with our darkness and our light to worship
you.
**The darkness and the light
are the same to you, O God.**
We come with those who long to know your presence
in the darkness and in the light.

A prayer of confession

Jesus said we are to love God with all our
heart and our entire mind and with all our soul.
Dear God, we bring our all to you. *(Pause)*
It is hard to believe that you want us to love you with
all that we are. *(Pause)*
There is goodness and badness in each of our lives.
There is darkness and light. *(Pause)*
It is no good to pretend otherwise.
We can be better than others think we are.
We can fail to be as good as we like to think we are.
(Pause)
There are times when we can hardly admit to
ourselves what kind of people we are. *(Pause)*
We do not want to make any excuses.
We come in the only way we can – just as we are.
We can hardly believe that you do not hold our
failures against us.
You forgive and set us free from the past.
Help us to believe in your forgiveness so we may
forgive ourselves and those who we feel have
wronged us.
So may we live in harmony with you, with ourselves
and with others.
Jesus declares that our sins are forgiven.
Pause
**Thanks be to God.
Amen.**

A prayer for all ages

*This prayer is found in the Galilee Chapel
of Durham Cathedral near Bede's tomb:*
Christ is the morning star
who, when the night
of this world is past
brings to its saints
the promise
of the light of life
and opens
everlasting day.
The Venerable Bede

A prayer activity

*Remind the group of God's longing to be close to us.
We don't have to impress when we pray. Put on some
background music and ask everyone to speak or
whisper their prayers, all at once. After all, 'the word
became flesh' so he could chat with us. Invite the
group to chat back.*

A prayer of intercession *based on John 1*

From the fullness of your grace
may we all receive one blessing after another.
Lord God, who made us your children in Jesus;
we pray for those on their own and lonely:
From the fullness of your grace
may we all receive one blessing after another.
Lord God, whose Son surpasses all others;
we pray for those who need a role-model:
From the fullness of your grace
may we all receive one blessing after another.
Lord God, whose Son is the life,
we pray for the sick and those close to death:
From the fullness of your grace
may we all receive one blessing after another.
Lord God, who gave the law through Moses,
but who sent Jesus to bring grace and truth,
we pray for those who follow other religions:
From the fullness of your grace
may we all receive one blessing after another.
Although no one has ever seen you, Lord God,
**may Jesus who is at the Father's side,
make you known to us and to those for whom
we pray.
Amen.**

A sending out prayer

May Christ take us back to the beginning with God,
remaking us in his life and light,
and fitting us to testify concerning that light;
and may the blessing of almighty God,
the Father, the Son and the Holy Spirit,
be with us all, evermore.
Amen.

Go in peace
to be channels of the love of God.
Amen.

Year A EPIPHANY 1

Isaiah 42.1–9; Psalm 29; Acts 10.34–43;
Matthew 3.13–17 *Then Jesus came from Galilee to John at the Jordan, to be baptized by him.*

Call to worship

Loving God, you call us to be your people,
you make us and fill us with your Spirit,
for you are our breath, you are our life.
Loving God, you call us to be your people,
to journey for the sake of love and to find, at every step, that we are full of you,
for you are our breath, you are our life.
Loving God, you call us to see your glory
in creation, your inspiration in our work, and your love in our lives,
for you are our breath, you are our life.
Loving God, you call us to be your people.
Refresh us here, rebuild us here,
renew us here as we offer you thanks and praise,
for you are our breath, you are our life.

A prayer of confession

For our failure to acknowledge you when the opportunity occurs and when you are being denied:
dear Lord, **forgive us.**
For our arrogance and ignorance in making you, our God, too small and in our own image, assuming we know you inside out just as you know us:
dear Lord, **forgive us.**
For our failure to celebrate all the blessings you give your people:
dear Lord, **forgive us.**
For our conceit in imagining that 'your people' are only us:
dear Lord, **forgive us.**
For ourselves when, as a church, we have not listened to you:
dear Lord, **forgive us.**
Dear Lord, forgive us for these and all our sins against you.
Amen.

A prayer of reflection and thanksgiving

Pause after each question to allow time to reflect:
Lord Jesus, there are so many things we do not understand.
Why do so many people get ill?
Why are so many people killed in wars?
Why are some people unkind to others?
Why are there so many things we do not understand?
Thank you that we can bring all our questions to you.
Thank you that no question is ever too foolish to ask you.
Thank you that you are always our friend.
Amen.

A prayer for God's blessing

Almighty God, you give us breath,
to praise you as our creator.
Lead us from praise to minds, hearts and spirits
sensitive to the world's injustices.
As we celebrate the baptism of your son,
Jesus Christ,
bless each of us in the ministry we share from him.
Amen.

A prayer for all ages

Lord, we are at the start of the year:
Thank you for new beginnings.
Lord, we are at the start of a month:
Thank you for new beginnings.
Lord, we are at the start of a new week:
Thank you for new beginnings.
Lord, we are at the start of another day:
Thank you for new beginnings.
Lord, we are at the start of the rest of our lives:
Thank you for new beginnings.
Amen.

A prayer activity

Set out a bowl of water. Swirl it around gently. Ask the group to think about the things they do for others, for example caring, helping, sharing and encouraging.
Say this or a similar prayer:
Lord, we want to praise you for all that you
are doing in our lives. We want to be more like you in everything we do. Help us to be caring and thoughtful with our friends and family.
Amen.
Invite everyone to take turns to dip their finger in the water and make a sign of the cross on the forehead of the person next to them.

A prayer of intercession

We pray for:
children and adults who have been baptized, that they will mature in every way as followers of Jesus Christ;
those who feel that they are on the edge of the church and are no longer comfortable with some of the church's teaching and practice;
those who have lost a sense of belonging to the Christian community.
May we examine ourselves so that we do not exclude those whom you welcome,
and may our Christian community be as gracious and as accepting as Jesus was.
Amen.

A sending out prayer

Wise God, thank you that you understand everything.
Give us courage to ask difficult questions
so that we can learn more about you
and the world you have created.
Amen.

Year A   EPIPHANY 2

Isaiah 49.1–7; Psalm 40.1–11; 1 Corinthians 1.1–9;
John 1.29–42 *Look, here is the Lamb of God!*

Call to worship

Arrange six candles to be lit during this prayer
Creator God, you spoke and your word was life
and light.
In God there is no darkness at all.
Light the first candle
In Jesus Christ, your living Word, you sent light
to the world.
In God there is no darkness at all.
Light the second candle
You have named us and we are a part of your light.
In God there is no darkness at all.
Light the third candle
You call us to your work in the world – to carry the light.
In God there is no darkness at all.
Light the fourth candle
You call us into growth, to become more than
servants of the light
but to live as light.
In God there is no darkness at all.
Light the fifth candle
We are one in the light of God.
We stand in the light of God.
We live in the light of God.
We belong in the light of God.
Strong in the light of God.
Where there is no darkness at all.
Amen.
Light the sixth candle

A prayer of confession and assurance of forgiveness

In silence, let us admit the faults and failures in our
lives, the times when through weakness and lack of
discipline we have let ourselves down;
for the times we have failed other people by
thoughtlessness and selfishness;
for the times when we have acted unjustly towards
others;
for ignoring our responsibility for what is wrong in our
lives;
for the times when we have deliberately ignored
the needs of others and selfishly pursued our own
interests;
for being unwilling to forgive others as we expect God
to forgive us.
We thank God that those who confess their sins will
know God's forgiveness.
Thanks be to God. **Amen.**

A prayer of thanksgiving and dedication

God who made the world, made me, shaped me,
filled me with life and talents.
God made me as part of a network of love that keeps
the world alive.
God knows the name of my heart, my true name,
the name that links me to God:
the name that says who I truly am.

My name lives in the mind of God just as I live in the
mind of God.
God gave me myself and I try to give myself back to
God, to use the freedom I have to choose God;
to place myself in God's hands,
trusting myself to his love and mercy,
trying to fill my life with him by giving my life to him
and acknowledging that God who made the world
made me.
I give thanks for myself and my place in God's world.
Amen.

A prayer of commitment

Lord Jesus, help us to follow you.
May our whole life entice others into your company.
Help us to let go of everything that keeps us from
being what you want us to be.
Amen.

A prayer activity

*Give several children an item to hold, each one
representing a different time of day. Pray, thanking
God that Jesus can be with us at all times. Then pray
specifically about each time of day, with the children
holding the items up, as appropriate. After each
section, everyone says:* **Thank you, Lord, that you
are with us always.**

A prayer of intercession

That the Spirit of Jesus will continue to guide all those
who have answered God's call to service, for all the
baptized and those who lead and direct God's people;
We pray to the Lord: **Lord, hear us.**
That the leaders of the nations of the world will treat
all of those entrusted to their care with justice and
respect;
We pray to the Lord: **Lord, hear us.**
That the sick, the terminally ill and those who are
grieving the loss of a loved one will place their lives in
the hands of the one who called them to himself;
We pray to the Lord: **Lord, hear us.**
For all the intentions which we hold in our hearts and
all our unspoken desires, we now recall in silence;
We pray to the Lord: **Lord, hear us.**
Gracious God, your Son has called us to be his
disciples and to follow his ways; grant us the grace to
remain faithful to his call.
Amen.

A prayer for insight

Loving Father,
When things are going wrong,
may we praise you, not blame you.
When the storm winds blow,
may we be strengthened by their power.
When the opportunity presents,
may we tell others fearlessly
of your grace and mercy.
Amen.

Year A EPIPHANY 3

Isaiah 9.1–4; Psalm 27.1, 4–9; 1 Corinthians 1.10–18;
Matthew 4.12–23 *Follow me, and I will make you fish for people.*

A prayer of approach

Lord, your call to us is:
'Will you come and follow me?'
Give me courage to respond.
Lord, your call to us is:
'Will you come and follow me?'
Give me strength to do my best.
Lord, your call to us is:
'Will you come and follow me?'
Give me the nerve to follow you immediately.
Open our ears to hear your call.
Open our eyes to see you before us.
Open our lips to respond.
And open our hearts to your love.
Amen.

A prayer of confession

Lord Jesus, when you called the fishermen, they responded immediately.
Forgive us for the excuses we make:
we are too young, too old, too busy.
Forgive us, Lord Jesus.
Lord Jesus, when you called the fishermen, they left their boats.
Forgive us for the things that we cling to and the things that hold us back.
Forgive us, Lord Jesus.
Lord Jesus, when you called the fishermen, they became fishers of men and women.
Forgive us for the chances we miss to fish for you, through our lack of courage.
Forgive us, Lord Jesus.
Amen.

A prayer of thanksgiving

Merciful One, gifting grace,
through offering us time,
through highlighting our poverty,
through drawing us out of securities,
through revealing our fearful inadequacies,
through challenging our selfish desires,
through illuminating our false motivations,
we worship you and give thanks.
Abundant One, lavishing life,
in Spring's invitation to grow,
in Summer's embrace of freedom,
in Autumn's encouragement of release,
in Winter's opportunity for reflection,
we worship you and give thanks.
Amen.

A prayer of adoration

Timeless One, ever-present in rhythms of tide and laughter of streams,
in sentinels of rock and ageless sands,
in rainbow colours and hedgerow beauty,
in brilliant night and confident day,
in distant stars and earth beneath,
in tang of tears and sweet-tasting love,
in squall of birth and visit of death,
we worship you and adore.
Amen.

A prayer of supplication

God, who comes among us as people move into our neighbourhood: help us to notice and reach out.
When new children join our class: help us to make friends. For those for whom this is a new country:
help us to accept and welcome.
When others bring new culture and customs:
help us to listen and to learn. If the language of others is different from our own: help us communicate in other ways, and walk alongside each other with respect, regard and genuine love.
Amen.

A prayer activity

Form a circle and ask the group to think quietly of something they are scared or worried about. Tell them you are going to be praying for each person, as they light a candle, a symbol of God as the Light. Take it in turns to light a candle each and all say together:
The Lord is my light and my salvation, whom shall I fear?

A prayer of intercession

When confusion reigns and questions lead to destruction rather than strength;
when the sky seems too dark and shadows appear too long;
when healing is not complete, and the crying will not stop;
Let there be light.
You came as one of us: lived, breathed, cried, laughed and brought your living light.
Where hunger is normal, where disease is widespread;
where children die through neglect; and the rest of your world looks on;
Let there be light.
Where money is exchanged; where deals are made; where policy is completed;
Let there be light.
In government, in school, in work, in play, in home, in university, in church;
Let there be light.
Jesus, light of the world, shine on us. Provide clear paths, well-lit journeys, and shimmering walkways towards your kingdom.
Amen.

A sending out prayer

Trusting God, grant us strength and inspiration to live up to your calling to follow our Lord, Jesus Christ, that together may we build communities of trust for the good of the world.
Amen.

Year A EPIPHANY 4

Micah 6.1–8; Psalm 15; 1 Corinthians 1.18–31;
Matthew 5.1–12 *Blessed are those who hunger and thirst for righteousness, for they shall be satisfied.*

Call to worship

All honour and praise and glory to you,
through whom we are created,
through whom we live and move,
through whom we have our being,
in whom we relate,
in whom we express and wonder,
in whom we find meaning,
with whom we shout our joy,
with whom we sing deep sorrow,
with whom we share all story.
All honour and praise and glory to you.

A prayer of confession

God of wisdom: we do not always do what is right or speak the truth; we are too quick to pass judgement on others. We are foolish, Lord, and we long to be wise. Forgive us and give us the strength to walk blamelessly all the days of our life.
Amen.

A prayer of thanksgiving

For the love of my family and friends,
Lord, thank you for this blessing.
For kind people who think of the needs of others,
Lord, thank you for this blessing.
For times when you give us a second chance,
Lord, thank you for this blessing.
For brave people who stand up for the poor,
Lord, thank you for this blessing.
For peacemakers who make wars cease,
Lord, thank you for this blessing.
For any who show me how to be like Jesus,
Lord, thank you for this blessing.
For each new day to love and serve you,
Lord, thank you for this blessing.
Amen.

A prayer of praise for all ages

God of all creation, you have woken us from our sleep and helped us out of bed.
You have given us breakfast to eat and have guided our journey to church.
You have called us here today and are delighted we have come.
You rejoice in our presence and we rejoice in yours.
You renew our joy and make us wonder-full.
So we praise you and we worship you,
O God and Lord of all.
Amen.

A prayer of acknowledgement

You lead us in the way we should go,
prompting us forward, challenging us in our stubbornness, calming us in our fear,
acknowledging us in our brokenness,
holding us in our fragility,
caressing us with comfort,
anointing us with courage,
saving us in yourself.
Amen.

A prayer of intercession

In your word, we hear how we are to live in this world as followers of Jesus.
You call us to hunger and thirst for justice, for the sake of the weak who suffer from the mistreatment of the strong.
Help us to act so that the hungry will be filled, the thirsty quenched and the downcast lifted up.
Lord in your mercy: **hear our prayer.**
In your word, we hear how we are to deal with others on our journey of faith.
Grow within us a sincere and considerate nature – to walk gently upon this earth, living at peace with nature and other people.
Lord in your mercy: **hear our prayer.**
In your word, we hear how we are to walk with you, in humility of heart.
Help us to seek those virtues that we see in the life of Jesus.
Shape our words and actions according to his commands, that we might learn to live as those who show mercy, who seek peace, who bear all manner of falsehood, and who look to the rights of others before our own.
Lord in your mercy: **hear our prayer.**
Father, in all that lies before us this week, bless our hearts and minds to do justice, to love kindness and to walk humbly with you. Through Jesus Christ our Lord.
Amen.

A sung prayer activity

To the tune of 'Wide, wide as the ocean':
Wise, wise is our Father, our Father in heaven above;
dear, dear is his care for me shown in Jesus' love.
I can be so foolish, I worry and then I don't pray.
I'm safe in your strength, Lord, your care and your love when I pray each day.

A prayer of blessing

God of the poor, bless us with your compassion.
God of the bereaved, bless us with your comfort.
God of the humble, bless us with gentleness.
God of the righteous, bless us with wisdom.
God of the merciful, bless us with forgiveness.
God of the pure in heart, bless us with kindness.
God of the peacemakers, bless us with understanding.
God of the persecuted, bless us with courage.
Amen.

Year A   EPIPHANY 5

Isaiah 58.1–9a, (9b–12); Psalm 112.1–9, (10);
1 Corinthians 2.1–12, (13–16); **Matthew 5.13–20**
You are the salt of the earth.

Call to worship

From the mountain, Jesus calls us to see life from a
different perspective.
From the mountain, Jesus teaches us to find our
place and live in each moment.
From the mountain, Jesus challenges us to reach out
and be the salt of God's kingdom.
We come to worship:
responding to God's call,
ready to learn God's wisdom.
ready to be sent back into the world
as salt and light.

A prayer of confession

You call us to be the salt of the earth,
yet we have lost the excitement of being called
disciples.
You call us to be the salt of the earth,
yet we have lost the vision of what the kingdom is
about.
You call us to be the salt of the earth,
yet we huddle in the safety of our church community.
You call us to be the salt of the earth,
yet we have become tasteless and indistinguishable
from the world.
From the mountain, Jesus challenges us to reach out
and be the salt of God's kingdom.
Amen.

An acrostic prayer

On four large cards draw each of the letters of the
word 'SALT' and ask four people to hold them up so
the congregation can read the word. Ask each person
to step forward as the line of the prayer related to
their letter is spoken:
S is for **Seasoning:** salt brings flavour to life.
May we add colour and taste to the world and help
others to enjoy life in all its diversity and beauty.
A is for **Antiseptic:** salt cleans, preserves and draws
out poisons.
May we be honest and open, enabling healing and
justice to our world.
L is for **Life-affirming:** salt is hidden yet essential
for life.
May we be constant and dependable, offering acts of
kindness without making a fuss.
T is for **Thirst-making:** salt creates a thirst for the
water of life.
May we thirst for a deeper relationship with God
and create a thirst for others to seek life in all its
fullness.
Amen.

A prayer activity

Place some coarse rock salt into a bowl. Pass round
the bowl and invite each person to take a salt crystal
and think of a situation or place in which they could
be God's salt of the earth. Invite people to place their
salt crystal on a map or on a series of newspaper
headlines and pictures cut out and placed on a table.
Or ask them to take the salt crystal home to remind
them to pray for that person or situation throughout
the week.

A prayer of intercession

We are called as his followers to continue the healing
ministry of Jesus Christ.
Let us ask God our Father for all the graces we need
to become healers in our world.
We pray for those who exercise a special healing
ministry in the church: that they may so use the
special gifts which God has given them.
Let us pray to the Lord: **Lord, hear our prayer.**
We pray for doctors, nurses and those with care of
the sick: that they may be given love in their hearts
and skill in their hands as they continue Christ's
healing work, bringing consolation to those in their
care.
Let us pray to the Lord: **Lord, hear our prayer.**
We pray for those who are ill: that they may have
confidence in those who treat them and know the
grace of God in their healing.
Let us pray to the Lord: **Lord, hear our prayer.**
We pray for an understanding of suffering: that we
may always see in it the loving hands of Jesus, who
wants us to be healed of all fears, even of death and
dying.
Let us pray to the Lord: **Lord, hear our prayer.**
Amen.

A prayer for all ages

God who has built salt into creation,
hidden in surprising places:
in salt lakes and seas,
in rocks hidden beneath the ground,
in our bodies and our food,
help us to be salt to those we meet,
adding flavour and healing to the world around us.
Amen.

A sending out prayer

May the God who creates the salt so essential to life
help us live in every moment of each day.
May the Son who used the metaphor of salt to
describe discipleship
help us to share the gospel of life.
May the Spirit who challenges us to be salt in the
world
help us to salt the world with justice and peace.
Amen.

Year A   EPIPHANY 6

Deuteronomy 30.15–20, or Sirach 15.15–20; Psalm
119.1–8; 1 Corinthians 3.1–9; **Matthew 5.21–37**
*Leave your gift there before the altar and go; first be
reconciled to your brother or sister.*

Call to worship

Read the *Prologue* to Shakespeare's *Romeo and
Juliet*, which reflects on the way an ancient grudge
between two families impacts on the lives of two
young people.

A prayer for all ages

God who loves us all:
We thank you when we are feeling happy.
We thank you for the fun things we can enjoy.
We thank you for all the people who love us.
We are sorry when we get angry or hurt other people.
We are sorry when we argue and fall out with one
another.
Help us to say sorry and make up again,
so we can feel good about ourselves and our friends.
Amen.

A prayer of thanksgiving and confession

We thank you, God, for families:
for parents and carers,
for husbands, wives and partners,
for step-parents and step-children,
for grandparents, aunts and uncles,
for friends, neighbours and all those who care for us.
We thank you that our families
come in all shapes and sizes;
in all ages, nationalities and cultures;
that sometimes we are close
and sometimes we have our space;
that we live nearby and see each other often,
or far away and visit on webcams and texts.
Forgive us when we don't get on with one another:
when arguments get out of control;
when we lose our temper and say things we
shouldn't;
when we hurt others and hold grudges.
Help us to say sorry, to forgive one another and to
make up.
Amen.

A prayer of inclusion

In the times when we exclude others,
Lord, remind us you are there.
In the times when we feel excluded,
Lord, remind us you are there.
In the times when we judge others,
Lord, remind us you are there.
In the times when we are judged by others,
Lord, remind us you are there.
Amen.

A prayer activity for very young children

*Invite the children to shake hands with each other
and say: 'Peace be with you.' They could suggest
different phrases or actions.*

A prayer of intercession

Lord, we stop and think about your beautiful earth
and our place in it, and we pray:
for our planet where climates are changing and fertile
land becomes desert or is devastated by flood; where
habitats are destroyed and species become extinct.
Lord, **grant us words of wisdom and life.**

We pray for areas of the world where conflict rages;
for people mourning loved ones and fleeing homes
and communities; for people who are imprisoned or
tortured or who live in constant fear.
Lord, **grant us words of wisdom and life.**

We pray for places where resources are scarce;
where the rich have and the poor have not; for people
setting out to make a new life and leaving families
and friends behind.
Lord, **grant us words of wisdom and life.**

We pray for families where relationships are strained;
where people are estranged or engaged in custody
battles; where children have two homes or no home
at all.
Lord, **grant us words of wisdom and life.**

We pray for families which are not happy, where
love has withered and regrets loom large; for those
struggling with illness or disability, who desperately
need some support.
Lord, **grant us words of wisdom and life.**

We pray for ourselves, in our relationships in our own
communities and churches, when disagreements
occur and people are excluded or not made to feel
welcome and accepted.
Lord, **grant us words of wisdom and life.**
Amen.

A sending out prayer

May God, who created us to live in relationship with
one another, go with us.
May the Son, who lived in relationships based on
inclusion and forgiveness, go with us.
And may the Spirit, who breathes wisdom and life into
community, go with us,
now and into the days ahead.
Amen.

Year A   EPIPHANY 7

Leviticus 19.1–2, 9–18; Psalm 119.33–40;
1 Corinthians 3.10–11, 16–23; **Matthew 5.38–48**
*Love your enemies and pray for those who
persecute you.*

Gathering words

Jesus calls us to a new way of living together marked
by justice, love and generosity. This is not easy as
we are asked to love not just our friends, but our
enemies too.

Prayer of Ignatius of Loyola

A medieval prayer about generosity
Dearest Lord, teach me to be generous.
Teach me to serve you as you deserve,
to give and not to count the cost;
to fight and not to heed the wounds;
to toil and not to seek for rest;
to labour and not to seek reward,
save that of knowing that I do your will.
Amen.

A prayer of confession

God, we're being honest here.
There are people we really don't like;
there are people we would rather not talk to;
there are people that seem unkempt
and strange;
there are people we might cross the road
to avoid;
there are people we label with our fears
and prejudice;
there are people we gossip about,
spreading the latest scandal.
God, we're being honest here.
There are times when we are not proud of
ourselves;
times when we let you down very badly.
There are times when we do not behave
like your disciples.
God, be honest with us.
Correct us gently
and challenge us passionately.
Forgive us and heal our faults.
Help us to forgive others and overlook
their faults.
Nurture us as we grow from childhood
into the maturity of your kingdom.
Amen.

A prayer for all ages

When someone loves us and cares for us,
Jesus, help us to **love them!**
When someone is kind to us and is a good friend,
Jesus, help us to **love them!**
When someone is just like us,
Jesus, help us to **love them!**
When someone is very different from us,
Jesus, help us to **love them!**
When someone is rude to us,
Jesus, help us to **love them!**
When someone is mean about us,
Jesus, help us to **love them!**
We pray for anyone who has been unkind to us
or hurt us.
Jesus, help us to **love them!**
Amen.

A prayer activity

*Look through newspapers and try to pray for those
for whom it can be difficult to pray: the criminal, the
terrorist, the gang member, etc.*

A prayer of intercession

God of all compassion:
Move us into action as we pray for people around the
world who are on their knees:
because of debt; because of drought; because of
disease.
They say: 'If you are willing – you can make me
whole.' Jesus is willing – are we?

God of all compassion:
Move us into action as we pray for people around the
world who are begging:
for a home; for food; for education.
They say: 'If you are willing – you can make me
whole.' Jesus is willing – are we?

God of all compassion:
Move us into action as we pray for people around the
world who are rejected by others:
because of belief; because of ethnicity; because of
behaviour.
They say: 'If you are willing – you can make me
whole.' Jesus is willing – are we?

God of compassion:
If we are not willing – please take away our heart of
stone and give us a heart that will be moved.
If we are willing but cannot see how to act, move us
to search until we find your way.
So we may be able to reach out and touch each other
until the whole world finds wholeness.
Through Jesus Christ.
Amen.

A sending out prayer

Father God,
Send us out to surprise others this week.
Help us to stand up to injustice, act generously,
sow seeds of love and pray for our enemies.
In the name of Jesus.
Amen.

Year A EPIPHANY 8

Isaiah 49.8–16a; Psalm 131; 1 Corinthians 4.1–5;
Matthew 6.24–34 *So do not worry about tomorrow,
for tomorrow will bring worries of its own.*

Call to worship

*Invite people to hold hands out, palms upwards, for
the response line*
The world is the Lord's and everything in it.
We worship you.
The mountains are his, the rivers are his.
We worship you.
The trees are his, the flowers are his.
We worship you.
The animals are his, the pets are his.
We worship you.
The nations are his, the towns are his.
We worship you.
Every person, every breath, every word is his.
We worship you.
God loves us all, God keeps us all.
We worship you today.

A prayer of confession

Lord God,
Sometimes we forget the work of your kingdom,
we forget to work for righteousness in the world.
Sometimes we work only to meet our own needs.
**Forgive us and help us to hear your word,
help us to follow your call,
help us to love your world.
Amen.**

A prayer of praise

Creator God, all your works are wonderful.
Creation sings of your might and power and whispers
of your compassion:
sunshine shouts of joy, darkness murmurs in mystery.
You are an awesome God.
We fall silent before you.
Silence
Redeeming God, all your works are wonderful.
In Jesus you showed us life and love.
You bring us health and healing, peace and love.
You care for each one of us in our sorrow, in our pain,
in our delight.
You are an awesome God.
We fall silent before you.
Silence
Sustaining God, all your works are wonderful.
Through your Spirit you build your Church and
transform your world.
You inspire us to worship and give us strength to work.
You provide all we need for our bodies, for our minds,
for our souls.
You are an awesome God.
We fall silent before you.
Silence
You are an awesome God.
Amen.

A prayer activity

*You will need: some pieces of thick string loosely
knotted (one per person). Invite the group to hold
the piece of knotted string. Ask them to focus on the
knot and think of something that they are worried or
anxious about at the moment. Ask them to untie the
knot. Pray that God will set them free from the worry
and give them peace.*

A prayer of intercession for children

*Remind the children that, because the Holy Spirit is at
work all over the world, bringing people to know and
follow Jesus, we belong to an enormous, worldwide
family of Christians. Pray together for that family:*
For all the Christians all over the world, we pray,
come, Holy Spirit.
Where Christians are happy and full of joy, we pray,
come, Holy Spirit.
Where Christians are sad because they are hungry,
come, Holy Spirit.
Where Christians are frightened of being hurt
because they follow Jesus, we pray,
come, Holy Spirit.
Where Christians are working to make the world a
fairer place, we pray,
come, Holy Spirit.
Wherever there are people just discovering how
much Jesus loves them, we pray,
**come, Holy Spirit.
Amen.**

A prayer for all ages

God, thank you for all the wonderful things you give us.
Thank you for our food and drink.
Thank you for our clothes.
Thank you for all the beautiful birds and flowers in the
world.
Amen.

A sending out prayer

God, our Father,
Thank you that you care for us
and provide for our every need.
Help us not to worry about the future,
but trust in you always
and enjoy living in the present moment.
Amen.

If Easter falls late, Proper 4 on page 33 may
be used as Epiphany 9.

Year A LAST AFTER EPIPHANY/ TRANSFIGURATION

Exodus 24.12–18; Psalm 2, or Psalm 99; 2 Peter 1.16–21; **Matthew 17.1–9** *This is my Son, the beloved, with him I am well pleased.*

Gathering words

Sometimes we experience things that go beyond words. Sometimes we see beauty that reduces us to silent wonder. Come let us worship Christ, beautiful beyond description.

A prayer of confession

Today, Lord, is your day, as was yesterday and as tomorrow will be, too.
My part in your timing is now, this time, this place, this moment.
Often I get lost in past remembrance or future plans, but none of these are right for me now.
May everything I do today give glory, honour and praise to you.
Amen.

A prayer of supplication

Merciful One, highlight our poverty.
Draw us out of securities.
Reveal our fearful inadequacies.
Challenge our selfish desires.
Expose our false motivations.
Lead us through reluctance.
Strengthen us in our weakness.
Lift us up again in failure.
Guide our tentative choices.
Grace us in our every breath.
Be with us in this moment and in all of time.
Amen.

A prayer of praise and thanksgiving

Thank you, God, that you journey with us,
up our own mountains!
You are with us as we struggle;
comfort us when times are tough.
You lift us up when we stumble;
give us strength we never knew we had.
You are with us every step of the way.
You teach us to take one step at a time.
Thank you, God, for the shifting clouds of faith.
You are in the midst, though we cannot see you.
Your presence is like the changing mist.
Faith can be transient and hesitant
but we do not journey alone.
When we enter the cloud we need not fear,
for you speak to us.
Thank you, God, that you spoke to Moses.
Speak to us in words we can hear:
in the words of prayer, in the verses of hymns,
in the teaching of Scripture, in the challenge of sermon,
in the fellowship of friends, in the love of family.
Amen.

A prayer activity

Read 2 Peter 1.16–19 prayerfully to the group, explaining briefly that this time obviously stayed in Peter's memory for many years because he is still writing and talking about it! Using the stillness, or using some background music, invite the group to remember the times in their lives when God seemed close; times when they have been protected; times when things have clicked into place and something in life makes sense; times when they know God was close. In the silence of their own minds and hearts, suggest they all give thanks to God.

A prayer of intercession

O God, your servant Moses heard your call and led your people Israel. He brought your commandments to help them live faithful lives. He gave direction and encouragement when they felt faint and weary and guided them on to your land of promise.
We pray for all leaders of your people, for all ministers of the gospel.

O God, your prophet Elijah spoke your word of truth with clarity and persistence. He called your people to purity of worship and faithfulness of living. He placed before them your demands for holiness of life and justice for all.
We pray for all your people, serving you in your world.

O God, your Son Jesus Christ laid aside his majesty and came to this world to live among us. He preached the good news of the kingdom. He called many to leave aside their daily tasks and come and follow him. He amazed with his authority to teach and power to heal. And he set his face to Jerusalem to complete his mission to seek and save the lost.
We open our lives to his words and power today.
Amen.

A prayer of praise for all ages

God of all gifts: **we adore you.**
God of all gifts: **we worship you.**
God of all gifts: **we honour you.**
God of all gifts: **we glorify you.**
God of all gifts: **we praise you.**
God of all gifts: **we thank you,**
now and for evermore,
Amen.

A sending out prayer

Lord Jesus, as we journey from here today,
let us remember the image of your radiant face,
on the mountain top, full of love and hope.
Inspire and guide us as we approach Lent and accompany you on your journey to Jerusalem.
Let your light and love transform us as we travel with you, so that we may transform the lives of others.
Amen.

Year A   LENT 1

Genesis 2.15–17, 3.1–7; Psalm 32; Romans 5.12–19;
Matthew 4.1–11 *Jesus was led by the Spirit into the wilderness.*

Gathering prayer

We gather today in Jesus' name.
Jesus who was tempted in the desert,
Jesus who was protected by God's angels,
Jesus who is with us now,
we offer you all we think, say and do.
Amen.

A prayer of approach

We come
to the creator of the dusty desert;
to the creator of the fertile fields;
to the creator of the teeming seas.

We come to the God
who is found in the wilderness
and yet in our hearts.

We seek that intimate conversation
that God would have with us
in the depths of our being,
and at the heart of our faith,
as we ask of Jesus, 'Who are you?'
and he replies, 'I am'.
Amen.

A prayer of confession

Gracious God,
forgive me when I see defeat and you see possibility;
when I see barriers and you see bridges;
when I see obstacles and you see stepping stones;
when I see deserts and you see resting places;
when I see temptations and you see opportunities;
when I see risk and am afraid,
and you see risk and go on.

Gracious God,
forgive me and be with me as I discover new territories,
new challenges, new friends.
Amen.

A prayer of intercession

Lenten God,
You knew the hardship of waiting in the desert.
Be with all those who are away from their homeland
as they seek to make a new life and wait for news
from home.

Lenten God,
You knew the temptation to turn stones into bread.
Be with all those who know the gnawing pain of
hunger as they struggle to survive in a world that
does not share.

Lenten God,
You knew the temptation to throw yourself off the
pinnacle.
Be with all those who know illness and despair
as they struggle to go on living as life passes them by.

Lenten God,
You knew the temptation to seize power for yourself.
Be with all those who hold and exercise power:
may they seek to make decisions that will bring
justice and peace.
Amen.

A prayer for all ages

*Invite people to put their hands on one another's
shoulders as this prayer is said:*
Angels came and waited on Jesus.
Lord God,
who loves each of us,
whose Son Jesus died for us
and whose Spirit helps us
at times of temptation,
help us to stand together,
so that we become angels
who wait on each other.
Amen.

A prayer activity

*Jesus was invited to turn stones into bread as a
symbol that he resisted temptation. Invite children to
decorate stones and hold them as this prayer is said:*
Jesus saw these stones and rather than thinking of
food he thought of God.
Help us this Lent to take these stones and to see
them as reminders of the time Jesus spent praying to
God.
God is with us and listens to us when we are happy
and when we are sad.
When we are lonely and when we are mad.
Forgive us when we try to do things ourselves and
forget about you, God.
Thank you for being with us and listening to us.
Amen.

A sending out prayer of blessing

Creator of the wilderness, go with us.
Jesus, who overcame temptation, go with us.
Spirit, strengthener of those who call, go with us.
Three in one, drawing all strands of life together,
go with us.
Amen.

Year A   LENT 2

Genesis 12.1–4a; Psalm 121; Romans 4.1–5, 13–17;
John 3.1–17 *For God so loved the world, that he gave his only Son.*

Call to worship

As Nicodemus came to see Jesus,
so we follow in his path.
As the Greeks said to Philip, 'Sir, we would see Jesus',
so we would see him too.
As Nicodemus had doubts in his heart,
so we too nurse them hidden.
So we come to meet the risen Christ,
as ourselves, with Nicodemus deep within.

A prayer of confession

God of new beginnings, when we have closed our ears to your call and not heard your invitation to move on, forgive us,
and help us to begin again.

When we have tried to keep our faith private and secret, and have not been willing to share it, forgive us,
and help us to begin again.

When we have taken your love for granted and lost the wonder of the abundant life you give, forgive us,
and help us to begin again.

When we have chosen to stick at a comfortable stage of faith and refused to tackle challenges, forgive us,
and help us to begin again.

When we have neglected opportunities to serve you through working for justice for others, forgive us,
and help us to begin again.

When we have been satisfied with maintenance ministry and have not been open to new ways of being church here, forgive us,
and help us to begin again.
Amen.

A prayer of intercession

God who so loves the world,
we bring to you the nations of the world.
Bring peace and love to our communities,
to our leaders, the politicians, both local and national;
to our teachers and all in our schools;
to all who work for peace, and all who seek peace in their lives.
God who so loves the world:
we bring you our nations.

God who so loves all people,
we bring to you those who are struggling,
refugees, the poor, the homeless;
families under stress, children with no families,
the elderly who are alone, infirm;
those we mention now…
God who so loves all people:
we bring to you those who are struggling.

God who died for the Church,
we bring to you the faith communities of the world,
whatever they believe.
May we all seek the truth that you bring, the love that you have, and the freedom of your Spirit.
May we move together, work together,
and so reflect the glory that you bring.
God who died for the Church:
we bring to you the faith communities of the world.
Amen.

A prayer for all ages

Lord of the night-time conversation, *(Cover eyes)*
be with me in the dark.
Lord of the question, *(Scratch head)*
be with me when I don't know.
Lord of the future and the past, *(All hold hands)*
help me to trust you.
Lord who brings love to the world: may I be your love, your life *(Raise joined hands together)*
at all times, in all places.
Amen.

A prayer for children

Dear God, we thank you for our minds, which we can use to think about the world around us.
Help us to ask questions when we are unsure, and to listen to the answers.
Help us to listen to the questions that others ask and to help them discover answers too.
Help us to use our minds wisely and to learn more about you through reading the Bible and talking to other people.
Thank you God for listening to us when we pray to you.
Amen.

A prayer activity

Read John 3.8. Pray some simple prayers as the group makes bubbles with bubble mixture: that God will bless people and help them to understand more. As you watch the bubbles float away, think about God's blessings being carried to others.

A sending out prayer

Jesus came to save the world and Nicodemus came to see Jesus. We came too.
Nicodemus was changed by Jesus and Jesus changes us too.
As we go out today may our lives show that change, the change within our hearts, our minds, ourselves.
May we go out to share the good news of the Spirit living within and around us.
Amen.

Year A LENT 3

Exodus 17.1–7; Psalm 95; Romans 5.1–11;
John 4.5–42 *… those who drink of the water that I will give them will never be thirsty.*

Call to worship

God meets the Israelites in the gushing of water from a desert spring. God meets a Samaritan woman by a well in the heat of the day. God meets us in the everyday meeting places of shops and playgrounds.

Come to encounter God.
Come to encounter one another.
Come to encounter yourself.

For it is here in this place, and in all places,
at this time, at all times,
with these people, and with all people,
that God encounters the miracles of creation.

A prayer of confession

Are you talking to me? Lord, I do not hear you.
Are you talking to me? Lord, I do not acknowledge you.
Are you talking to me? Lord, I do not see you.

You talk to me: I confess my deafness.
You talk to me: I confess my hardness of heart.
You talk to me: I confess my blindness.

Talk to me, Lord, in the depths of my being.
Help me to hear, help me to recognize, help me to see, that your life, and love and living water,
may flow through my life into the world.
Amen.

A prayer of praise for all ages

Pour water into a bucket or bowl before you begin
Give me this water, so I may never be thirsty.
God of the living water, we praise you.
God of the living water, we give you thanks,
for you alone can quench our thirst.
God of the living water, we worship and adore you:
for you are found in the places where others do not go.
You are found by the well of our sin.
You are found in our hearts and in our lives, where your love and your living water have refreshed, renewed and cleansed us.
Lord of the living water, we sit at your feet today.
Amen.

A prayer of intercession

Jesus was in a Samaritan city, scorned by the Jews, avoided by the good.
So we hold before God the places where we fear to walk:
the street corners where drugs are sold, the parks where muggings are rife, the house where the ASBO is relished.
May your Spirit walk the places where we fear to tread, and embolden us to take your love there too.

Jesus spoke to a woman of ill repute, who knew who she was and sought to change.
So we hold before God all those who live and work on the edges of society:
the refugees, scared and homeless, the sex workers, addicted and desperate, the children who have no families.
May your Spirit love where we fear to love, and move us through your love in our hearts.

She shared her new-found joy, and others came to meet the Lord.
May we be bold to speak of your love
through action and through words.
May we be bold to go to places where we fear,
full of your love for others.
May we be bold to work for your kingdom,
and find it where we did not expect to.
Amen.

A prayer for children

We love water.
Thank you, God, for the gift of water.
We love water in the sea and in the swimming pool.
Thank you, God, for the gift of water.
We love water to drink after running around.
Thank you, God, for the gift of water.
We love water for washing our bodies, hair and clothes.
Thank you, God, for the gift of water.
We love water for cooking and making ice cubes.
Thank you, God, for the gift of water.
Thank you, God, that the gift of Jesus is more special than every other gift.
Thank you for loving us.
Amen.

A prayer activity

Cut out water-drops shapes on paper or card and ask the group to write prayers on them, thinking especially of those who struggle to find water for their daily living.

A sending out prayer

We have heard for ourselves –
the great love of Jesus.
We have drunk for ourselves –
the living water of God.
We have seen for ourselves –
the new life of the Spirit.
May the great love, living water and new life go with us this week –
into our lives and the lives of others.
Amen.

Year A   LENT 4

1 Samuel 16.1–13; Psalm 23; Ephesians 5.8–14;
John 9.1–41 ... *though I was blind, now I see.*

Call to worship

Creator God, you made the world and all that is in it –
and saw that it was good. Let us say together with the
man born blind: **Lord, I believe.**

Saviour Christ, you healed the blind and set them
free to worship you. Help us here today, to worship
you in body, mind and spirit. Let us say together with
the man born blind: **Lord, I believe.**

Living Spirit, we see your work in the world in all that
is good and true and just. Give us grace to proclaim
your good news to everyone. Let us say together with
the man born blind: **Lord, I believe.**

A prayer of approach

God of all creation, your dream for us is of life lived to
the full.
As we come confidently before you today, help us to
acknowledge our dependency on you for all things
and our need of your healing touch to help us see.
As we come hesitantly before you today, draw us
closer to you, so that, as we travel with you towards
the cross this Lent, we may be enabled to live more
fully the life you have given us.
As we come uniquely as ourselves before you today,
assure us of your love for each one of us.
Amen.

A prayer of confession

Creator God,
We remember before you today the times when we
take you for granted and the times when we take your
gifts for granted.
We know that we do not love as Jesus loved.
We know that we do not act as Jesus acted.
We know that we do not think as Jesus thought.
We are truly sorry, and we turn from what is wrong in
our lives. But we know also that you are a forgiving
God: and so we claim for ourselves today the promise
that in Jesus all our sins are forgiven.
Amen.

A prayer for all ages

Lord Jesus, you spent your time on earth healing,
comforting and teaching people about the kingdom.
I wish I had been there. I wish you had spoken to me.
But I know that you are here, and that you do care
about my needs, and wants, that you do want me to
be your disciple.
Help me to listen for you, even though I can't see you.
Help me to know how special I am to you.
Help me to know how very much you love me.
Heal what is painful and sick in my life, and I will
spend my life gratefully, loving you in return, and
learning to do the things and say the words that
others need from me.
Amen.

A prayer of intercession *with a focus on sight*

Use any familiar pattern with a response such as:
Lord hear us. **Lord graciously hear us.**
Pray especially:
For all for whom seeing is a particularly important part
of their job, people such as surgeons or pilots. Give
thanks for the technology that enables them to see
even more clearly.
For those who literally cannot see – and for those
whose perception is limited and who metaphorically
cannot see.
That the Church – local, national and international
– may see more clearly its role in God's mission to
today's world; that the leaders of the nations may see
how to work for peace and justice.
That those in need may see and experience help,
both human and divine, in their troubles; and that we
may see where we can be the hands and eyes and
feet that offer help.
Finally pray with those we see no more, whose prayer
is joined with that of all the saints in glory.
Amen.

A prayer for children

Dear Lord Jesus,
The man was born blind. *(Cover eyes with hand)*
You put mud on his eyes. *(Rub fingertips over eyes)*
You sent him to wash. *(Mime splashing eye)*
He could see. *(Take hands away, open eyes wide)*
Hallelujah!
Amen.

A prayer activity

*Ask people to bring in pictures of people to pray for.
Place a large candle on a table and light it. Give each
person a tealight. Invite everyone to put their picture
on the table and light a tealight near it, saying the
name out loud if they would like to. When everyone
has had their turn all pray together:*
**We bring you our friends, our families, those
whom we love. We ask for healing for them within
your will and your peace for those who love them.
Amen.**

A sending out prayer

Lord, help us to learn how to see, and how to believe:
and help us to put what we see and what we believe
into practice, today and tomorrow and for the rest of
our lives.
Amen.

Year A   LENT 5

Ezekiel 37.1–14; Psalm 130; Romans 8.6–11;
John 11.1–45 *Jesus cried with a loud voice,
'Lazarus, come out!'*

A prayer of approach

We come to worship as we are, known by God and
called by name. We come with our doubts and our
fears to a Lord who knows doubt and fear too. We
come weary and weighed down, to the Spirit who
breathes new life into us and sends us on our way
rejoicing.
Amen.

A prayer of confession

Read Psalm 130 then after a silence, pray:
As our souls and minds wait for you, O God, we offer
all of our lives: the things we have done and the
things we have not done; the things of which we are
ashamed and the ways in which we have hurt other
people. In your steadfast love, forgive and redeem
us, as we claim the promise that in Jesus our sins are
forgiven.
Amen.

A prayer of praise

Eternal God, source of all life and all love, we praise
you for your gifts to us and to all people.
In creation you gave life to the world.
In Christ you redeemed the world, offering the
promise of resurrected life for all, foreshown in his
rising from the dead.
In the Spirit you give us new life here and now, and
challenge us to live as resurrected people in the
Church and in the world.
Give us hearts and minds ready to hear your voice
and to do your will, day by day.
Amen.

A prayer for all ages

When we hide away because we don't want to do
what we should be doing (*shout*) **come out!**
When we hide away because we are sorry and
ashamed (*speak reassuringly*) **come out!**
When we hide away because we are afraid (*whisper*)
come out!
Jesus loves us (*shout*) **we are free!**
Jesus saves us (*shout*) **we are free!**
Jesus gives us life (*shout*) **we are free!**
Amen.

A prayer of intercession

Lord of life and light and love, we ask you to call out
from their tombs all who are barred from fullness of
life, not only because of the sin that besets us all, but
because of our inhumanity towards each other.

To those whose lives are narrowed by extreme
poverty, who have been compelled to leave their
homes because of war or persecution, say,
'Come out.'

Say it by showing our world leaders paths of justice
and of peace. Say it through us, our attitudes, actions
and commitment.

To those who live on the margins of society, restricted
by homelessness or unemployment, confined to
prison, facing discrimination due to colour, disability
or sexuality, say, 'Come out.'
Say it through legislation that will help us become a
fairer society for people to live in. Say it through us,
our attitudes, actions and commitment.

To those we know and love, who struggle to make
sense of their lives, who face sickness or loss or
loneliness or depression, or who have to make
difficult decisions, say, 'Come out.'
Say it through us, through our understanding and our
willingness to listen and to take whatever action will
be most helpful.

To us, Lord, as we seek to be your disciples, your
church, in our own daily lives and in the life of this
community, this and every week, say, 'Come out.'
Help us to hear and to have the peace and the
courage and the boldness to step into the new thing
that you are calling us to, for Jesus' sake.
Amen.

A prayer for children

Dear Jesus, thank you for bringing Lazarus back
to life. That was amazing! You are wonderful and
powerful and mighty. We praise you.
Amen.

A prayer activity

*Invite the children to make long thin strips of paper
or cloth, like those taken off Lazarus when he was
raised, and to write their own prayers about the story
on these strips. Read them out.*

A responsive prayer

Dear God, please bless all those who face death.
Let them know your presence and your comfort.
Jesus, you are the resurrection and the life.
Please help us when someone we know and love
dies.
Jesus, you are the resurrection and the life.
Help us, like Martha, to believe in you even when life
is hard.
Jesus, you are the resurrection and the life.
Thank you for raising Lazarus from the dead, and
showing everyone that
Jesus, you are the resurrection and the life.
Amen.

A sending out prayer

May all that binds you fall away so that you may
believe and see the glory of God. Then go out, and
declare the good news.
Amen.

Year A   LENT 6/PALM SUNDAY

Palms: Psalm 118.1–2, 19–29. *Passion*: Isaiah 50.4–9a; Psalm 31.9–16; Philippians 2.5–11; **Matthew 21.1–11 and 26.14–27.66** *Blessed is the one who comes in the name of the Lord!*

A prayer of approach

Humble Lord, you chose to ride on a donkey into Jerusalem, a beast of the field and dusty road; an animal used to carrying heavy burdens, a creature overlooked by most – used and abused. Help us to live simply too, to carry the burdens of others; to notice and pay attention to those ignored and unheard. Help us to follow in your footsteps.
Amen.

Prayer over palm crosses

Bless to me this palm cross, loving God.
May it help me to praise you from my heart today.
May it help me understand how much it cost you to die for me. As I live through this Holy Week, and all the coming year, may it remind me that you have promised to be with me always, and that I have promised always to follow you.
Amen.

A prayer of invocation

Lord of Palm Sunday, who walked the path of pain and died the death of costly sacrifice, you love beyond measure; Lord of Palm Sunday,
come among your people.

Lord of Palm Sunday, who humbled yourself before people and suffered the agony no one can imagine, you offer us hope beyond measure;
Lord of Palm Sunday,
come among your people.

Lord of Palm Sunday, God became man for us, who was mocked and scorned and hated, you come to us always, beyond measure; Lord of Palm Sunday,
come among your people.

Lord of Palm Sunday, come to us and all God's people; Love beyond measure, Lord of Palm Sunday,
come among your people.
Amen.

A prayer of confession

Jesus, still centre of the universe, we come to you battered and weary, acknowledging that our lives are full of inconsistencies and weaknesses. Our lips give you praise, but our lives contradict what we say. We claim to be your loyal disciples, but so often when things get tough we run away. We say we are willing to suffer with you and for you, but so often we don't recognize your call to stand by you. Yet still we long for your truth and your love to direct our lives.
So we ask you to forgive the hurt we do to you, to others, to our own integrity.

Give us hearts that are full of praise, open to your call, and impatient with whatever stands between us and the things you want from us, so that we may follow you into Jerusalem and to what lies ahead, closely, in peace, with tenderness and awe, this Holy Week and every week.
Amen.

A prayer of intercession

Suffering, servant God, as we listen again to the story of your Passion, move our hearts within us to weep over Jerusalem and all the places of conflict, to mourn those who die unnoticed and to lament the damage done to your world.
Lord, mercifully hear us.

Stir our wills to stand firm when we meet injustice, to work for reconciliation, at home and in the world, and to transform what is, to what shall be.
Lord, mercifully hear us.

Embolden our lives to stand up for the voiceless, to be advocates for the bullied and to protect all of your creation.
Lord, mercifully hear us.
Amen.

A prayer for all ages

On Palm Sunday the crowds flocked to Jesus in worship. *(Move outstretched arms towards you)*
They celebrated him as king. *(Place 'crown' on head)*
On Good Friday they rejected him. *(Arms outstretched in front, hands raised as a barrier)*
We worship Jesus the Lord, *(Arms outstretched with hands open)*
who is king. *(Place 'crown' on head)*
But we too reject Jesus, and we push him out. *(Arms outstretched in front, hands raised as a barrier)*
We want to go our own way. *(Point to self)*
Lord, when we are mean, *(Make a mean face)*
come to us with your love we pray. *(Hands together in prayer)*
Amen.

A prayer activity

Give children a picture of a donkey or let them draw one. Invite them to write or draw on the donkey someone they want to pray for. Then pray:
Dear Jesus, the crowds were very excited to see you, the day you rode the donkey. There are some people who need to meet with you today too. Please bless...
(Read all the names)
Amen.

A sending out prayer

Lord, you know the dusty road, the fickle crowd, the pushing and pulling of everyday life.
Be beside us as we journey on.
Amen.

Year A   EASTER DAY

Jeremiah 31.1–6, or Acts 10.34–43; Psalm 118.1–2, 14–24; Colossians 3.1–4, or Acts 10.34–43; Matthew 28.1–10, or **John 20.1–18** *Mary of Magdala went to tell the disciples, 'I have seen the Lord.'*

Call to worship

The night has been long, but now the morning is here.
Be with us, loving Lord.
Let us go to the garden where our Lord is laid.
Go with us, leading Lord.
We come to the place, but he is not there.
Be with us, surprising Lord.
The stone is moved, the tomb is empty.
Be with us, risen Lord. Alleluia!

A prayer of confession

Dear God,
Today we celebrate the good news of Jesus, and yet so often we keep that good news to ourselves; we fail to share it with others, for we are worried about what they will think of us.
We are sorry, Lord, when we have let you down.

There have been times when we have forgotten you, when we have not loved you with our whole heart. When we have tried to do things our own way, rather than spend time listening to you.
We are sorry, Lord, when we have forgotten and not listened to you.

There have been occasions when we have ignored the needs of our neighbours, putting ourselves first, ahead of those who need our love and support.
We are sorry, Lord, for our selfishness.

Help us to show the love that you have for us in all that we do and think and say in the coming days.
Amen.

A prayer of adoration

Risen Lord on this Easter Day,
we celebrate the joyful news that Christ is alive.
We celebrate the amazing love of God shown in the giving of his Son for all humanity.
We celebrate that death has been overcome and new life is a gift to all who believe.
We worship and adore you.

Living, loving, risen Lord,
we worship and adore you.
Amen.

A prayer of intercession

Risen Lord, we praise you for changed lives and new hope, for sins forgiven and peace in our hearts.
Give us a sense of your risen presence abiding with us always.

Risen Lord, conqueror of evil, we pray for all those who experience darkness and destruction. We pray for nations in turmoil, for those without hope.
Give to your people the power to overcome and to live with the assurance of your living hope.

Risen Lord, we welcome you this Easter Sunday. Enter our lives and the lives of all people, that we may experience your new life within us.
We pray for your world, that there might be peace on earth. Make us your peacemakers.

We pray for all those who suffer and those who are struggling with life, those who are dying, those whose lives are shattered and torn apart.

Risen Lord, who greeted Mary in her despair, we pray for all those trapped by their circumstances in lives that give them little hope. May they know the comfort of the risen Lord, and the peace of the Christ who came and stood with Mary, transforming despair to hope.

Risen Lord, we praise you and rejoice in your resurrection.
Alleluia, alleluia,
Amen.

A prayer for all ages

Risen Lord, we meet you at the tomb.
We find it hard to believe, hard to recognize that someone who was dead, could be alive again.
Help us to believe.

Risen Lord, we move from your tomb towards our lives. Help us to know
that you are with us.

Risen Lord, we take the empty tomb to share with those we love. May we celebrate your new life
with all we meet today.
Amen.

A prayer activity

Invite the children to draw a picture of Jesus or write his name with a candle or wax crayons on thick paper. Now paint all over the paper with watercolour and watch the drawing/writing appear.
Say together:
We are joyful because Jesus is risen.
He is risen indeed, alleluia.
Amen.

A sending out prayer

Almighty God,
We thank you for helping us to worship you on this joyful Easter Day.
Help us, we pray, to continue in our worship throughout the coming week, by living our lives, filled with love, both for you, and for all people.
Alleluia!
Amen.

Year A EASTER 2

Acts 2.14a, 22–32; Psalm 16; 1 Peter 1.3–9; **John 20.19–31** *Jesus said to Thomas, 'Do not be faithless, but believe.'*

Call to worship

We have come to worship a risen Lord.
Be with us as we praise your name.

We have come as a group of people ready for what you have to tell us today.
Give us hearts ready to respond to what we hear.

We have come knowing that you are a loving, listening God.
We ask that you will hear our prayers and accept all that we do in your name.

A prayer of confession

Jesus came among his disciples and said, 'Peace be with you!' Forgive us when we do not seek your peace.

Jesus came among his disciples and said, 'Receive the Holy Spirit.'
Forgive us when we are unwilling to accept your gifts for ourselves and the gifts of others.

Jesus came and said to Thomas, 'Stop doubting and believe.'
Forgive our doubts, but help us to see that doubting is a part of believing.

Jesus stood among his disciples and said, 'Blessed are those who have not seen and yet believe.'
Forgive us when we criticize rather than support those who struggle with doubts. When we make it hard for people to be part of the church community.

As he came to the disciples, Jesus comes to us, holds out his nail-pierced hands, welcomes us into his love and forgives our sins. Thanks be to God.
Amen.

A personal prayer

Lord, I am resistant like Thomas and long to be as brave as Peter. So breathe into my heart the prophetic voice of the psalmist, the confident voice of the transformed Thomas and the spirit-filled voice of Peter. That through me others may know that you live, to save, forgive and empower at Eastertide and always.
Amen.

A prayer of intercession

We pray for those for whom faith is difficult, for the persecuted, for those living in fear of persecution.
On them, **Lord breathe your Spirit.**

We pray for the frightened, the timid, the very old and the very young, the housebound and those imprisoned by fear.
On them, **Lord breathe your Spirit.**

We pray for the bullied, children in schools, those in workplaces, all who are at the mercy of tyrants in places of power, governments, police forces, armies or militias.
On them, **Lord breathe your Spirit.**
Amen.

A prayer for all ages

All: Lord, we thank you for Thomas.
Children: When we see someone bothered and confused, help us to listen.
Adults: When we see someone dubious and argumentative, help us to comfort them.
Older people: When we see someone wrestling with doubt and fear, give us faith to support them.
All: We thank you for all the disciples, whose stories of faith and doubt have helped us to grow nearer to you, the one certainty on which our faith rests.
Amen.

A prayer activity

As a reminder of Jesus' gift of peace, make some stress busters. Invite the children to cut small sponges into fat cross shapes, write 'Peace' on both sides and decorate them brightly. Suggest that when faced with situations of fear and unhappiness the children could squeeze the sponge into a ball and then watch it unroll to display the word 'Peace', as a reminder of Jesus' Easter promise.
Use this prayer:
When I am scared and feel like running away.
When I am lonely and feel trapped by everything.
Jesus says, 'Peace be with you.'
When I am full of doubt and feel that no one understands.
When I do not know what to do and feel like giving up.
Jesus says, 'Peace be with you.'
This is God's promise for me and for us all.
'Peace be with you.'
Amen.

A sending out prayer

Jesus stood among them and said,
'Peace be with you.
As the Father has sent me, so I send you.
Receive the Holy Spirit.'
Go and do the Father's work,
in the name of the Son
and in the strength of the Spirit.
Amen.

Year A EASTER 3

Acts 2.14a, 36–41; Psalm 116.1–4, 12–19; 1 Peter 1.17–23; **Luke 24.13–35** *Jesus took the bread and broke it … and their eyes were opened.*

Call to worship

We come to find the risen Lord, in our hymns and our prayers.

In the readings and the preaching.
In our times of conversation and fellowship,
make yourself known, Lord Jesus.

Whenever bread is broken among those who seek to follow you,
make yourself known, Lord Jesus.

A prayer of confession

Lord, as we travel the journey of life, sometimes we are sad and discouraged and don't recognize your presence.
Forgive us and help us, loving Lord.

As we travel through new experiences, sometimes we are confused and afraid and forget to look for you among the unfamiliar.
Forgive us and help us, loving Lord.

As we meet new people, who have different ideas and views from our own, who challenge us and make us feel uncomfortable, we fail to see you at work in them.
Forgive us and help us, loving Lord.

As we listen to familiar Bible stories, sometimes we neglect to look for the new opportunities among the well-known words.
Forgive us and help us, loving Lord.

As we share food at your table, sometimes we do not go out with joy in our hearts.
Forgive us and help us, loving Lord.

When we come before our Lord and confess our sin, God forgives us. We hear then God's word of grace, our sins are forgiven.
Amen. Thanks be to God.

A prayer of intercession

We pray for travellers, for refugees and asylum seekers, for the homeless victims of war and natural disasters.
Draw closer. Be known to them and to us, as you were in the breaking of the bread.

We pray for those involved in the processes of justice, for police officers, lawyers, magistrates and judges.
For those imprisoned, whether justly or unjustly.
Draw closer. Be known to them and to us, as you were in the breaking of the bread.

We pray for the bereaved. For those who are concerned about their own health or that of others.
Draw closer. Be known to them and to us, as you were in the breaking of the bread.
Amen.

A prayer for all ages

When we feel sad, you draw near.
Wipe away tears or dab eyes with tissue
Thank you, Jesus, that you are here.
When we talk with our friends, you draw near.
Pretend to talk to your neighbour
Thank you, Jesus, that you are here.
When we hear stories, you draw near.
Open a Bible or hold your hands in the shape of an open book
Thank you, Jesus, that you are here.
When we break bread at your table, you draw near.
Mime breaking bread or break a real bread roll
Thank you, Jesus, that you are here.
When we welcome the stranger, you draw near.
Shake hands with someone
Thank you, Jesus, that you are here.
Amen.

A prayer of thanks

Thank you, Jesus, for being patient with us when we don't understand.
Thank you that you take time to show us who you are, and give us people to help us see you more clearly.
Amen.

A prayer activity

Give each child a piece of net-type fabric and invite them to place it on their heads and to cover their eyes with their hands. Pray:
Lord, we begin in the dark, not knowing who you are. Open our eyes and help us to see you.
Invite the children to put the veils over their faces and open their eyes. Pray:
As we learn more about you, you show us your goodness. Take the veil from our eyes and help us to understand.
Finally ask the children to take their veils off and have their eyes wide open. Pray:
We open our eyes wide to see you. Help us to open our lives wide to let your Spirit in.
Amen.

A sending out prayer

Lord, we thank you for our time of worship: for our fellowship, for the opportunity to listen to your word, and to one another. Help us to take what we have learned about you today, and to use it to your glory in the coming week.
Amen.

Year A EASTER 4

Acts 2.42–47; Psalm 23; 1 Peter 2.19–25;
John 10.1–10 *Jesus said, 'He who enters by the door is the shepherd. The sheep hear his voice … and follow him.'*

Call to worship *based on Psalm 23*

The Lord is my shepherd, I shall not want.
To those who come in need, in the name of Jesus:
Come and worship, for all are welcome here!

He makes me lie down in green pastures, he leads me beside still waters.
To all who come in peace, or with a longing to be still, in the name of Jesus:
Come and worship, for all are welcome here!

Even though I walk through the darkest valley, I will fear no evil. To those who are sad and burdened, in the name of Jesus:
Come and worship, for all are welcome here!

You prepare a table before me in the presence of my enemies. To those who are confident in the strength of God, rejoicing in God's goodness and love, in the name of Jesus:
Come and worship, for all are welcome here!

Come and worship the living God, whose goodness and mercy shall follow us all the days of our lives.
Come and worship the living God, who gathers us to his side, as a shepherd gently gathers in the flock, in the name of Jesus:
Come and worship, for all are welcome here!

A personal prayer for all ages

O good shepherd,
guide my feet with your ways,
hold my heart with your truth,
fill my life with your love.
For your kingdom is for all creation.
Amen.

A prayer of adoration

God, we are your people.
You count each one of us as your own.
You call us brothers and sisters of Christ.
You know us by name and by nature.
Shepherding God,
we worship.

God, we are your people, we know your voice.
The voice that draws us closer,
the voice that sends us out,
the voice that injustice cannot silence,
the voice that sets the prisoner free.
Shepherding God,
we worship you.
Amen.

A prayer of confession

God who is like a good shepherd,
We are your people and we have wandered from your presence.

We have turned our ears from your voice and listened to other voices – the voice of greed, of selfishness, of arrogance and pride.
You have offered us abundance of life, but we have settled for much less.
Forgive us. *(Allow silence for reflection)*

Assurance of pardon

Our God is like a good shepherd,
never giving up on those who are lost,
always ready to welcome the wanderer home.
Hear these words and take them to heart.
You are already forgiven.
Therefore live as one who is forgiven,
in the name of Christ.
Amen.

A prayer of thanksgiving

Grace is God's gift:
we welcome this gift from the giver of life.
A sure foundation:
building on the Word of Life.
A guiding shepherd:
living in hope through the Word of Truth.
Grace is our gift:
to be welcomed and shared, with friend and stranger,
for now and for ever, a hope for the world.
Amen.

A prayer activity with prayers of intercession

Create a 'sheep' pen using chairs. One child is the gatekeeper who must protect the sheep and stop others getting in. Have a supply of balloons that the other children try to throw into the pen. If a balloon does get in, that child becomes the new gatekeeper. Then invite everyone to be silent and to reflect on those who look after them and on the call of Jesus in their own life. Say together:
Jesus, shepherd of the sheep, help us to hear your call and follow you into abundant life.
Pray for those who need protecting in the local community.
Jesus, shepherd of the sheep, help us to hear your call and follow you into abundant life.
Pray for those who need help around the world and for wisdom to know how to help.
Jesus, shepherd of the sheep, help us to hear your call and follow you into abundant life.

A sending out prayer

May God's blessing be with us as we go:
a blessing from the one who calls us together;
a blessing from the one who never deserts us;
a blessing for life, in all times, in all places,
a blessing from our Gracious God.
Amen.

Year A   EASTER 5

Acts 7.55–60; Psalm 31.1–5, 15–16; 1 Peter 2.2–10;
John 14.1–14 *Jesus said, 'I am the Way, the Truth and the Life.'*

Call to worship

O God, you are our rock and our fortress,
for the sake of your name, lead and guide us.
Jesus, our Way, our Truth and our Life,
for the sake of your name, lead and guide us.
Spirit of our God, our inspiration, our comforter,
for the sake of your name, lead and guide us.

A prayer of adoration

O Lord our God, we bless and praise you for the life you lived.
We praise and adore you for the truth you teach.
We praise and adore you for the way you call us to follow.
O Lord our God, we bless and praise you.
Amen.

A prayer of confession

Jesus is the way…
Yet I have gone my own way.
My way is better, less costly, quicker, it doesn't make any hidden demands,
and I know my way is the wrong way.
Lord, forgive me.

Jesus is truth…
Yet I prefer to cobble together my own truth.
My truth always offers me comfortable answers,
and I know my truth is a poor substitute for God's truth.
Lord, forgive me.

Jesus is life…
Fullness of life. Yet I am quite happy with a half-life, without risk, a life turned inwards, that avoids the real depths of love,
and I know my life could be so much more.
Lord, forgive me.

Jesus is the way…
The way of forgiveness, of peace of reconciliation.
Jesus is truth.
You may confidently believe that you are forgiven.
This is a moment of new beginnings.
Jesus is life.
You are called to live as those forgiven.
Alleluia. Thanks be to God.
Amen.

A prayer of intercession *based on 1 Peter 2.2–10*

We pray for the living stones in your world, O God.
Living stones who speak out and face persecution;
who stand up and get beaten down;
who stay with the ones everyone else ignores, with no thought to their own lives.
God, you are our refuge, let us not be put to shame.

We pray for your living stones who work for peace;
whose lives change the world, whose words inspire us.
God, you are our refuge, let us not be put to shame.

We pray for your living stones who are in need at this time; those who are hungry and homeless,
who are lost, alone, sick or bereaved.
Living stones whom we love who come to us for help, and for those who help us.
God, you are our refuge, let us not be put to shame.

Let us hold fast to your promises,
and know your call is true.
Let us be strong.
Let us be built up for you,
that your kingdom may come.
Amen.

A prayer of thanksgiving for all ages

Jesus, thank you for those who show me the way when I am lost: mums, dads, grans and granddads…

Jesus, thank you for those who teach me your way when I get mixed up: family, friends, teachers…

Jesus, thank you for those who give us life:
for farmers who grow our food, doctors who keep us well, for friends who make life fun.

Jesus, thank you for being you and for helping me to be the me you want me to be.
Amen.

A prayer activity

*Make or draw a house. Talk about how fortunate we are to have a place to live on earth, and for the promise of a place in heaven. During the prayer time invite each child to touch the house and to say:
'Thank you, God, for my home, especially…'
The leader who finishes the prayers can also thank Jesus for preparing a big house in heaven for everybody who loves him.*

A sending out prayer

May the God who blesses all
who travel the way of faith,
bless us on our way.
May the God who blesses all
who thirst for truth and justice,
bless us with an insatiable thirst for the truth.
May the God who longs for us
to enjoy life in all its fullness,
bless us with a child-like delight in life in all its wonder.
Amen.

Year A   EASTER 6

Acts 17.22–31; Psalm 66.8–20; 1 Peter 3.13–22;
John 14.15–21 *Jesus said, 'I will ask the Father and he will give you another to be your advocate … the Spirit.'*

Call to worship

Jesus says, 'I will not leave you orphaned.'
God our mother, father, sister, brother and friend is here among us.
Let us worship the one who loves us, who nurtures us.
Let us worship the one who challenges us, who calls us out of loneliness into community.
Let us worship our God.

A prayer of thanksgiving and confession

'If you love me you will obey my commands.'
Lord Jesus, we love you, and want to love you more.
Yet we acknowledge that we have not obeyed you and have made mistakes.
Help us to begin again.

'I will ask the Father, and he will give you the Advocate.'
We thank you, loving God, that you have not left us alone, but have given us your Spirit.
But we acknowledge that we have been deaf to the Spirit's counsel.
Help us to begin again.

'You know him, because he abides with you, and he will be in you.'
We thank you for opening up a new relationship through your Son and that through your Spirit you live in us.
Yet we acknowledge that we have wanted to shut you out when your truths are inconvenient.
Help us to begin again.

'Because I live, you also will live.'
We bless and thank you, loving God, that in spite of our mistakes, negligence and disobedience, your love is so vast, so generous; that because you live, we live too, forgiven, loved and free.
We thank you for your love.
As you live in us, so help us to live in you,
to the Father's glory.
Amen.

A prayer of intercession *based on 1 Peter 3.13–22 and Acts 17.22–31*

Gracious God, who holds all creation.
We hold before you now in prayer, our world,
in fear and turmoil; our hungry, war-torn, unfair world.
In you we live and move and have our being.
We hold up our world in need.

We hold before you our country, for all those in the news…
In you we live and move and have our being.
We hold up our world in need.

We hold before you those whom we want to pray for this day,
the ones we love, the names you know, the people known to us in our hearts…
In you we live and move and have our being.
We hold up our world in need.

We hold before you the worldwide church,
her needs, and the needs of the fellowship in this place…
In you we live and move and have our being.
We hold up our world in need.

Gracious God, who holds all creation,
hold now our prayers.
Teach us to have hope in you that we might not despair, but share your love and grace with all creation.
In the name of Jesus our loving Saviour we pray.
Amen.

A prayer for all ages

Sometimes we find ourselves on our own and are frightened. *(Stand alone)*
But our families can make us feel safe. *(Stand in small groups)*
Sometimes we feel sad, lonely, left out. *(Stand alone)*
But our friends cheer us up. *(Stand in small groups)*
Sometimes, we feel our friends and family have left us. *(Stand alone)*
But God is with us always and we are never alone.
(Move into one big group)
All shout:
Amen.

A prayer activity

Fill a large jar with water and add some glitter. Swirl it round and place it on a tray with four tealights around it. Ask everyone to watch the swirling stop and the glitter settle. Say:
God as Spirit can be busy, swirly and beautiful, and also still, just like in us.
Then pray together:
Spirit of truth, stay with us.
We want you, we need you.
Today and every day, stay with us.
Amen.

A sending out blessing

Jesus said, 'I will not leave you orphaned:
I am coming to you.'
Even so, come, Lord Jesus.
Come, Lord Jesus, and bless us with the Father's love. Bless us with the Spirit's inspiration and bless us with your presence.
Come, Lord Jesus.
Alleluia! Alleluia! Alleluia!
Amen.

Year A   EASTER 7

Acts 1.6–14; Psalm 68.1–10, 32–35; 1 Peter 4.12–14, 5.6–11; **John 17.1–11** *Jesus said, 'Father, the hour has come. Glorify your Son that the Son may glorify you.'*

Call to worship *using Psalm 68*

Sing to God, sing praises to his name and be glad in his presence:
lift up a song to him who rides upon the clouds.

Sing to God, bring your whole life before him, because he cares for you:
lift up a song to him who rides upon the clouds.

Sing to God, the companion of the lonely, the strength of the weak, the light of our darkness:
lift up a song to him who rides upon the clouds.

A prayer of confession

Loving God, we humble ourselves before you. We are not worthy even to call upon your name, but we know that you are merciful in judgement.
Forgive us our false pretences, our prejudices and our disregard for the world you created and for the people you give us to love and respect. Turn us away from the sins we have committed. Amend what we are and help us to walk with you.
In Christ's name we pray.
Amen.

A prayer of intercession

Jesus, you sought to alleviate pain and suffering. You challenged oppressive powers and questioned beliefs about God.

Help us to be with those who struggle physically or mentally.
To offer support to the weary.
To notice those who are quietly suffering…
Help us to release love and mercy into people's lives.

Help us to challenge the structures that keep people chained to poverty, that create suffering and harm and unfair trading rules…
Help us to release love and mercy into the world.

Help us to be sensitive in disagreements about Christian faith.
To listen to one another with humility and to be able to live in creative tension…
Help us to release love and mercy into the church.

Help us to follow faithfully in your footsteps and to work with you to build God's kingdom.
Amen.

A prayer for all ages

Dear Jesus,
When we are tempted to do the wrong thing,
protect us and help us.

When friends laugh at us for coming to church,
protect us and help us.

When we can't find the words to tell others about you,
protect us and help us.

When we don't understand your words in our Bible,
protect us and help us.

When we are not sure what you want us to do,
protect us and help us.
Amen.

A prayer of thanksgiving

Father God,
we give you thanks that you empowered your Son and that your glory was revealed on earth through him.

Christ Jesus,
we accept with gratitude the mission you have passed on to us and as a sign of our faith, we are honoured to be called 'Christian'.

Spirit of Truth,
we are part of a community of faith that transcends time and space.
Make us one in our belief – a unity grounded in heavenly glory.
Amen.

A prayer activity

Talk about worries and how they can feel like a heavy weight we carry. Give out cloud-shaped cards and invite people to write down, anonymously, anything they are worried about. Collect the cards in a bag. Pass it around and invite each person to select a card and read it out. After each worry, pray together:
Jesus, please restore, support, strengthen and establish us with you.
Amen.

A sending out prayer

Send us out, O God,
to travel towards Pentecost.
Waiting for your Spirit, we look for signs of your life.
Restore, support, strengthen and establish us,
this week and in the weeks to come.
Amen.

Year A   PENTECOST

Acts 2.1–21, or Numbers 11.24–30; Psalm 104.24–34, 35b; 1 Corinthians 12.3b–13, or Acts 2.1–21; John 7.37–39, or **John 20.19–23** *Jesus breathed on them saying, 'Receive the Holy Spirit.'*

Call to worship

The spirit of the Lord is with you:
and also with you.

Strengthening God, send forth your Spirit upon us:
may your breath give us life.

Welcoming God, send forth your Spirit upon us:
may we be one with you and with each other.

Challenging God, send forth your Spirit upon us:
may we break down the barriers that divide us.

Healing God, send forth your Spirit upon us:
may we use our gifts to heal this broken world.

Loving God, send forth your Spirit upon us:
may we sing your love for ever.

An active prayer of confession

As music is played, invite people to use water-soluble, non-permanent pens to write their confessions on small strips of OHP acetate or similar. Then invite them to dip the film into a bowl of water, with washing-up liquid added, or in water in the baptismal font if your church has one, symbolically washing away sins.

A reflective prayer *based on Acts 2.1–21*

Speak to us through the tongues of Pentecost.
Stir our longings with the excitement of Pentecost.
Unite our communities with the inclusiveness of Pentecost.
Bless our nations with the surprise of Pentecost.
Until our lives overflow with the gifts and the grace of your Spirit, and we serve one another and you in your strength and to your glory.
Amen.

A personal prayer *based on Acts 2.1–21*

Ignite our prayers with the life-giving fire of Pentecost.
That we may not fear our inadequacy,
our hesitancy, our doubt.
But bring before you all that we are, all that we have been, all that we can be.
Believing that we can never aim high enough,
and never conceive anything complete enough,
to prepare us for all you would bless us with,
individually,
as communities, as nations,
if we would but gather together and wait for you afresh.
Amen.

A prayer of intercession

As we seek to share your word:
come, Spirit of God, empower us.

As we care for those in need
and try to show your love:
come, Spirit of God, empower us.

As we treasure every gift:
come, Spirit of God, empower us.

As we challenge injustice and wrong:
come, Spirit of God, empower us.

To all your people, those in authority,
and those who feel insignificant:
come, Spirit of God, empower us.
Amen.

A prayer for all ages

One finger pointing upwards
Come Holy Spirit, make us one.
Join hands

One finger pointing upwards
Come Holy Spirit, give us your gifts.
Open hands to receive

One finger pointing upwards
Come Holy Spirit, hear our prayers.
Put hands together

One finger pointing upwards
Come Holy Spirit, now and for ever.
Roll hands over each other
Amen.

A prayer activity *based on Acts 2.1–21*

Bring in a range of empty boxes. Stick a label on each one and invite the children to write on them things that create boundaries between people in the world and in the church. Build the boxes into a wall. From today's reading, talk about how the power of love can blow away barriers we create. Knock down the wall of boxes in a symbolic gesture. Then pray together:
Fill us with your Spirit, Lord.
Please, God, make us brave.
Let us show the power of your love.
Amen.

A sending out prayer

Loving God, as you have poured out your Spirit, may those through whom it flows make our world, our neighbourhood, and our church better places for all to grow, develop and reach their potential.
Amen.

Year A   TRINITY SUNDAY

Genesis 1.1–2.4a; Psalm 8; 2 Corinthians 13.11–13;
Matthew 28.16–20 *Jesus said, 'Go to all nations and
make them my disciples: baptize them in the name of
the Father, and the Son and the Holy Spirit.'*

A prayer of approach

God of the Holy Trinity, three in one, one in three,
ever present mystery, be present in our midst
as we offer you our worship, our wonder and our
praise.
Amen.

A prayer of intercession

God, three in one and one in three,
we pray for your church,
for leaders, learners and workers…
Weave us together:
to strengthen our witness.

We pray for all leaders,
of communities, nations, in cities, in hamlets,
those who elect and those elected…
Unite us together:
to strengthen our solidarity.

We pray for our own community,
for those we know, for those who are strangers,
for the young and energetic, for the old and wise…
Bring us together:
to serve one another.

We pray for the suffering, the sick,
for the homeless and alienated,
for those seeking a living far from home, for those
who are afraid…
We pray together:
may they know your love.

Great God, the Holy Trinity,
three in one and one in three,
to your strength, your love, your insight,
we offer our prayers.
Amen.

A blessing for Trinity Sunday

You are the breath of this summer morn.
You are this day newly born.
You are our hope and our delight.
You are our joy, our strength, our light.
The Holy Three be over you and over me
The blessing of the Trinity.

God be with us through this day.
God be in the words we say.
God be in the bread we share.
God be in our deepest prayer.
The Holy Three be over you and over me
The blessing of the Trinity.

To each of us give grace to grow.
On each of us your love bestow.
Inspire our lives, set longings free.
Be with us now, O Holy Three.
The Holy Three be over you and over me
The blessing of the Trinity.

A prayer for all ages

May this Trinity Sunday be an opportunity to rest and
reflect on the interconnectedness of all creation.
And may it be the day we pledge to honour it for love
of you.
Amen.

A prayer of thanksgiving

Holy and undivided Trinity, one God,
we give you thanks and praise,
for a world full of wonder,
for all you have made good and for our lives in your
service.
We give you thanks and praise.

We give you thanks and praise,
for the communities of faith we form together,
bearing witness to your eternal Trinity of love.
We give you thanks and praise.

We give you thanks and praise,
for your love revealed in our frailty,
for your faithfulness in calling us back again and
again to your open heart.
We give you thanks and praise.

We give you thanks and praise,
for your love without limit, constantly poured out.
We give you thanks and praise.
Amen.

A prayer activity

*Children make a bracelet, anklet, or necklace, to
represent the Father, Son and Spirit, by twisting or
plaiting three coloured threads or ribbons together,
or by threading three different shaped or coloured
beads. Then pray:*
May the love of our good Father keep you safe.
May the friendship of Jesus his Son give you
courage.
And may the joy of the Holy Spirit live within you as
you go out in God's name.
Amen.

A sending out prayer

In the name of the Father:
let us love the world like parents.
In the name of the Son:
let us serve the world with justice.
In the name of the Spirit:
let us share our world with all people.
Amen.

Year A   PROPER 4

Deuteronomy 11.18–21, 26–28; Psalm 31.1–5, 19–24; Romans 1.16–17, 3.22b–28 (29–31); **Matthew 7.21–29** *Jesus said, 'Whoever hears these words of mine and acts on them, is like one who builds their house on rock.'*

Call to worship *based on Psalm 31*

Be for me a rock, O Lord,
a rock on which to build,
a rock where I may hide.
Be for me a rock, O Lord,
to save me from the storm,
on which to ground my faith.
Be for me a rock, O Lord,
in which to find your gold.
Blessed are you, O Lord,
our rock and our salvation,
for you give courage and hope
to all who wait on you.

A prayer of petition

Lord, sand is so much more convenient to work with:
we can mould it to our own design,
and make beautiful patterns which give us delight.
But it doesn't stand up to the storms of life,
and anything we construct with it is liable to collapse.
Help us to be willing to work with the rock of your faithfulness, which gives us something to cling on to when life gets rough.
It's not so comfortable to rest on – but comfort is not about cosiness –
at the heart of the word is strength.
Lord, help us always to make you the bedrock of our lives.
Amen.

A prayer of confession

Lord, forgive us when we seek comfort in the familiar:
the easy words, the regular patterns.
Forgive us when we get annoyed by even small changes that upset our routines.
How can you transform our lives when we are so attached to what we have created for ourselves?
Lead us to seek the gifts of your Spirit – Faith, Hope and Love – knowing that it is on these things alone that we can truly rely.
Amen.

A prayer of intercession

God, our rock, bless your Church,
that it may be built on the sure foundation of your word. May your people be so deeply rooted in the promise of your love that they may be good news for a broken world.
God of justice,
hear our prayer.

God, our rock, bless your world with the gifts of justice and of peace.
Hear the cry of the poor;
humble the rich and the powerful;
bind up the wounds of those whose lives are scarred by famine, disease and war.
God of justice,
hear our prayer.

God, our rock, bless this community, gathered in your name. Help us to dig deep foundations for our life in you, and be a blessing for those among whom we live.
Make us attentive to the ways you speak to us, especially in the voices and the lives of unexpected people, and help us to make better connections between our worship and our lives.
God of justice,
hear our prayer.
Amen.

A prayer activity

As each line of the prayer is said, place one fist on top of the other:
Help us, Lord, to build our lives on you.
Help us to build up our faith.
Help us to build up our friendships.
Help us to build up our families.
Help us to build up our community.
Help us, Lord, to build our lives on you.
Amen.

A prayer for all ages

In times of happiness and excitement
help us to stand firm, Lord Jesus.
In times of sadness, and uncertainty
help us to stand firm, Lord Jesus.
When there is growth and fruitfulness
help us to stand firm, Lord Jesus.
When there are storms and wilderness
help us to stand firm, Lord Jesus.
In the busyness and in the stillness
help us to stand firm, Lord Jesus.
In public, and alone with you
help us to stand firm, Lord Jesus.
Amen.

A sending out prayer

God who is our strength and refuge,
the rock of our salvation,
build us up on the firm foundation
of the word made flesh,
who calls us into life,
and fills us with his blessing.
Amen.

Year A   PROPER 5

Sunday between June 5 and June 11 inclusive (if after Trinity Sunday)

Hosea 5.15–6.6; Psalm 50.7–15; Romans 4.13–25;
Matthew 9.9–13, 18–26 *Jesus said, 'I did not come
to call the virtuous but sinners.'*

Call to worship

God, lover of the lost and healer of the broken,
you reconcile those divided by sin and you call the
outcast to be a guest at the banquet of salvation.
Be with us here in this place today,
teaching us mercy and love.
Help us to praise, love and serve you
in our worship and in our lives,
through Jesus Christ our Lord.

A prayer of confession

Lord, the words of Scripture remind us that you
were often angry. We get angry too and take out
our frustrations on others. Teach us that your anger
comes out of love and not hate. You never reject
those you correct but instead you heal and cleanse.
Turn our hearts back to love so that we may lay aside
our anger and learn to honour those who annoy
us. Even in the most difficult of moments may we
find your calm and mercy so that we can ask for
forgiveness and start anew.
Amen.

A prayer of intercession

Pour your compassion, Almighty Father,
on *(Name the person or people)*, and all those whom
we know who are ill.
Each one is precious to you and each one carries a
special burden of doubt, pain, frustration and inner
loneliness.
Give the strength that will take them one more step
on their journey.
May they receive the attention and the skills of
the professionals and be spared the delays and
uncertainties that all health care brings.
Most of all, we pray that they will be accompanied
by people who really understand their needs
and who are willing to share the sympathy
that makes everything possible,
through Jesus Christ our Lord.
Amen.

A prayer for all ages

For those of us, like Matthew,
lost in the world, wandering away,
help us to hear your voice
calling out once more, 'Follow me.'
Give us the courage to change
and the knowledge of your grace to help us.
For those of us, like Jairus,
trying to follow, but weighed down with anxiety or
grief, help us to trust in you knowing that your will is
perfect.
Give us the faithfulness to hold on
and the knowledge of your grace to help us.

For those of us, like the woman,
lost in the crowd, going unnoticed,
locked in our private world of pain,
help us to seek your face and see once again the
Father's love.
Give us the strength to ask
and the knowledge of your grace to help us.
For each and every one,
for the public face and the private life,
help us to seek you, trust you, hear you
and to encourage one another.
Show us all the next steps in our journey with you
and the knowledge of your grace to help us to take
them.
Amen.

A responsorial prayer of petition

For those who disagree with me,
For those whom I find it difficult to love,
For those who are rejected and placed on the
margins of society,
I desire mercy not sacrifice.
For those who are worlds apart from me,
For those who have contrary ideas and lifestyles,
For those whom I would disregard,
I desire mercy not sacrifice.
For those who are my enemies,
For those whose values are different from mine,
For those who most annoy me,
I desire mercy not sacrifice.
For myself,
I desire mercy not sacrifice.
Amen.

A prayer activity

*Gather around the 'party' table. Add an uncut loaf.
On place cards invite everyone to write their name
and the name of a person Jesus would want at his
party. Place these on the table. Say something like:*
Jesus accepted invitations to eat with different people
as a sign of his friendship and acceptance. We break
and share this bread in friendship with Jesus, each
other and those on the margins of society.
*Pass the bread around, inviting each person to break
off a small piece and give it to the next person.*

A sending out prayer

Redeeming Lord,
You have fed us at the table of your word,
and called us to be your people once again.
Send us out now as bearers of your healing word,
to live, to serve and to praise,
through Jesus Christ our Lord.
Amen.

Year A   PROPER 6

Sunday between June 12 and June 18 inclusive (if after Trinity Sunday)

Exodus 19.2–8a; Psalm 100; Romans 5.1–8;
Matthew 9.35–10.8 *Jesus said, 'The harvest is plentiful but the labourers are few.'*

Call to worship

Voice 1: Come, people of the Lord, and gather together in prayer.
Voice 2: Come, people of the Lord, and listen to God's word.
Voice 1: Come, people of the Lord, and be open to God's presence.
Voice 2: Come, people of the Lord, and praise God's holy name.
All: Enable our hands, Lord, to gather in your plentiful harvest.
Voice 1: Hear, people of the Lord, the call to be labourers.
Voice 2: Hear, people of the Lord, the needs of the harassed.
Voice 1: Hear, people of the Lord, the needs of the helpless.
Voice 2: Hear, people of the Lord, the needs of the shepherdless.
All: Enable our hands, Lord, to gather in your plentiful harvest.

A prayer of confession

For the times when we have not listened to you,
Lord, we are sorry.
For the times we have let you down,
Lord, we are sorry.
For the times we have not shared our story,
Lord, we are sorry.
For the times you have trusted us,
Lord, we thank you.
For the times you have answered our prayers,
Lord, we thank you.
For the times our lives have been blessed by others,
Lord, we thank you.
Amen.

A prayer of petition

Lord God, you call us to be holy.
But often that word brings negativity.
We don't like people we call 'Holy Joe',
or the 'holier than thou' attitude that diminishes others.
Teach us, holy God, that true holiness is beautiful.
True holiness means being so full of your love
that others are attracted to holiness in their turn.
Give us that as our mission task, Lord,
and give us grace to be faithful in loving as we are loved.
Amen.

A prayer of intercession

Dear Jesus, for those who have never heard of your name or know of your Good News –
we want to spread your word.
Help us to reap your harvest, Lord.

Dear Jesus, for those who are harassed in our society, we want to offer your comfort.
Help us to reap your harvest, Lord.

Dear Jesus, for those whose faith is weak,
we want to encourage renewal.
Help us to reap your harvest, Lord.

Dear Jesus, for all who struggle with change,
we want to assist where transition is needed.
Help us to reap your harvest, Lord.
Amen.

A prayer for all ages

Lord Jesus, you sent the disciples out
without a training course, or a manual.
They were not to take extra clothes, or food,
but to rely on God's provision.
Like the disciples, we feel vulnerable
when we go to do your work, with our hands free, and our mouths empty.
Give us confidence to follow the example set by the disciples.
Lead us to depend completely on God
rather than relying on our own resources.
Make us trusting, courageous and faithful messengers.
Amen.

A prayer activity

Gather around a mosaic or jigsaw that has a piece missing. Look at the design or picture. Ask the group what difference the missing piece would make. Explain that no other stone or piece is the right shape, size or colour; that would be Jesus' team without any one of us. No one else can take on the role we are called to. Allow a minute of silence while each person thinks of one act of care they can do this week.

A sending out prayer

Send us out with nothing to rely on.
No gold or silver, no copper, or bag.
No sandals or coat or staff.
Make us open and vulnerable, give us empty hands and hearts, that uncluttered, we may receive from others.
Expose us to compassion, so that we may be at one with those who are struggling, or stressed,
with those who are burdened or troubled, or pressured, with those who are helpless, or in danger.
Release the healing.
Amen.

Year A   PROPER 7

Sunday between June 19 and June 25 inclusive (if after Trinity Sunday)

Jeremiah 20.7–13; Psalm 69.7–10, (11–15), 16–18; Romans 6.1b–11; **Matthew 10.24–39** *Jesus said, 'Are not two sparrows sold for a penny, yet without my Father's knowledge not one can fall to the ground?'*

Call to worship

Come to worship, you children of the Lord.
Come to hear God's holy word.
Teach us, Lord, to teach others your teaching.
Come to this house, the house of the Lord,
Come and dwell as God's guest.
Teach us, Lord, to teach others your teaching.
Come singing and dancing in praise of the Lord.
Come raise your minds and voices.
Come open your hearts to learn from the Lord,
come open your hearts anew.
Teach us, Lord, to teach others your teaching.
Come to worship, you children of the Lord,
come to hear God's holy word.
Teach us, Lord, to teach others your teaching.

A prayer of confession

The Bible tells us, Lord, that we love because you first loved us; but sometimes our love for you is not as strong as it should be.
There are people, and even things, in our lives that sometimes mean more to us than you.
We know that this is wrong, Lord, and we ask your forgiveness.
Give us the will and the strength to put your purposes before our own interests.
Amen.

A prayer of thanksgiving

Thank you for today.
Lead us into tomorrow.
Praise you for your love.
Spill our love widely.
Bless you for forgiveness.
Bend us to forgive.
Glory to you for being here.
Take us where you go.
For your sake.
Amen.

A prayer of intercession

'Do not think I have come to bring peace to the earth; I have not come to bring peace, but a sword.'

Lord, we find these difficult words to use in the same sentence as 'good news' and yet they are part of it. They make us think, Lord, of our fellow Christians around the world having to make that choice between prayerful and grace-filled non-action, and of fighting back in some way against tyranny, oppression, violence and bullying.

And so, Lord, we pray for Christians everywhere.
We pray for those who make difficult decisions in dealing with people who oppose their faith…

We pray for those who are imprisoned for their public expression of faith.

We pray for those who are left isolated and alone, rejected by their families for their Christian beliefs.

We pray for those who are too afraid to acknowledge that they may be encouraged by God's word today.

We pray for those who serve in the armed forces.

We gather all our prayers as we ask for the guidance of the Holy Spirit in living with the sword that our Lord sometimes brings.
Amen.

A prayer for grace for all ages

We face a world that is sometimes hostile.
Grace us with courage, Lord.
We face a world that can be very superficial.
Grace us with depth, Lord.
We face a world that is full of greed and envy.
Grace us with simplicity and humility, Lord.
We face a world that can be silent about you.
Grace us with wise words, Lord.
Help us to remember, Lord, the strength and power of your fullness, Father, Son and Holy Spirit, and to ask for all the grace we need, day by day.
Amen.

A prayer activity

Draw, write or use symbols on sparrow-shaped cards, to symbolize people that the children want to pray for. When they are ready, invite the children to place the birds in a round basket that has been lined with crumpled newspaper to look like a bird's nest. When all the birds have been placed into the nest, say a prayer for all the people thought of or mentioned.

A sending out prayer

Leave, now, with holes in your heart,
that your love for others may spill out easily.
May God give you sores on your feet,
that you may feel the pain of those who have no rest.
Let your hands be calloused and pierced,
that your blood may mingle with that of those you greet,
just as Christ mingled his life with ours.
And may the Spirit of God blind you to yourself,
and pull your soul free.
Amen.

Year A   PROPER 8

Sunday between June 26 and July 2 inclusive

Jeremiah 28.5–9; Psalm 89.1–4, 15–18; Romans 6.12–23; **Matthew 10.40–42** *Jesus said, 'To receive me is to receive the One who sent me.'*

Call to worship

We welcome you in the name of Christ, and we welcome Christ who has come in you.
In your faces we see his face.
In your voices we hear his voice.
In your touch we feel his touch.
In our gathering we feel his presence.
Come let us worship Christ, who walks among us!

A prayer of approach

Generous God, we come to this place of worship and hope to be welcomed.
We come to this time of worship and hope to welcome you.
Come among us and open our hearts and minds this day, so that we are ready to receive a word from you, and ready to receive all whom you love and welcome.
For in doing so we gain a reward more valuable than any this world can offer: the reward of better knowing you and our fellow human beings.
Amen.

A prayer of confession for all ages

Invite the young people to sit in such a way as to make it impossible for anyone to join them. Pray:
For the times we have not welcomed others.
Lord, we are sorry.
For the times we have not welcomed you.
Lord, we are sorry.

Invite the group to move positions so that they are welcoming to others and pray:
At the times we can welcome others.
Lord, make us open.
At the times we can welcome you.
Lord, make us open.
Amen.

A prayer of thanksgiving

Dear God,
Thank you for all the times
people make us really welcome,
in all sorts of places.
Please help us to welcome people,
even those we don't like.
Thank you that you see
every kind thing we do,
big or small,
even the secret ones.
Amen.

A prayer of intercession

Use a congregational response that is familiar to your congregation:
We pray for those in power,
may they be hospitable to those who need support and help,
as well as to those who will pay and flatter them.

We pray for the Church,
that it may be hospitable to its critics,
to people of other faiths and traditions,
to those who express doubt.

We pray for ourselves,
that we may be hospitable neighbours.

We pray for those who care for the weak,
that they will be hospitable
whatever the needs that confront them.

We pray for the marginalized,
that they will encounter hospitality,
that the world will become a hospitable place
where they are noticed.
Amen.

A prayer of petition

Your prophets, O Lord, do not always come to church,
yet they can be known by the way they express the truth that reflects you.
Open our minds to hear your prophecy, however it is communicated.
Open our hearts to welcome your truth even if it makes us uncomfortable.
Help us, Lord, not to be blind or deaf to any who carry your message in a new way for our world today.
Amen.

A prayer activity

Ask the children for imaginative ideas for what they would do if Jesus was coming to visit. Then incorporate them into the following prayer:
If you came to visit, Lord,
I would roll out the red carpet,
I would bake a cake,
I would break open a bottle of champagne,
I would raise a flag.
Add other suggestions
Nothing would be too much trouble.
Help me to welcome, in the same spirit of joyful enthusiasm and exuberant support
all those called by you and sent to do your work.
Amen.

A sending out prayer

Whoever gives even a cup of water to one of these little ones will not lose their reward. Go in faith and love to serve the world God loves.
Amen.

Year A   PROPER 9

Sunday between July 3 and July 9 inclusive

Zechariah 9.9–12; Psalm 145.8–14; Romans 7.15–25a; **Matthew 11.16–19, 25–30** *Jesus said, 'Come to me all who are weary and whose burden is heavy and I will give you rest.'*

Call to worship

Almighty God, we gather in your name and bring ourselves before you:
your burden is light.

When we are heavy of heart, and the pressures of life push us down, we bring ourselves before you.
When we are in need of rest, tired from the activities of the past week, we bring ourselves before you:
your burden is light.

Jesus, gentle, humble Lord,
we leave behind that which holds us back,
and devote ourselves to celebrating the wonder of your love, Father, Son and Holy Spirit.

A prayer of confession

Almighty God, when we do not understand why we do the things we do.
When we speak out of spite and not in love.
When we act out of anger and not in mercy,
forgive us.
In Christ there is freedom:
set us free.

When pride overcomes humility.
When jealousy is more important than generosity,
forgive us.
In Christ there is freedom:
set us free.

Lord, by your Spirit forgive us our sins and transform us by the perfect law of freedom.
Amen.

A prayer of intercession

From the community of faith, in the strength we give each other in Christ, we pray for those who have no community or sense of belonging.

We pray for those who carry burdens,
lives disturbed by the past, by guilt.

For those whose burden is responsibility,
those in government and positions of power.
For all those lost in the complexity of modern living.
Lord of all life and experience, touch the lives of those for whom we have prayed and in the unity of Jesus build your kingdom.
Amen.

A prayer of thanksgiving *based on Psalm 145*

Holy God,
Thank you for your righteous rule in our lives.
That mercy triumphs over judgement.
That compassion overcomes anger.
That those who fall are lifted up.
Use us as instruments of your gracious power, that the hungry may be fed and all eyes turn towards you.
Amen.

A prayer for all ages

Loving Jesus,
Your invitation here sounds so good.
Can we really come to you for rest?
Can we really trust you with our burdens?
Can we trust you with our sinfulness, our worries, our broken relationships, our responsibilities and our disappointments?
Can we live so closely with you that instead we share your burdens and your concerns for the world?
And discover that they are light
because we share them with you.
It sounds like a wonderful way to live:
lost in your purposes and freed from our own.
Loving Jesus, please show us how to do it.
Amen.

A prayer activity

Someone stands up weighed down with many burdens: a rucksack could represent worries we carry; a clock, our time; a mobile phone, things we buy; a luxury food item, the food we don't need. As each concern is mentioned, the item is taken from the bag and laid on a table. Finally a small cross can be picked up to represent the light burden of Christ taken at the end of the prayer:
Life can get so heavy, so many worries to carry.
Gentle Lord, **lighten us.**
Work and school can be hard: do we have enough time? Gentle Lord, **lighten us.**
So many things to buy, do we really need them all? Gentle Lord, **lighten us.**
So much food to eat, are we ever that hungry? Gentle Lord, **lighten us.**
Jesus, you carried the cross, yet you lighten us with joy and peace. Gentle Lord, **lighten us.**
Amen.

A sending out prayer *based on Psalm 145*

Go and tell:
God is gracious and merciful and full of love.
Go and live:
God's compassion embraces us all.
Go and give thanks:
God is faithful and blesses us.
Amen.

Year A PROPER 10

Sunday between July 10 and July 16 inclusive

Isaiah 55.10–13; Psalm 65.(1–8), 9–13; Romans 8.1–11; **Matthew 13.1–9, 18–23** *Jesus said, 'The seed sown on good soil is the person who hears the word and understands it.'*

Call to worship

Loving Creator, as we come to worship you,
we offer you our whole lives:
Lord, soften the soil of our hearts.
May the words we hear and the words we speak take root, and change the way we are.
Lord, soften the soil of our hearts.
May we worship you not only with our minds and mouths but in everything we do.
Lord, soften the soil of our hearts.

A prayer of confession

O Word of life, made flesh in Jesus Christ,
we confess our failure to receive, and to live the word.
O Word of life, generously sown in human experience,
we confess when our lives have been like the pathway, the rocky place or the thorns, and your word has found scant response from us.
O Word of life, given in love to change the world,
we confess that even when your word is rooted in us, we have not flourished or brought in the harvest that we could.
O Word of life, forgiving and renewing,
forgive us, and set us free from the past,
that we may go forward in the light of your word.
Amen.

A prayer of intercession

Let us pray to God that we may welcome his word and respond to his call.
We pray for those who spread the Word of God in our world,
for church leaders, evangelists and teachers,
that they may sow the good news with energy and joy.
Lord of the harvest,
hear our prayer.

We pray for all Christian communities,
and especially for the people of God gathered in this place,
that we may not let the cares of the world choke the Word of God in us.
Lord of the harvest,
hear our prayer.

We pray for those who have not yet seen and understood the Word of God,
that they may be enlightened and recognize God's power in their lives.
Lord of the harvest,
hear our prayer.

We pray for those who have remained deaf to the Word of God,
that they may begin to hear and comprehend the Word of Life in all its fullness.
Lord of the harvest,
hear our prayer.

We pray for the sick, the sad and the suffering,
for doctors, nurses and for all who work for healing,
that God's strength and power may be with them.
Lord of the harvest,
hear our prayer.
Amen.

A prayer for all ages

God helps us grow!
(Crouch down) We all start small – you can hardly see us at all!
But God helps us grow!
Thank you, God, for helping us grow.
(Kneel) As you can figure – soon we get bigger!
God helps us grow!
Thank you, God, for helping us grow.
(Stand) Then it is known, that we are full grown!
God helps us grow!
Thank you, God, for helping us grow.
Thank you, God, that you help us grow,
both in our bodies and in knowing you.
Thank you that however big we get, there is still more we can learn about you.
Amen.

A prayer of faith

Sowing God, grow our faith, embrace us in your vision, to see growth when all is bare, to make your kingdom come.
Working God, silent and hidden, yet growing, alive and active, your miracles of grace confound us.
Generous God, giving abundantly more than we can know or ask, our promise is to justly share ourselves in celebration of your word.
Amen.

A prayer activity

Prepare a large tub of soil, and give everyone a drinking straw/garden cane and a cut-out paper flower. Invite them to write prayers on the flowers, e.g. thanking God for people/situations that have helped them grow. Then stick the flowers to the canes/straws, and plant their prayers in the soil.

A sending out prayer

Thank you, Lord, for all your gifts
and especially for the seed of your word planted in our hearts.
May we take your message of love and use it to bear good fruit in our lives,
serving others for your name's sake.
Amen.

Year A   PROPER 11

Wisdom of Solomon 12.13, 16–19, or Isaiah 44.6–8;
Psalm 86.11–17; Romans 8.12–25;
Matthew 13.24–30, 36–43 *Jesus said, 'Let the wheat and the weeds grow together until harvest.'*

Call to worship

The good and the bad grow together.
The strong and the weak worship together.
We are your complex people.
Accept our worship in Jesus' name.

A prayer of confession

Almighty God, we are your harvest.
As we stand before you we give thanks for the fruit of our lives, we also remember where we have fallen short of the ideals of your kingdom,
where weeds have grown up among the good you have planted in us.

Where we have spoken without thinking, causing hurt to others. Where our hearts have turned to malice and jealousy:
Father, forgive us.
Where things have been more important to us than people:
Father, forgive us.
Where we have neglected you for the sake of the busyness of our lives:
Father, forgive us.

Lord of the harvest, forgive us where we have fallen short. Tend us gently, that we may learn to imitate your Son, our Saviour, Jesus Christ.
Amen.

A prayer of thanksgiving

We thank you, loving God, for giving your Son, Jesus Christ and for making us your own. Help us to live as your children, treating as your family all those whom we meet. Keep us faithful to your gospel and help us to serve our neighbour as ourselves, now and always.
Amen.

A prayer of intercession

We pray for farmers throughout the world, for all who work in field and farm,
especially those whose labour is great
and whose reward is small.

We pray for those who till the ground
to produce our tea, coffee, and other foods and fruits.
Your rule is theirs, Lord.

We pray for those who are working towards a fairer world, where people are not burdened by debt, disease, or poverty.
Your rule is theirs, Lord.

We pray for those who are victims of oppression, injustice, poverty or war, for those who feel hopeless, helpless, or forgotten.
Your rule is theirs, Lord.
Amen.

A prayer for all ages

Dear God, maker of the world,
creator of all that is good in our lives,
**help us to grow in strength and goodness
like healthy wheat.**

Dear Lord Jesus, Saviour of the world,
giver of all that is good in our lives,
**help us to grow in strength and goodness
like healthy wheat.**

Dear Holy Spirit, breath of God in the world,
sustainer of all that is good in our lives,
**help us to grow in strength and goodness
like healthy wheat.**
Amen.

A prayer activity

Invite the children to write prayers on slips of paper for themselves or for others who face difficult situations. Give each child a balloon with a string and ask them to stick the prayer to the string with tape. Allow some time for playing with the balloons, then pray:
Lord Jesus, thank you that you are with us when things get tough. Thank you that you help us to deal with difficult situations, and that we can trust you to keep us safe.
We pray now for all the people and situations we have written about.
Amen.
Afterwards, the children take the prayer from the balloon nearest them and pray it. They could take the balloons home to help them remember to pray during the week.

A sending out prayer

May our lives yield a rich harvest through our good works for others and may we learn to live with our weeds and those of others and leave the act of judging to you alone.
Amen.

Year A   PROPER 12

Sunday between July 24 and July 30 inclusive

1 Kings 3.5–12; Psalm 119.129–136; Romans 8.26–39; **Matthew 13.31–33, 44–52** *Jesus said, 'The Kingdom of Heaven is like this…'*

Call to worship

Lord, our God and our king,
you show your love to those of faithful heart.
May we be citizens in your kingdom of love.
Give to us an understanding mind:
that we may recognize your kingdom.
Lead us to a disciplined life:
that all we do will be for your kingdom.
May we be able to separate right from wrong
and live at peace in your kingdom.
So we come before you now,
to worship you in body, mind and spirit,
bought at great cost:
your kingdom people.

A prayer of confession

Lord Jesus, you have won for us the treasure of life and you bring us the treasure of the Father's love. Forgive our ingratitude when our hearts are fixed on ourselves and not on the kingdom of heaven.
Lord, in your mercy, **hear our prayer.**

In the family of your Church you give us the treasure of your presence and strength; forgive our apathy when we fail to spend time with you.
Lord, in your mercy, **hear our prayer, forgive our sins and lead us into everlasting life.**
Amen.

A prayer of intercession

Lord, we pray for those involved in the highly competitive race of life; for those who give their time and energy to your kingdom:
that you may bless their efforts and reward their faithfulness.

For those who offer a support network for others, who pray for and encourage those able to take a more active role:
that you may bless their efforts and reward their faithfulness.

For all new disciples who are full of energy; for all who yearn to take everyone into the kingdom:
that you may bless their efforts and reward their faithfulness.

For those who strive to do your will but fall back, the challenge too great, the cost too high:
that you may bless their efforts and reward their faithfulness.

And for ourselves, that we may win the prize that Jesus has bought for us at great cost,
and take our place with him as we cross the final line.
Amen.

A prayer for all ages

God of the tiny baby and the oldest pensioner,
help us to seek your kingdom together.
God of ancient stories and of new life,
help us to seek your kingdom together.
God of the Olympic gold winner and the last across the line,
help us to seek your kingdom together.
God of who we are and who we can be,
help us to seek your kingdom together.
In times of struggle and times of celebration,
help us to seek your kingdom together.
Amen.

A prayer of petition

O God, you are the seed planter, fish netter, bread baker and pearl hunter. Make us living parables, that we may become creative and life-giving stewards of the world you have entrusted to our care.
Amen.

A prayer activity

Prepare a container with compost and have some seeds ready. Invite the group to reflect on where signs of the kingdom may be visible in their lives. Give each person a seed to hold and say:
The seed you hold has within it all it needs to reproduce its own kind. Plant the seed in some soil. As you do, feel the moist texture of the earth. Think of the darkness the seed goes into before it can spring to life. On the brink of creation there is darkness. As you plant the seed you are participating in one of the greatest mysteries of the cosmos. You are co-creating with God. Together you give birth to life. As the seed grows and flowers, remember it as a symbol of your love and of your care of nature, creation, the planet and home.

A sending out prayer

Go in peace,
live the kingdom,
share its treasures,
keep the faith.
And now may God the Father bless you,
God the Son inspire you,
and God the Holy Spirit enlighten you,
today and always.
Amen.

Year A   PROPER 13

Sunday between July 31 and August 6 inclusive

Isaiah 55.1–5; Psalm 145.8–9, 14–21; Romans 9.1–5; **Matthew 14.13–21** *They all ate and were satisfied.*

Call to worship

If you are hungry, come to feast on the bread of life.
If you are thirsty, come to drink the water of life.
If you are weary, come to enjoy God's refreshing grace.
Come to enjoy the feast that God provides.

A prayer of confession

Extravagant God, forgive us when we do not value the riches of your gospel.
When we cling tightly to what we have and do not share it with others.
Forgive us when we are anxious and afraid and do not trust you to meet our needs.
Faithful God, forgive us, that in joy we may take risks for your kingdom.
Amen.

A prayer of intercession

Let us keep a short time of silence as we join the crowd on the hillside, eager to get close to Jesus.

Lord God, our loving, giving Father, we bring before you our needs and the needs of those around us.

Those who feel they have nothing to share, and ourselves as we encourage and value them.
The communities which need to learn how to work together, starting with us, our own commitment and involvement.

Those who feel they must hold on to what they have, praying that we may demonstrate and reflect your generosity.

The many who do not know the love of Jesus that doesn't count the cost, that we may share our blessings and our message of good news.
And today we particularly bring before you…
Silence

The crowd has become quieter now. All have been fed and satisfied. All have been blessed by being in the presence of God.
We too have been fed, renewed and touched by our generous, loving God.
We go out to share him in our world.
Amen.

A prayer for all ages

Jesus, you took a little bread,
Jesus, you took two fish,
you blessed them, broke them,
and fed many people,
until they were full.
Jesus, take us,
Jesus, take our little lives,
please bless them, break them,
and feed us,
until we are full.
Jesus, take our small resources,
Jesus, take our precious days.
Please bless them, use them,
to bring many, many people
into your kingdom.
Amen.

A prayer of thanksgiving

Lord God, our creator and provider,
you give us all we need and much more beside.
Thank you for opportunities we have to make a difference in our world, to share what we have and what we believe with those you have given us.
We can never have enough baskets to contain all you give us.
As we think about the miracle of Jesus feeding so many people, we recall that baskets are full of holes:
Lord God, make us people through whom your blessings leak out.
And thank you that as we share your word and your love, they will grow in us.
May we be people of the kingdom, whose passion is to fill the kingdom with all those who will come to be fed.
Thank you for Jesus, who shared with us the gift of his life: give us your Holy Spirit to enable us to share Jesus with others.
Amen.

A prayer activity

Cut out bread and fish shapes. Invite everyone to take a shape and write/draw on it something or someone they would like to pray for. Then place all the shapes in a basket and pray together:
Lord Jesus, you provided food for those who followed you all those years ago.
Please help us to trust you to provide for us and all we have prayed for.
Amen.

A sending out prayer

Go out into the world rejoicing in God's generous love; and may you be fed by the living God, who makes, feeds and sustains the world.
In the name of Jesus Christ.
Amen.

Year A   PROPER 14
Sunday between August 7 and August 13 inclusive

1 Kings 19.9–18; Psalm 85.8–13; Romans 10.5–15;
Matthew 14.22–33 *Jesus said to them, 'Take heart! It is I, do not be afraid.'*

Call to worship

Do not be afraid, for Jesus is here.
Listen to his living word and respond to his call. Look to him and step out in confidence and faith. Reach for his outstretched hand and be held in his love.

A prayer of approach

As Jesus went up a mountain to pray, so we come together in this place of God's presence, to pray and to worship.
We come from lives that are stormy or calm, rough or smooth, far from secure or somewhat becalmed.
Here in this holy place we see Jesus and he calls us to come. He calls us to follow him out of this safe place and into the difficult waters of life.
We need have no fear, as he takes our hand, lifts us up and saves us. However small our faith, we need not doubt, for he truly is the Son of God and we come to worship him.
Amen.

A prayer of confession

Lord, bring us not to the time of testing unless you give us the means to get through it.
Forgive us when we test you, for we are poor in faith and weak in spirit.
Forgive us when we set out with good intentions and lose our way.
Forgive us when we take our eyes from you and sink beneath our doubts.
Forgive us when you say 'come' and we 'go' instead.
Forgive us when you say 'go' and we stay still.
Lord, we lay before you our testing times and thank you for carrying us through them all.
Amen.

A prayer of adoration

Blessed are you, Lord our God, king of the universe, you come to us in our need; comfort us in our fear and rescue us when we are sinking.
We offer you the praise of our thankful hearts.
Blessed be God for ever.
Amen.

A prayer of intercession

Faithful God, we bring you our prayers for all who are fearful.
We pray for those who face physical danger as part of their work.
For ....
God our refuge,
we ask that in the daily dangers they face you will give wisdom, care, and protection.
Amen.

We pray for those who are fearful for the future.
For ....
God of hope,
we pray that you will give them strength to face their fears, and to trust you for the way ahead.
Amen.

We pray for those who live with the fear of violence day by day.
For ....
God of freedom,
we pray that you will give them confidence and courage, and help them and others to work for places and communities of safety.
Amen.

We pray for ourselves, when we are fearful and uncertain, conscious of the forces that threaten us and aware of our own vulnerability.
God of encouragement,
we ask that we will find confidence and strength in your faithfulness.
Amen.

A prayer for all ages

Stepping out, faithful God, we worship you.
On outstretched arms you catch us, bringing us into security and love.
Stepping out, creator God, we worship you.
In one breath, you sent us on the great adventure of life.
Stepping out, father God, we worship you.
With an offered hand, you support us as we face the seemingly impossible.
Stepping out, loving God, we worship you.
Giving words of encouragement, you brush us down to start again when we fall.
Stepping out, faithful God, we worship you.
Amen.

A prayer activity

Cut out footprint shapes from paper. Ask the group to write on them something about which they would like to ask Jesus to help them step out in faith. Everyone holds their footprint in their hand. Say a short prayer. If appropriate you could make a collage of the footprints.

A sending out prayer

Living God, you have met us here and calmed our fears. May we step out into your world strong with the hope and courage you give. Ready to meet you in faith.
Amen.

Year A   PROPER 15

Isaiah 56.1, 6–8; Psalm 67; Romans 11.1–2a, 29–32; **Matthew 15.(10–20), 21–28** *Jesus said, 'What faith you have, let it be done for you as you wish!'*

Call to worship

Come to meet the God who embraces the outsider.
Come to pray to the God who hears the cries of the voiceless.
Come to listen to the God who calls us to change.
Come to worship the God who brings life and healing to all.

A prayer of confession

Forgive us, O God, if, in our enthusiasm, we have overlooked the limitations of our understanding.
If, in our narrowness, we have overlooked the enormity of your love.
If, in our haste, we have overlooked the needs of our neighbour.
Forgive us, O God, and may we partner you, and others, more fully in all endeavours to establish your sovereign rule.
God forgives all who are truly sorry and frees them to live more fully in light and love.
Thanks be to God.
Amen.

A prayer of thanksgiving

God who gives a welcome to all, we thank and praise you. We praise you that in your love those who think themselves worthless find themselves called by name and welcomed at your table. We praise you that in your strength those who challenge exclusion find the courage to speak up for justice. We praise you that in faith in you all our barriers are broken down, and all are made welcome in your love.
Amen.

A prayer of intercession

We pray for those parts of the world
where religious law seems to promote conflict rather than love.
God of wisdom, **bless your children we pray.**

Where anger flows between nations
and scripture is used to justify bloodshed,
we pray for people of power, whose words and actions can incite violence or promote peace.
God of wisdom, **bless your children we pray.**

Where it is not safe to go to worship
or religious prejudice leads to fear,
we pray for ordinary people trying to find a way through life in a threatening world.
God of wisdom, **bless your children we pray.**

Where old scars and divisions run deep,
where memories of injustice and outrage are fresh,
we pray for children born into a fragile peace. May they, and those who teach them, grow into a new and better place.
God of wisdom, **bless your children we pray.**
Amen.

A prayer for all ages

When life is terrible, out of control,
Lord, let me be like the woman
to whom Jesus said,
'Woman, great is your faith!
Let it be done for you as you wish.'

When it seems as if you are not listening,
not caring,
Lord, let me persist like the woman
to whom Jesus said,
'Woman, great is your faith!
Let it be done for you as you wish.'

When there is a prayer,
a desperate, life-or-death prayer,
Lord, let me be determined like the woman
to whom Jesus said,
'Woman, great is your faith!
Let it be done for you as you wish.'

When there are obstacles,
arguments, things in the way,
Lord, let me be feisty like the woman
to whom Jesus said,
'Woman, great is your faith!
Let it be done for you as you wish.'
Amen.

A prayer activity

Ask everyone to think quietly about situations where they know someone is excluded. It could be someone at school, or someone they know (of) who's excluded because of disability, race, gender, sexuality, language, fashion, and so on.
Allow some silence for their prayers for these people, then pray:
O God, you hear the cry of all who call on you. Please give us faith like the Syro-Phoenician woman, who refused to remain an outsider. Grant that we, too, may have the wit to argue and demand that all are made welcome, through Jesus Christ.
Amen.

A sending out prayer

Go out into the world rejoicing in the God who brings challenge and hope; and may the blessing of the living God, Creator, Redeemer and Sustainer, give you confidence and strength to live the life of the gospel.
Amen.

Year A PROPER 16

Sunday between August 21 and August 27 inclusive

Isaiah 51.1–6; Psalm 138; Romans 12.1–8;
Matthew 16.13–20 *Jesus said to Peter, 'You are rock, and on this rock shall I build my church.'*

Call to worship

Come all you rock people, come together and let's rock.
Come all you followers, come together and let's follow.
Come all you seekers, come together and let's look for a key, a key to a new way, a key to life.

A prayer of confession

Lord, when times are hard and we forget your presence, **forgive us.**
When all seems lost and hope is a long way off, **forgive us.**
When we overlook our past wrongdoing to avoid our responsibilities in the present, **forgive us.**
When we seek to shame others by dwelling on their mistakes, **forgive us.**
When we think only of ourselves, our needs and our dreams, **forgive us.**
Forgive us, and remind us of your constant love.
Amen.

A prayer of intercession

O God, you call us into relationship with each other, so we take time to pray for your Church.
We, who are many, **are one body in Christ.**

We pray for the church in this place,
for our weaknesses and strengths.
Give us a life together rooted in wisdom and faith,
that we might not only speak of your love,
but share it with others.
We, who are many, **are one body in Christ.**

We pray for the other churches in our community.
Help us, together, to reflect to those around us that difference does not have to mean division,
and that we are united in our love for you.
We, who are many, **are one body in Christ.**

We pray for your worldwide Church,
for millions of Christians, in thousands of places,
following you in myriad different ways.
Help those whose faith is costly and those who try to express your hope in the face of hardship.
We, who are many, **are one body in Christ.**

By your Spirit strengthen your Church,
through our care and prayer for each other.
We pray in the name of Christ, the head of the Church.
Amen.

A prayer of thanksgiving for all ages

Lord Jesus, thank you for giving us a place where we are welcome and where we belong.
Thank you for your Church.

For giving us all sorts of people to learn from, and to share with, and somewhere to gather to sing to you and hear about you.
Thank you for your Church.

For giving us a family all around the world,
bigger than we can imagine, who share our love of you.
Thank you for your Church.

For showing us yourself through each other,
giving us love, joy, faith and hope to celebrate.
Thank you for your Church.
Amen.

A prayer activity

Put out a selection of stones and rocks and let everyone choose one, then say:
Thank you, God, for the Church.
Help it to be solid as a rock.
Help us to be willing to be changed for you.
Help us to use all that we have and all that we are to make your world as you want it to be.
Help us to dream dreams and truly to believe that things can be better for everyone.
Amen.

A reflective prayer about Peter

Sometimes he got things gloriously right,
sometimes he got things spectacularly wrong.
Sometimes he got them right, and wrong all at once,
like when he walked on the water…
then sank.
But, Jesus, you could never ignore him,
because there he was, eager to learn,
eager to discuss, argue, find out, and try out,
eager to do whatever it took.
And you made some amazing promises
to Peter, of all people, Jesus –
funny, muddled, brave, kind Peter,
sometimes right and sometimes wrong.
And they were promises you kept, too, Jesus.
Here we are, all these years later,
sometimes right, sometimes wrong.
Amen.

A sending out prayer

God has a purpose for you.
You are given a part to play in the Body of Christ.
Go then in peace, and serve God with faith.
Amen.

Year A   PROPER 17

Sunday between August 28 and September 3 inclusive

Jeremiah 15.15–21; Psalm 26.1–8; Romans 12.9–21;
Matthew 16.21–28 *Jesus said, 'Whoever wants to save his life will lose it. But whoever loses his life for my sake will find it.'*

Call to worship

We come before God to worship
with our voices and our lives.
We trust the Lord our God
and seek to love as we are loved.
We walk in God's light
and rejoice in the hope we are given.
We sing of God's goodness
and give thanks for God's love.
We want to be worthy of God's name
and to serve the Lord in our lives.
We rejoice in the house of God
and bring our sacrifice of praise.
Amen.

A prayer of confession

O God, we confess that we want to follow you, but get easily put off by the twists and turns of the journey. There are times when we are willing to carry the cross, but there are also times when we want to lay it down and let someone else pick it up. We are willing to speak your word, but sometimes do so quietly, so that it will not disturb anyone.

Forgive us for our lack of trust in ourselves, in each other, and in you. Help us to learn how to reach out when we are struggling and to open our hearts so you can empower us. For, however much we stumble, we want to walk with you.
Amen.

A prayer of dedication

Lord Jesus, when we are tempted to save ourselves and expect money or possessions to bring us happiness: remind us that you alone fulfil our deep desire and bring us eternal joy.
For those who want to save their life will lose it, and those who lose their life for my sake will find it.

When we are tempted to follow our own desires, becoming deaf to your call: remind us that you need us to share your love in this world.
For those who want to save their life will lose it, and those who lose their life for my sake will find it.

When we are tempted to save ourselves through deeds, in which we find honour, and prestige: remind us that you chose the way of humility.
For those who want to save their life will lose it, and those who lose their life for my sake will find it.

Lord Jesus, we are yours, we have chosen to walk with you, denying ourselves, taking up our cross to follow you.
Save us and help us, Lord, we pray.
Amen.

A prayer of intercession *based on Romans 12.9–21*

The passage seems to suggest a very diverse community and hints at some of the challenges to be prayers in such a place. Offer prayers for the people we find difficult and the attitudes we struggle with – our own and those we encounter.
For example:
We pray for those we reject,
may they find a welcome.
Make us welcomers too.

We pray for those we don't have time for,
may they find genuine commitment.
Make us loving too.

We pray for your enemies,
may they be well fed and watered.
Make us generous too.
And so on…

A prayer activity

Ask everyone to cut out a cross shape from card or paper then to look through the Gospels to find a saying of Jesus to write on it. Lay the finished crosses around a candle. In quietness, invite everyone to reflect on their commitment to follow Jesus. Finish with this prayer:
Dear Jesus, you showed passionate love for us in all you did on earth. Here we offer you our love in return. Help us to take up our cross too.
Amen.

A prayer for all ages

O God, it must have been so hard for Jesus to keep going to Jerusalem, when he knew it could all go so badly wrong for him.
But he had to keep going.
His friends did not want him to go. His family did not want him to go. They did not understand.
But he had to keep going.
Help us to keep going when things are hard.
Help us to know what is important – and to support each other, even if we do not always understand.
Amen.

A sending out prayer

Send us out, Cross taker, to be cross takers too.
Send us, Cross chooser, to choose the cross too
and lose a life that is worth little for one that is worth much. Send us out to see your kingdom coming and all your glory.
Amen.

Year A PROPER 18

Ezekiel 33.7–11; Psalm 119.33–40; Romans 13.8–14; **Matthew 18.15–20** *Jesus said, 'Where two or three are gathered in my name, I am there also.'*

Call to worship

Reconciling God,
We gather together to worship you, to affirm you,
not only as the God of love, but as the God who
understands our hurts and our divisions.
May we recognize your image in us,
welcome the stranger among us, and celebrate your
presence with us.

A prayer of approach

Loving God, calm my heart and still my mind.
Fill me with a spirit of understanding.
Let me be slow to take offence and quick to forgive.
As water finds its way through cracks, let your peace
find its way through hardened hearts.
Let your grace flow through all our dealings, your love
flow through all we do together,
through Jesus Christ our Lord.
Amen.

A prayer of confession for autumn

O God, as the days grow shorter and the evenings
darken, we bring before you any negative thoughts
and feelings that add to the darkness.
Forgive us and heal us.

As the wind blows the bright leaves from the trees
and strips the branches bare, we bring before you
the times we have stripped away the dignity of others
with a hurtful word.
Forgive us and heal us.

As the fallen leaves are gathered into piles,
we bring before you the times we have carelessly
swept away the needs of others without consideration
of their feelings.
Forgive us and heal us.

Forgive us and heal us, O God.
Restore the light and colour to our lives and to the
lives of those we have hurt.
Amen.

A prayer of intercession

War is an evil, on this we agree;
people are hurt and killed.
Let us pray to our God for peace in the world,
and let it begin in our own hearts.

Poverty is an evil, on this we agree;
people struggle, suffer and starve, children die
unnoticed by the world, day after day after day.
Let us pray to our God for an end to poverty,
for a fair sharing of the world's resources,
and let it begin with our generosity.

Oppression is an evil, on this we agree;
people are enslaved to terror.
Let us pray to our God for an end to oppression,
let us pray for freedom for all people,
and let it begin with our willingness to serve.

Hatred is an evil, on this we agree;
people are crushed and broken beneath its weight;
love withers, security perishes…
Let us pray to our God for an end to hatred,
let us pray that God's love may be known to all
people, and let it begin as we share it.
Amen.

A prayer for all ages

Loving God,
Sometimes we upset each other.
Sometimes we don't want to share.
Help us remember **Jesus is with us.**

Sometimes we are bad-tempered.
Sometimes we are not very gentle.
Help us remember **Jesus is with us.**

Sometimes we are unkind.
Sometimes we lose faith in the important things.
Help us remember **Jesus is with us.**

But other times, when we are happy
and kind and helpful and big-hearted,
help us remember **Jesus is with us.**
Amen.

A prayer activity

*Ask the group to pray together by using a chain
of words: each person can say only one word of a
prayer at a time. This might cause great hilarity. Allow
the group to enjoy the prayer, but also to recognize
that it only works because the individual parts make
up the whole. Conclude by prayerfully reflecting on
the closing words of the Gospel passage: 'where two
or three are gathered in my name'.*

A sending out prayer

May the love of God be yours.
May the gentleness of Christ be yours.
May the peace of the Spirit be yours.
And may the Trinity bless you today and always.
Amen.

Year A   PROPER 19

Genesis 50.15–21; Psalm 103.(1–7), 8–13; Romans 14.1–12; **Matthew 18.21–35** *Peter came to Jesus and asked, 'How often am I to forgive my brother?'*

Call to worship

We stand before God. We open our hearts.
Knowing our need.
We offer our thanks. We pour out our praise.
Knowing our need.
In faith we come, in trust we come, in hope we come, offering all that we are,
Knowing our need.

A prayer of confession

Help me, God,
for you will forgive as I have forgiven.
Help me, God,
because I have judged harshly
when I sought kindness;
I have condemned quickly
when I required patience;
I have hated easily
when I needed loving.
Help me, and forgive me
as I hope to forgive.
Amen.

A prayer of thanksgiving

How difficult it can be to 'settle accounts' with each other. 'Sorry' can be the hardest word to say,
but even when we have said it to each other
the feelings can remain: fear, mistrust, suspicion, unease.
Merciful and compassionate God,
thank you that you do not treat me as my sins deserve.
Thank you that you do not go on accusing me when I confess my sin.
Help me to know, accept and feel your forgiveness and to be forgiving in turn.
Root out the feelings of fear, mistrust, suspicion and unease and may your strong, compassionate love flow into and through all my relationships.
Amen.

A prayer of intercession

We pray for people around our world
caught up in situations of conflict and violence
or suffering from famine or disaster.
We are embodied with them now.

We pray for those who are sick or bereaved
and those who are homeless.
We are embodied with them now.

We pray for the broken and torn fabric of the earth
as it yearns for healing.
We are embodied with Christ in creation now.

And because you are one with us, O Christ,
enable us to share your life with the world by sharing our own lives.
**May we live together in harmony and peace.
Amen.**

A prayer for all ages *based on Genesis 50.15–21*

Dear God, sometimes families seem to be just such hard work. Big families, small families – they all have their hard times, their hard moments, their hard words said, their hard actions taken.
Sometimes families get broken into pieces, and I hate that, because people get broken into pieces too. It seems to be that there are lots of families in the Bible who get broken too – Abraham and Lot, Jacob and Esau, David and his sons … and loads more. Today, it's Joseph and his brothers. They really blew it big time. They got really broken into bits. And yet, and yet, the brothers said sorry, and Joseph forgave. He forgave ALL that stuff…
And lots of people were saved – that whole, huge family, did not starve. That forgiveness was a breakthrough. Please help me to be ready to say sorry, to be ready to forgive, in my family too.
Please help us all when we are broken into pieces.
Amen.

A prayer activity

Roll hands over and over each other during the first and third line of each verse:
Over and over and over again,
Forgive the wrong things I do.
Over and over and over again,
When I've been unkind to you.

Over and over and over again,
Forgive the cross things I do.
Over and over and over again,
Disobedient to you.

Over and over and over again,
Forgive the selfish things I do.
Over and over and over again,
Help me, God, to follow you.

Over and over and over again,
God forgives the wrong I do.
Over and over and over again,
God loves **ME**, and God loves **YOU**.

A sending out prayer

Go in the steadfast love of the Lord.
Keep Christ in your heart always.
Bless the Lord and do his will.
Amen.

Year A PROPER 20

Sunday between September 18 and September 24 inclusive

Jonah 3.10–4.11; Psalm 145.1–8; Philippians 1.21–30; **Matthew 20.1–16** *'Why be jealous because I am generous?*

Call to worship

Generous God, your love embraces and welcomes all people.
In our lives and our worship:
help us to share your hospitality.
Generous God, your salvation is a gift, not a reward for labour.
In our lives and our worship:
help us to show your generosity.
Generous God, your Son taught that your kingdom is open to all.
In our lives and our worship:
help us to teach your message.
Generous God, your Spirit is at work in the world today.
In our lives and our worship:
help us to live as your disciples.

A prayer of confession

For those times when we have judged others to be less worthy of your love than we are:
Gracious God, **forgive us.**

For those times when we have judged people by the world's view of success and value:
Gracious God, **forgive us.**

For those times when we have ignored your call to follow you and gone our own way:
Gracious God, **forgive us.**

In silence we remember all the things for which we are truly sorry.

Hear God's gracious word: your sins are forgiven.
Thanks be to God.
Amen.

A prayer of thanksgiving

Thank you, God, for being so generous.
You have created a world full of beauty,
with more animals and plants than we can count.
Thank you for your generous love.

You have created a world full of people,
who sing and giggle, talk and pray.
Thank you for your generous love.

You have created a universe full of wonder,
where planets spin and stars sparkle in the skies.
Thank you for your generous love.

You have given us Jesus to show your love,
who taught us that there is no limit to your grace.
Thank you for your generous love.

You have given us your Holy Spirit,
to help us live as your people today.
Thank you for your generous love.

Give us grace to share the wonderful news of your love with our friends and all the world.
Thank you for your generous love.
Amen.

A prayer of intercession

Generous God, we pray for our world, in which your gifts are meanly kept by some from others. Cure our poverty of spirit, that your abundant love may flow throughout the world.
We pray for the poor in every land.
For those caught up in violence and war.
The Lord hears our prayer. **Thanks be to God.**

For those known to us who have particular needs.
For our church as it seeks to live and speak of the good news you gave.
The Lord hears our prayer. **Thanks be to God.**

Lord Jesus, you hear our prayers, welcome our concern and invite us to share in your work of changing the world.
Give us generous hearts, that we may work, and pray, and live to your praise and glory.
Amen.

A prayer for all ages *based on Jonah 3.10–4.11*

Lord God, you are always calling people to spread your love and share your word with others.
You call ordinary people to do the most unexpected things. You need so many people to do your work here on earth.
Help us always to be ready to listen to your call, and to know that you will give us the gifts, courage, energy and enthusiasm to do the things you need us to do.
Help us to overcome the worries, doubts and anger that Jonah had, and be ready to respond to your call, like the disciples did when Jesus called them to follow him.
Amen.

A prayer activity

Give everyone a vine leaf cut from green paper. Encourage them to think about times when God has been generous to them, and to write a thank you for these times on the leaf. Place the leaves on a picture of a vine branch drawn on a large sheet of paper.

A sending out prayer

Go into the world filled with grace and generosity.
Rejoice in the profusion of creation and make peace.
Be more than fair, showing the tender compassion of God who created and redeemed you.
Amen.

Year A   PROPER 21

Sunday between September 25 and October 1 inclusive

Ezekiel 18.1–4, 25–32; Psalm 25.1–9; Philippians 2.1–13; **Matthew 21.23–32** *The chief priests asked Jesus, 'By what authority are you acting like this?'*

Call to worship

The power is yours: to shape and to teach;
to mend and to raise; to love and to forgive.
Come, Spirit of power.
The truth is yours: to live out in life;
to lead the humble; to proclaim to all.
Come, Spirit of truth.
The authority is yours:
to challenge the unjust;
to bring down the arrogant;
to judge the world.
Come, Spirit of authority.

A prayer of confession

Between our words and actions there is a gap.
A gap filled with indecision and lack of care;
fear-filled but empty of love.
The larger this gap grows, the further away you
seem, O God of active word and loving deed.
Forgive us, and help us to fill the empty space
with love that flows from you through us.
Help us who sing 'We worship and adore you',
to find a way to live our praise and adoration,
to find ourselves in you.
Amen.

A prayer of thanksgiving

God, creator and giver of all wisdom, we thank you
for the gift of story in Scripture. We thank you that
Jesus challenged his listeners to think for themselves,
and that we too are challenged to think about your
word and apply it to our lives today.
Amen.

A prayer of intercession

We pray for all in authority:
for governments and leaders:
let the same mind be in them
that was in Christ Jesus.

For teachers, for parents and carers:
let the same mind be in them
that was in Christ Jesus.

For those with power over life and death:
for military leaders and those who direct them:
let the same mind be in them
that was in Christ Jesus.

For NGOs and charities and those that make a
difference:
let the same mind be in them
that was in Christ Jesus.

We ask these prayers in the name of Jesus Christ
who humbled himself and became obedient to the
point of death – even death on a cross.
Amen.

A prayer activity

*This prayer involves movement. Prepare two cards,
one with the words 'Towards God' and the other with
'Away from God'. Two people hold these up opposite
each other, with the children standing in-between. As
the words of confession are said, the children face
the 'away from God' sign, and then turn 'towards God'
as they say the response together:*
When we are facing away from you, dear God,
turn us back towards you.
When we say we love you but don't show it in our
actions, dear God,
turn us back towards you.
When we ignore what you tell us in the Bible,
dear God,
turn us back towards you.
When we forget about you at home or school,
dear God,
turn us back towards you.
Children stay facing the 'towards God' sign
**Thank you that you are always there, dear God.
Help us to keep facing towards you.
Amen.**

A prayer for all ages *based on Philippians 2.1–11*

Jesus, we worship and praise you,
who, though he was in the form of God, did not
regard equality with God as something to be
exploited. But emptied himself, taking the form of a
slave, being born in human likeness.

Jesus, we worship and praise you.
And being found in human form, he humbled himself
and became obedient to the point of death – even
death on a cross.

Jesus, we worship and praise you.
Therefore God also highly exalted him
and gave him the name that is above every name.
So that at the name of Jesus every knee should
bend, in heaven and on earth and under the earth.
And every tongue should confess
that Jesus Christ is Lord,
to the glory of God the Father.

**Jesus, we worship and praise you.
Amen.**

A sending out prayer

Go in peace. Do what is honourable, just and pure.
Remember all that you have learned and received
and heard that is of God, and do his will.
Amen.

Year A   PROPER 22

Sunday between October 2 and October 8 inclusive

Isaiah 5.1–7; Psalm 80.7–15; Philippians 3.4b–14;
Matthew 21.33–46 *Jesus said, 'There was a
landowner who planted a vineyard…'*

Call to worship

Restore us, O God of hosts:
let your face shine, that we may be saved.
We gather to ponder on your word;
to hear the whisper of your Spirit
and the shout of your prophets.
Restore us, O God of hosts:
let your face shine, that we may be saved.
We gather to reflect on our lives;
to see the needs of the world,
and to glimpse your glory.
Restore us, O God of hosts:
let your face shine, that we may be saved.
We gather to worship you; to sing your praise,
to talk of your wonderful deeds.
Restore us, O God of hosts:
let your face shine, that we may be saved.

A prayer of confession

God of the vineyard, you have entrusted your world to
us. Forgive us when we let you down.
When food is bought through unfair trade,
leaving workers to go hungry:
**save us and help us, that we may praise you as
we share with our neighbour.**
When interest is gained through questionable
business, putting your world in jeopardy:
**save us and help us, that we may praise you
through our care for the earth.**
When security is found through warfare,
taking the homes and lives of others:
**save us and help us, that we may praise you in
peace and respect for all.**
Silence
God of the vineyard, call us back to your way;
turn us to love our neighbour;
let us face you, that we might hear your words of
grace when you say to us:
'Your sins are forgiven.'
Amen. Thanks be to God.

A prayer of intercession

Creator God, we thank you for all your gifts,
for our beautiful, productive earth.
Help us to steward it well
and share all we have with others.

Make us faithful, **bearing good fruit.**
Sustainer God, make us grateful for your gifts
and generous to others.

Make us faithful, **bearing good fruit.**
Redeemer God, thank you for your love,
for your son who came to show us what you are like,
and how we should live.

Make us faithful, **bearing good fruit.**
Eternal God, may we live as though we believe in
tomorrow, so that there will be a harvest for our
children and joy in the faces of all your people.

Make us faithful, **bearing good fruit.**
Amen.

A personal prayer

Walls and vines: building and planting,
planning and tending, measuring and pruning,
protecting and nurturing, waiting and watching –
God is at work.
Walls protect but also separate;
demolish all that separates me from you, O God.
Vines can flourish or fail;
help me to respond to your loving care, O God.
Grapes can be sweet or sour;
may I bear fruit that brings you joy, O God.
People can be honest or corrupt;
make me a responsible tenant of this bit of your
world, O God.
Amen.

A prayer for all ages

God the gardener and carer of the vines, we praise
you for the breath of life. We thank you for the love
and care you give us. We are sorry that our words
and our actions are not always like sweet wine. We
ask you to help and encourage each one of us to play
our part in creating a fruitful vineyard.
Amen.

A prayer activity

*Remind the group that we are a bit like the fruit of the
vineyard, God's kingdom, so in this activity you are
going to use the grapes to pray for one another. Invite
people to take turns to pull off a grape from a bunch
and, as they do, pray for someone in the group or in
another context in their lives. After you have finished
praying, let everyone eat the grapes and pray:*
Lord of the vineyard,
we thank you for each other.
Help us to look after each other
so we can grow more and more as you want us to be.
Amen.

A sending out prayer

May God who plants vineyards
call you to work for justice and righteousness.
May God who breaks down walls
release you to work for justice and righteousness,
and sustain you as you work.
And may you be blessed in the knowledge that you
are a child of God.
Amen.

Year A   PROPER 23

Sunday between October 9 and 15 inclusive

Isaiah 25.1–9; Psalm 23; Philippians 4.1–9;
Matthew 22.1–14 *The kingdom of heaven is like a banquet…*

Call to worship

The food has been gathered.
The meal is prepared.
The table is set.
Your place is ready.
Come to the party: take bread without money,
and drink without cost.
Our host is calling and welcomes us all.

A prayer of confession

For the times we have turned down your invitation.
Generous God, **forgive us.**
For the times we have taken your invitation for granted.
Generous God, **forgive us.**
For the times we have feasted on fine food but ignored the plight of the hungry.
Generous God, **forgive us.**
For the times we have chosen our way not yours.
Generous God, **forgive us.**
Remove all our self-centredness and help us to be worthy guests of your banquet.
Amen.

A prayer of response

For the one who is a place of refuge and shelter for the poor.
Rejoice in the Lord always: **again I say, rejoice.**
For the heavenly banquet prepared for all people.
Rejoice in the Lord always: **again I say, rejoice.**
For the power of love over hatred and life over death seen in the resurrection.
Rejoice in the Lord always: **again I say, rejoice.**
For the end of tears and of the disgrace of God's people.
Rejoice in the Lord always: **again I say, rejoice.**
For sharing in the commonwealth of God's love.
Rejoice in the Lord always: **again I say, rejoice.**
Amen.

A prayer of intercession

Loving God, from before time began you planned a plentiful feast to which all would be invited.
Hear us as we pray for a world that needs a party, and longs for your presence.

Let all be called, **for the feast is ready to begin.**
We remember those for whom life is hard and difficult. We pray that they may have all that they need, in a just and fairer world.

Let all be called, **for the feast is ready to begin.**
We remember those who suffer from ill health, their families and friends, and those involved in their healing. We pray that they may have comfort and courage, and find wholeness.

Let all be called, **for the feast is ready to begin.**
We remember those who feel unloved, or unsafe in their families and communities. We pray that they may find love, and be safe.

Let all be called, **for the feast is ready to begin.**
We remember your Church, called to the party, but sometimes slow in coming, and nervous of joining in. We pray for your joy to flood through our church in this place.

Let all be called, **for the feast is ready to begin.**
Amen.

A prayer for all ages

Feasting God, we thank you for food to eat and friends to share it with.
May we welcome others as you welcome us.

Hungry God, we remember those who don't have enough to eat, or who eat alone.
May we welcome others as you welcome us.

Out-of-place God, we remember those who feel rejected or who are bullied for being different.
May we welcome others as you welcome us.

Inclusive God, we thank you for the many different cultures that brighten up our world.
May we welcome others as you welcome us.
Feasting God, help us to share your feast with the world.
Amen.

A prayer activity

A prayer to be shared around the table. This prayer is a chance to say thank you to God for the feast that we are invited to. On a large sheet of paper write FEAST in big letters. Ask the children to write around the letters things that they can thank God for, beginning with the letters in the word. So around the 'F' they may write 'friends' or 'food' and so on. When everyone has contributed several things stop and say a big thank you to God. End with a feast!

A sending out prayer

God, we came at your invitation, send us out into our streets to invite others.
You fed us at your feast, send us out into our streets to feed others.
Help us to remember that you are with us in our streets, always.
Amen.

Year A   PROPER 24

Sunday between October 16 and October 22 inclusive

Isaiah 45.1–7; Psalm 96.1–9 (10–13);
1 Thessalonians 1.1–10; **Matthew 22.15–22**
*Jesus said, 'Pay to Caesar what belongs to Caesar
and to God what belongs to God.'*

Call to worship

Holy is the Lord our God:
The Lord our God is holy.
Holy is the Lord our King:
The Lord our God is holy.
Holy is our God who reigns:
The Lord our God is holy.
Holy in justice, holy in peace:
The Lord our God is holy.

A prayer of confession

When we fail to recognize your authority, Lord, forgive
us for not seeing you. When we are angry and we
turn to you for answers, forgive us for not thinking
of you first. When we seek signs and look to you
for proof, forgive our lack of trust in your everlasting
presence. When we turn to other influences, forgive
our lack of confidence in you.
Amen.

A prayer of offering

Gracious God,
We acknowledge that all we have comes from you.
We offer back to you these notes and coins,
symbols of our work, our benefits and our devotion.
May we always be honest and faithful with our
offerings and our taxes.
May we not begrudge giving that which blesses
others.
And may these gifts be used wisely and well to bring
blessing in the Church and in the world.
For Jesus' sake,
Amen.

A prayer of intercession

It is not your will that some should be hungry and
others full, that some should have much, and others
little, that some should suffer, and others be sad, and
others still long and long for your kingdom to come.
And so we pray:
Our Father in heaven,
let your kingdom come.

Where there is utter poverty, desperate misery, and
terrible unfairness:
Our Father in heaven,
let your kingdom come.

Where there is sadness and tears, where grief is
fresh and people mourn:
Our Father in heaven,
let your kingdom come.

Where there is sickness and pain, where depression
and illness rule:
Our Father in heaven,
let your kingdom come.

Where we fail to be the people you long us to be:
Our Father in heaven,
let your kingdom come.
Amen.

A prayer for all ages

Lord Jesus,
They were always trying to trap you,
and make you say something they could jump on,
stamp out, criticize and gloat over.
But it never seemed to work like that.
Somehow, you always went to the heart of the matter.
Your answers often left them puzzled,
or amazed, or angry.
Please help me to be like you –
wise when those tricky moments come,
when people ask difficult questions,
or try to trap me.
Lord Jesus, as I try to follow you with my life,
help me to see things clearly,
as you do,
and speak wisely,
as you do.
Amen.

A prayer activity

*This coin-rubbing exercise provides time to think
about what we can give to God. Place a coin
underneath a piece of paper and using the side of
a crayon, rub over the coin to make an impression
on the paper. Invite everyone to write on the paper
things they can offer to God.*
End with this prayer:
We thank you, creator God, that you give us good
things.
We thank you for the gift of patience.
Today we have identified some of the things you have
given us, and we would like to give them back to you.
Help us to use the things we are good at to serve you
in our homes, schools, church and in the community.
Amen.

A sending out prayer

We leave in your name, Lord,
we leave as your people.
Help us to recognize all that is yours,
to give you all that is yours,
to protect all that is yours.
Amen.

Year A PROPER 25

Sunday between October 23 and October 29 inclusive

Leviticus 19.1–2,15–18; Psalm 1; 1 Thessalonians
2.1–8; **Matthew 22.34–46** *Love the Lord your God,
with all your heart, with all your soul and with all your
mind. This is the greatest commandment.*

Call to worship

Come, love the Lord your God
with all your heart, all your soul,
and all your mind.
Come, love your neighbours
with all your heart, all your soul,
and all your mind.
Come, love yourself with all your heart, all your soul,
and all your mind.
For this is the greatest commandment.

A prayer of confession

Loving God, we bring to you in our prayers all those
who make up our family circle.
We love them but we know your love for them is
much greater.
Thank you for all who love us and for your special
loving care. Help us to love our friends and
neighbours with your kind of gentle love.
Help us when we are annoyed or tired to control our
behaviour so that we do not hurt other people by
what we say or do.
You forgive us, dear God; help us to forgive others
even when we are hurt, and to dry our tears and trust
in you when life is sad.
Help us to bring love, wherever we go.
Amen.

A prayer of intercession

Out of the generous love you pour upon us,
the hope you hold before us, and the faith that you
inspire in us, we offer you our prayers for the healing
of creation.
We pray for a world battered by human greed, and
desperate to be cared for…
God of love who calls us to love:
Pour out your generous love upon us.
We pray for communities shattered by war and
violence, and longing for peace…
God of love who calls us to love:
Pour out your generous love upon us.
We pray for people suffering in body, mind and spirit,
and seeking wholeness…
God of love who calls us to love:
Pour out your generous love upon us.
We pray for those we know with particular needs, and
hope for the assurance of your comfort…
God of love who calls us to love:
Pour out your generous love upon us.
We pray for ourselves in our need and desire to love
you with all our heart, soul and mind…
God of love who calls us to love:
Pour out your generous love upon us.
Amen.

A prayer of praise and adoration

God of love, love is your being, love is your nature,
love is your purpose, you are love.
You are the source of all love and we praise you, we
worship you, we adore you. We offer afresh to you all
the love of our heart, our soul and our strength.

We rejoice in the love that you have for us and in
the delight that you find in us as we express our love
for you. We are amazed at the love you have for us
and thank you from the depths of our being for the
freedom that gives us to enjoy being the people you
have made us to be.

As we rejoice in your love for us, help us to
demonstrate the integrity of our love by loving our
neighbours as ourselves.

May our love for you be as sincere on Monday
morning as it is on Sunday morning. May our offering
of heart, soul and mind be as complete in the home
and workplace as it is at Communion.

God of love, we celebrate again the wonders of your
love and pray that the worship and service we offer
may truly be filled with your love.
For Jesus' sake we pray.
Amen.

A prayer for all ages

Love the Lord your God *(Point to the sky)*
with all your heart, *(Point to your heart)*
with all your mind, *(Point to your head)*
with all your soul. *(Move your hands to make a circle)*
Come, love your neighbours *(Point at everyone
around you)*
with all your heart,
with all your mind,
with all your soul.
Come, love yourself *(Hug your arms around yourself)*
with all your heart,
with all your mind,
with all your soul.
Amen.

A prayer activity

*Children of all ages could be helped to write on
smiley faces the name of someone they love and
want to pray for. Older children may want to add
some distinguishing features. Each child holds their
smiley face while someone says a prayer.*

A sending out prayer

Go into the world following the law of love:
delight in it and reflect upon it
so that you yield good fruit.
And know that the Lord watches over you always.
Amen.

Year A PROPER 26

Sunday between October 30 and November 5 inclusive

Micah 3.5–12; Psalm 43; 1 Thessalonians 2.9–13;
Matthew 23.1–12 *Jesus said, 'The greatest among you should be your servant.'*

Call to worship *based on Psalm 43*

O Lord my God, send out your light and truth to lead me. Let them bring me to your holy house and to this time of worship.
I will come before your altar with joy.
I will come and sing your praises.
Nothing will stand in my way, for my hope is in you.
My God, I shall praise you, for you are my help and my God.

A prayer of confession

Lord Jesus, we confess to you the times when we don't practise what we preach.
When we burden others and do nothing to help.
When we parade our good works in public and try to hide our bad works.
We confess to you our own love of status,
our grasping after the best seats or pews or positions of power, the ways in which we put others down and deny them opportunity.
Forgive us, we pray, and help us to change,
recognizing that we all are children of the same Heavenly Father, and keep us humble as you were humble. For your name's sake.
Amen.

A prayer of petition

Lord Jesus, teacher and friend,
you are with us when we take our first steps in the discoveries of life.
And you are in our last steps,
however faltering they may be.
Bless those near the beginning of their journey.
Strengthen those who have come a long way.
And cherish those whose steps of life have all been trodden.
Help us to encourage one another as we travel,
and to know that although it seems as if we are for ever students, for ever learning
and for ever making mistakes,
there is nowhere we can go
where your love will not surround us,
and no mistake that can separate us from you,
not in life, not in death, not ever.
For you are our gracious redeemer,
not our menacing judge.
Amen.

A prayer of intercession

Lord God, we pray for all who have the responsibility of teaching, whether in church, school, college or business life. Theirs is an exacting task.
May they discern that imparting skills is more important than the acquisition of knowledge.

May they appreciate that nurturing wisdom
is more precious than passing on information.
May they understand that empowering people
is more valuable than gaining academic success.
May they acknowledge that cultivating skills for life
is more useful than learning abstract facts.
May they bear in mind that education can impart spiritual values as much as material ones.
May they never forget that they are relating
to fragile human beings with genuine needs.
May they always be open to learn from those they are teaching.
Specific teachers and learning situations may be named at this point
Gracious God, hear our prayers
as we offer them in the name of the master-teacher, Jesus Christ, your Son.
Amen.

A prayer of thanksgiving for all ages

For the good news of the gospel,
thanks be to God!
For God's word at work in us, **thanks be to God!**
For those who have made God's word known to us,
thanks be to God!
For those who encourage us in our living for God,
thanks be to God!
For the times when God has used us to bless others,
thanks be to God!
For those who inspire us through their humble service, **thanks be to God!**
For the humility of Jesus, **thanks be to God!**
For God's calling us into his own kingdom and glory,
thanks be to God!
Amen.

A prayer activity

Sit in a circle with a cross in the middle. The children write their names on heart-shaped pieces of paper. Play a song such as 'I, the Lord of Sea and Sky'. Invite them to place the hearts around the foot of the cross to form a circle of hearts. Then pray:
Dear Jesus, we are here…
Each child says their name in turn
We want to serve you by serving one another.
Please help us to care for one another like you care for us. Please help us to love one another like you love us.
Amen.

A sending out prayer

Lord Jesus, lead us this week into opportunities where we can serve you by serving one another. Help us to walk the week humbly with our God, uplifted by your presence, guided by your Spirit, and cherished in your love.
We go in peace.
Amen.

Year A   PROPER 27

Sunday between November 6 and November 12 inclusive

Wisdom of Solomon 6.12–16, or Amos 5.18–24;
Psalm 70, or Wisdom of Solomon 6.17–20;
1 Thessalonians 4.13–18; **Matthew 25.1–13**
*Keep awake, for you know neither the day nor the
hour when the bridegroom will come.*

Call to worship

The bridegroom is coming!
Wake up! Get ready!
See, he is here,
the feast can begin.
**Joyfully we greet him,
our waiting is over,
and our hearts burn brightly
with the light of his love.**

A prayer of confession

Lord Jesus, we come before you
as those who would bear your light
to shine in the darkness.
Forgive us the times when we have been
too unready and uncaring,
too unprepared and slothful,
too lazy and selfish,
to know your voice,
to listen to your word.
We would come before you now
as the wise bridesmaids,
supplied with the everlasting oil
of your love.
Amen.

A personal prayer

God who calls,
There are so many things going on around me
demanding my attention, that it is easy to be
distracted and fail to keep my eyes on you.
Deep down I know that you are the source of all my
happiness.
So I pray, give me the wisdom to know and live in the
truth of your love for me, so that when you call
I will hear and answer readily.
Amen.

A prayer of intercession

God who is in all things and sees all things,
open our eyes to the needs of the world around us,
that we may respond with love and generosity.
Loving God, **keep us awake.**

We pray for our leaders and all in authority,
that they may serve the good, and be protected from
pride and arrogance.
Loving God, **keep us awake.**

We pray for our churches, that the doors may be
open, and the welcome warm to all.
Loving God, **keep us awake.**

We pray for servicemen and women, for those far
from family and friends, as they keep the peace in
other nations.
Loving God, **keep us awake.**

We pray for the hungry and homeless,
that their cries will not be left unheard.
Loving God, **keep us awake.**

We pray for the vulnerable and sick,
that they may find comfort and strength through the
acts of those who care for them.
Loving God, **keep us awake.**

We pray for those who have died. Comfort those
who mourn, that they may share in the hope of the
resurrection.
Loving God, **keep us awake.**
Amen.

A prayer for all ages

Everyone holds a lighted candle:
Lord Jesus, you are the light of wisdom.
Lord Jesus, you are the light of love.
Lord Jesus, you are the light of truth.
Lord Jesus, you are the light of peace.
Lord Jesus, you are the light of hope.
Lord Jesus, you are the light of joy.
May we always be ready to keep the lights of our
lives alight and ready for you, so that every day – and
when you come again in glory – we will be ready to
enter the door of your love.
Amen.

A prayer activity

*Play Yolanda Adams' 'I'm Gonna Be Ready', or
another track or piece of music. Invite the group to
write down areas of their life they want to give over to
God. Place a bowl in the centre of the room and ask
everyone to throw their papers into it as a symbolic
act of offering them to God.*

A sending out prayer

Be prepared to do the work of God.
Lord, prepare us.
Be prepared to serve your neighbour's needs.
Lord, prepare us.
Be prepared to fight for justice and support the
oppressed.
Lord, prepare us.
Be prepared to speak words of comfort.
Lord, prepare us.
Be prepared to meet Jesus in any situation.
Lord, we are prepared.
Amen.

Year A   PROPER 28

Sunday between November 13 and November 19 inclusive

Zephaniah 1.7, 12–18; Psalm 90.1–8 (9–11), 12;
1 Thessalonians 5.1–11; **Matthew 25.14–30**
*Well done, good and faithful servant. You have
proved trustworthy.*

Call to worship

This day God summons us.
God calls us to account.
We bring our joys and sorrows.
We bring our success and failure.
We lay our lives open
to God's judgement and mercy.
This day God summons us.
God gives precious gifts to us.
Our hearts and hands are open
for all that God would give us.
Our trust is in the Lord,
who puts his trust in us.

A prayer of confession

This is the season of remembering, and along with all
the good things, we also remember the bad things,
and our part in them.
So in a moment of quietness we say sorry for those
things we have done, said and thought, that have let
you down and hurt other people.
We are truly sorry for these things.
We remember them with shame and ask that you
forgive us and remember them no more.
Heal us from the pain of these memories as we
are forgiven.
Because of what Jesus did, our sins are forgiven.
Thanks be to God.
Amen.

A prayer for faithfulness

We thank you, Lord, that whatever our age,
experience, wealth or status, you call us simply to
trust you, and to be worthy of the trust you place
in us.
Make us wise and careful stewards, but also faithful
and courageous ones, willing to take risks for you and
open to the reward that you have prepared and long
for us to receive.
Amen.

A prayer of intercession

Gracious God, we pray for all who are afraid:
for those facing violence in places of war, or in the
home; for those facing ill health or disability;
for those facing the loss of their job, their home, or
someone they love.

We pray for those who are afraid because they have
done great wrong and fear the consequences;
for those who become paralysed by their sense of
failure or inadequacy.

We pray for those whose fearlessness brings pain
and anxiety to others;
for those whose complacency causes suffering;
for those whose recklessness endangers the lives
of others.

From all these and from ourselves, replace the
darkness of dread with the light of your presence.
Give protection from evil and despair with the armour
of faith, love and hope.
So may we all take our place in your kingdom,
where love casts out fear,
and where we enter into your joy for ever.
Amen.

A prayer for all ages

Dear God, it is so easy for us to hide our talents –
to be shy, scared or intimidated.
Lord Jesus, help us to use our gifts to honour you.
It can feel as if our gifts are worth nothing –
that next to others, they are useless.
But to you, our gifts are precious.
Lord Jesus, help us to use our gifts to honour you.
It can feel very dangerous –
exposing our talents to the world.
Even when it feels like a big risk,
Lord Jesus, help us to use our gifts to honour you.
We are critical of each other.
Help us to encourage rather than crush,
help us to grow together.
Lord Jesus, help us to use our gifts to honour you.
With use, our talents develop –
they grow and blossom and bless others
to the glory of your name.
Lord Jesus, help us to use our gifts to honour you.
Amen.

A prayer activity

*Give everyone a shiny or chocolate coin. Ask them to
think about what it represents. Then pray:*
Lord, you have given us so many gifts and talents.
Make us trustworthy.
Lord, you gave us Jesus to teach us and save us.
Make us trustworthy.
Lord, make us generous with all your gifts.
Make us trustworthy.
Invite everyone to give their coin to someone else.

A sending out prayer

Generous God, as we are sent out bearing the wealth
of riches that you have entrusted to each one of us,
may our thankful hearts become brave hearts, ready
to risk everything for your kingdom.
Amen.

Year A   PROPER 29/CHRIST THE KING

Sunday between November 20 and November 26 inclusive

Ezekiel 34.11–16, 20–24; Psalm 95.1–7a; Ephesians 1.15–23; **Matthew 25.31–46** *The King will say, 'Anything you did for the least of my brothers, you did for me.'*

Call to worship

As we draw together to worship,
let us remember that we are in the presence of a King, not a King for whom we have to dress up and paint the building, but a King who loves us and comes to us just as we are.
So come, Holy Spirit; come, enter this space,
enter our hearts and minds and draw us into the presence of our King, the King of kings.

A prayer of adoration

Jesus our king,
there you are, in the emptiness of the hungry.
We humbly adore you.
There you are, in the parched craving of the thirsty.
We humbly adore you.
There you are, in the naked shame of the poor.
We humbly adore you.
There you are, in the loneliness of the stranger.
We humbly adore you.
There you are, in the pain and fear of the sick.
We humbly adore you.
There you are, in the humiliation of the prisoner.
We humbly adore you.
Jesus our king, in your greatness you cradle our vulnerability, and by your indwelling you bless our deepest need.
As we are humbled by your love,
so may we be moved to love by your humility.
Amen.

A prayer of confession

God our shepherd,
we are both sheep and goats,
unselfish and selfish,
loving and indifferent,
compassionate and cruel.
Cast out from within us
the prejudice and pride
that separates us from one another and from you.
And welcome us all into the one fold, your Son, our Saviour, came to prepare and open and be.
Amen.

A prayer of intercession

Welcoming God, we pray for those
who are strangers to your word.
Help us to reach out to them with your love.
On the day of judgement,
may we be found righteous.

Truthful God, we pray for those who hunger for justice and peace. Help us to stand beside them.
On the day of judgement,
may we be found righteous.

Loving God, we pray for those who are thirsty for human kindness. Help us to seek out the lonely and be a refuge for the abused, so that they might be refreshed in you.
On the day of judgement,
may we be found righteous.

Caring God, we pray for those who are sick in body, mind or spirit. Help us to do those things that will help them be open to your healing love.
On the day of judgement,
may we be found righteous.

Transforming God, we pray for those
who are imprisoned by their addictions.
Help us to support them until they can break free.
On the day of judgement,
may we be found righteous.

Searching God, we pray for ourselves, knowing we are naked before your gaze. In our acts of witness and service, remind us of our dependence on your love, so that we might find our strength in you alone, and on the day of judgement, be found righteous.
Amen.

A prayer for all ages

When the hungry cry for food: take us there.
When the thirsty need clean water: take us there.
When the stranger needs a friend: take us there.
When the sick need care: take us there.
When the imprisoned need a visit: take us there.
Amen.

A prayer activity

Encourage the children to think of people or situations that need God's healing and to write or draw them on craft sticks. Break the sticks in half. Give children sticking plasters still on their backing and ask them to write on the plaster one thing they could do to make things better for others. Then bind the broken sticks together using the sticking plasters. Pray together:
Help us, Lord, to treat others as we would treat you.
Amen.

A sending out prayer

Christ awaits us in the world, hungry, homeless, lonely and afraid. Go, love him and cherish him, tend him and care for him, and the blessing of God rest upon you.
Amen.

58   *A ROOTS resource*   PRAYER & PRAYER ACTIVITIES   © ROOTS for Churches Limited

Year B

Year B   ADVENT 1

Isaiah 64.1–9; Psalm 80.1–7, 17–19; 1 Corinthians 1.3–9; **Mark 13.24–37** *Heaven and earth will pass away, but my words will not pass away.*

Call to worship

We gather together at the beginning of Advent to wait for the coming Messiah.
We look up to the darkness of the heavens, and we see the first faint glimmer of the sunrise creeping over the horizon.
The day is not yet upon us, but its dawning is announced.

A prayer of confession

Forgive us, Lord, because we tie you down.
We think we can fathom and understand you.
We try to place you in a straitjacket of our creation, and so try to limit what you can do.
Forgive the smallness of our minds, and help us to broaden them to see you in your fullness.
Amen.

A prayer of adoration

You are a God of surprises.
Your arrival on earth was expected,
you had told us you were coming,
but none of us could have guessed how it would be –
in a stable rather than a palace.
Lord, we worship and adore you,
because you are a God of surprises.

You are a God of surprises.
As Jesus you grew and developed,
but not into the man we would have expected,
not a warrior king, but a gentle healer and preacher,
who didn't keep the company we would have admired.
Lord, we worship and adore you,
because you are a God of surprises.

You are a God of surprises.
When you were here you told us you would come again.
We may think we have an idea of how that will happen,
but as we stand back and think about your nature,
we realize that you will surprise us again.
Lord, we worship and adore you,
because you are a God of surprises.
Amen.

A prayer of thanksgiving

We cannot help but see that Christmas is coming.
The shops are full of decorations and presents.
We are counting the days to go, thinking about what to buy for everyone, and drawing up our card and present lists.
Children are practising for their plays, making their lists, too, and day by day getting more excited.
In all of this excitement, we thank you for Christmas, not the wrappings that we have put around it, but the deep truth at the centre – that you came to share this earthly life with us.
Lord, we thank you that you love us so much, that you did all this just for us.
Amen.

A prayer activity

Ask the group to write a private letter to God. In the letter they can tell God how they are feeling, what their worries are, and news of things good and bad going on in their lives. Give each member an envelope and have a 'post-box' for them to 'send' their prayer-letter. Assure them they will be removed and destroyed after the meeting. Or, they may prefer to take the letters home to keep, and look at in a few months' time, to see how things have moved on.

A prayer of intercession

Lord God, we pray for the world in which you have placed us. We affirm before you that we believe you are the creator God, and we believe that the coming of Jesus Christ is good news to the world.
But we are frustrated that it seems that so many people are deaf and blind to this good news. We long for you to open the ears and eyes of the world to the good news of the coming of Jesus.
Amen.

A prayer for all ages

God, sometimes you seem far away,
but you are our Father.
You love us and want the best for us.
You are the potter and we are the clay.
You hold us in your hands.
Help us to trust you.
We are all your people.
Amen.

A sending out prayer

How beautiful are the feet of those
who bring good news.
Go, believing that Christ will come,
and proclaim it to those who have not heard.
Take the Word to all the earth,
that it may be heard at the ends of the world.
Amen.

Year B   ADVENT 2

Isaiah 40.1–11; Psalm 85.1–2, 8–13; 2 Peter 3.8–15a; **Mark 1.1–8** *The one who is more powerful than I is coming after me.*

Call to worship *based on Psalm 40.1–4*

I waited patiently for the Lord;
he inclined to me and heard my cry.
He drew me up from the desolate pit,
out of the miry bog,
and set my feet upon a rock, making my steps secure.
He put a new song in my mouth,
a song of praise to our God.
Many will see and fear,
and put their trust in the Lord.
Happy are those who make the Lord their trust,
who do not turn to the proud,
to those who go astray after false gods.

An Advent prayer for all ages

God of comfort,
we want to be ready for you.
Help us to build a good road for you.
Help us to make it straight and level.
Walk with us along our road
and lead us to your kingdom.
Amen.

A prayer of praise and proclamation
based on Psalm 136

Praise to the Lord for he is good,
his love endures for ever.
Praise and thanks to the God of gods,
his love endures for ever.
Praise to the one who does great things,
his love endures for ever.
Praise to the one who made all things,
his love endures for ever.
Praise to the God who made the earth,
his love endures for ever.
Praise to our God who made the skies,
his love endures for ever.
Praise to our God who loves us all,
his love endures for ever.
Praise to our God who rescues us,
his love endures for ever.
Praise to our God who cares for us,
his love endures for ever.
Praise to the Lord of heaven and earth,
his love endures for ever.
Praise to the Lord for he is good,
his love endures for ever.
Amen.

A prayer of adoration

I see the world…,
you see the world differently.
I see people…,
you see children.
I see racial diversity…,
you see glorious differentiation.
I see men and women…,
you see sisters and brothers.
I see clever and intellectual…,
you see puffed-up pride.
I see small and insignificant…,
you see precious and unique.
I see judgement…,
you see forgiveness and grace.
I look for you…,
and sometimes I cannot find you.
I look at your world…,
and see you staring back at me.
Amen.

A prayer activity

This action prayer reminds us of the continuing journey. Ask the group to stand in a circle.
March on the spot as you speak the first line
John came out of the desert.
Put your hands either side of your mouth
He spoke to the people out loud.
Open your hands palms up in front of you
Someone special is coming.
Bring praying hands together
Get ready to come close to God!
Repeat the actions for the second verse
March on the spot as you speak the first line
I am listening to John.
Put your hands either side of your mouth
I want to do things that are good.
Open your hands palms up in front of you
I'll do what I can to get ready
Bring praying hands together
to come very close to God!

A prayer of intercession for all ages

Lord, you have given us people to show us the way,
be with us now and every day.
Teach us to be kind to others,
be with us now and every day.
Give us patience when things go wrong,
be with us now and every day.
Help us to do your will on earth,
be with us now and every day.
Amen.

A responsive prayer

The word of our God will stand for ever.
We come and go,
but your word stands for ever.
We rush around,
but your word stands for ever.
We sometimes get too busy to think about you,
but your word stands for ever.
Help us to remember you this Christmas.
Your word stands for ever.
Amen.

Year B   ADVENT 3

Isaiah 61.1–4, 8–11; Psalm 126, or Luke 1.46b–55;
1 Thessalonians 5.16–24; **John 1.6–8,19–28**
He came as a witness to testify to the light.

Call to worship

A voice cries in the wilderness,
'Prepare the way of the Lord.'
God's anointed is coming, good news for the world:
the broken hearts will beat with strength,
the feet in shackles will dance with freedom,
the eyes that weep will cry no more, for hope is
restored.
And today, in this place, we hear heaven's call.
The angels proclaiming, the prophets telling: God's
anointed is coming, good news for our world.
And our voices shall sing, for God's covenant is sure,
the promise is for ever.
God's word is for us. We are ready to hear.
To find ourselves, in the light that is coming.

A prayer of confession

Lord, forgive us when we seek to repay evil with evil.
Forgive us when we give in to the temptation of
retribution.
Forgive us when we seek vengeance against our
fellow human beings.
We recognize that all humanity is fallen, ourselves
included.
We recognize that others will seek to do to us what
they would not want to receive.
We recognize that our immediate desire is to repay
like with like, and to implement our own perception
of justice.
Lord, forgive us, and help us to live differently.
May we meet hurt with grace.
May we model a new way led by your Spirit.
May we heal hurt in the name of Christ.
Amen.

A prayer of dedication

Almighty God,
We ask that you will help us to keep our attention
fixed on you alone.
Too often we focus on others, or on ourselves, giving
glory to others, or seeking glory for ourselves.
Yet you alone are worthy of all glory and honour
and praise.
Help us to resist the subtle voices that call us
towards idolatry, and give us a renewed sense of
your awesome presence, revealed through your Son,
Jesus Christ, working in our lives by the power of
your Spirit.
Amen.

A prayer activity

*It is wise to recognize our strengths and limits and not
try to be someone we can't be. Look at, sing or listen
to the song 'Jesus, take me as I am'. As you do, invite
the group to pray quietly, asking God to use them as
they are and to help them know their strengths and
limits.*

A prayer of intercession

*You will need a newspaper, a few coins, a cardboard
box*
In our prayers today we remember those who
struggle to keep or find their identity in this complex
world.

We take this newspaper to remember those who are
in the headlines today: for those who have allegations
against them or who face personal trauma that has
become public property.
Lord, in your mercy,
hear our prayer.

We take these few coins to remember those whose
identity is shaped by money: for those who face the
problems of debt or those whose only identity is in
what they have.
Lord, in your mercy,
hear our prayer.

We take this cardboard box to remember those who
have no place to call home: for the refugee robbed of
his or her homeland or the rough sleeper we so easily
pass by.
Lord, in your mercy,
hear our prayer.

We offer these prayers and, with them, our hands,
that we might be the voices who proclaim hope, and
lives of action that point to the light.
Amen.

A prayer for all ages

Jesus, light of the world,
thank you that we can look around and see many
different faces,
people of different ages and different callings.
Help us each to shine as a light in the world,
confident in our faith and pointing others to you,
the true Light.
Amen.

A prayer for children

What shall I wear?
What shall I buy?
What shall I ask for?
Who shall I be friends with?
Where should I go?
Decisions. Decisions. Decisions.
Help us, Lord, to choose you.
Amen.

Year B   ADVENT 4

2 Samuel 7.1–11, 16; Luke 1.46b–55, or Psalm
89.1–4, 19–26; Romans 16.25–27; **Luke 1.26–38**
Do not be afraid, for you have found favour with God.

Call to worship

Bless, O Lord, our questions.
Bless, O Lord, our thoughts.
Bless, O Lord, our fears,
and, bless, O Lord, our joy.
May we bless you, O Lord,
pondering as Mary did.

A prayer of confession

As Mary pondered, O Lord,
we gasp with embarrassment.
As Mary pondered, O Lord,
we rely upon common sense and intelligent
conversation.
As Mary pondered, O Lord,
we look to what is achievable at the most efficient
cost.
As Mary pondered, O Lord,
we expect more of an answer to the mystery
than a cross.
Lord, in your mercy hear our confession,
and may your forgiveness change our confession
into newness of living.
Amen.

A prayer of anticipation

Gracious God, you accepted David and gave him
purpose through your covenant.
Mary identified your generosity and mercy in her
words which we know as the Magnificat.
May we recall the mystery, wonder and obedience
this week in the advent adventure of faith.
Amen.

A prayer of thanksgiving and intercession

Thank you, God, for all those Gabriels who delight
and astound us with your good news. We praise you
for the richness and complexity of the world in which
surprise and joy constantly await us.
For we too have found favour with God.
Too often we close our minds to new or fresh starts.
Too often we bring your kingdom down to our level.
Too often we fail to grasp how much you cherish us.
For we too have found favour with God.
We pray for those who live in conditions of such
want, exclusion, fear or bigotry that they have little
chance of being surprised or of living in hope. We
pray for ourselves when we are crabby or feel sorry
for ourselves.
For we too have found favour with God.
We resolve to take nothing for granted, to see nothing
as immutable; not people, not systems, not your
kingdom. Give us a passion for your Gospel and
a vision of your kingdom in which all are included.
For we too have found favour with God. Amen.

A prayer activity

*Put the items below in different bags or boxes. Invite
the children to open them in turn. Use the items as a
focus for a prayer.
Angel figure/feather: Pray for people who deliver
messages, news and surprises.
Mary from a nativity set: Pray for everyone receiving,
wanting and waiting for a surprise.
Baby doll or crib Jesus: Pray for people expecting
children.
Toy fire engine/ambulance: Pray for those who help,
save, and rescue.
Toy crown: Pray for leaders.
Glitter: Pray for people who need to be showered and
surprised with God's love.*

A prayer of intercession for all ages

When you want us to be nice to the people we don't
like, dear God, please help us.
Please help us to say 'yes'.
When you want us to keep quiet and we want to
argue, dear God, please help us.
Please help us to say 'yes'.
When you want us to stand against things that are
wrong, dear God, please help us.
Please help us to say 'yes'.
When you want us to spend time with you and we
think we're too busy, dear God, please help us.
Please help us to say 'yes'.
When we want to fight back and you want us to turn
away, dear God, please help us.
Please help us to say 'yes'.
Amen.

A prayer for all ages

Dear Lord,
You called Mary and she was willing.
You call us also.
Help us to say 'yes' when you call
and give us the faith to follow your leading.
Help us to see that you can achieve great things
through those who trust you.
Help us not to try to be everything in the story or
picture or patchwork,
for as individuals, unique and precious to you,
we join together in playing the parts you ask of us.
Amen.

A sending out prayer

As Mary questioned, Lord, may we not be afraid to
ask.
As you gave her your Holy Spirit, fill us too.
As you assured her of your power and presence, be
with us always.
As you gave her companions to share her journey,
send us others to support us.
As Mary said: 'yes', help us to say: 'yes'.
Amen.

Year B   CHRISTMAS 1

Isaiah 61.10–62.3; Psalm 148; Galatians 4.4–7;
Luke 2.22.40 *The child grew and became strong,
filled with wisdom; and the favour of God was upon
him.*

Call to worship

We worship the God of time and eternity.
We worship the God who existed before creation
leapt into being:
our beginning, our present and our future.
We worship the God who has been with us in this
closing year:
our beginning, our present and our future.
We worship the God who will be with us as our
stories continue:
our beginning, our present and our future.
We worship the God who is with us today and will be
for ever.

A prayer of praise and thanksgiving

God our Saviour,
as Mary and Joseph brought Jesus to the Temple
to present him before you,
we, too, come just as we are,
with praise and thanksgiving in our hearts,
to offer our lives to you, our gracious God.
Amen.

A prayer of confession

Gracious God, we come before you, realizing that we
are not as perfect as we sometimes think we are.
We are sorry for the times when we fail to take care
of your creation, when we use it for our own needs
and not for all people.
Lord, forgive us.

We are sorry for the times when we have hung on to
the past, trying to remain there rather than be led by
you into new ways and a new relationship with you
and our neighbours.
Lord, forgive us.

We are sorry for the times when we have turned our
back on your ways of love and care, and have hurt
those we love.
Lord, forgive us.

Gracious God, may we know your forgiveness and
your new life flowing through our whole lives.
Amen.

A prayer of intercession

Lord, we are aware that humankind is capable of
thinking wonderful things and imagining ways to
express them.
**Help us to give respect to you, the creator, and to
all that you have created.**

Lord, we are aware that humankind is capable of
making huge discoveries in this world and beyond,
searching into the heights and down to the depths,
measuring size and dimension, large and small.
Help us to give respect to the earth that we share.

Lord, we are aware that humankind is capable of
relationships with family and friends, of finding similar
aspects of personality and inclination in all races,
religions and nation groupings.
**Help us to express this sense of togetherness
rather than discordant themes and inclinations.**

Lord, we are aware that humankind is capable
of achieving many things through ingenuity and
intelligence.
**Lord, help us to give glory to you who are more
than we can be by ourselves.**
**Lord, you have chosen us to be. May we be
known to be of you by the choices that we make.
Amen.**

A prayer for all ages together

Praise the Lord, you are close to him.
Praise the Lord! *(Raise hands)*
Praise the baby in the manger.
Praise the Lord! *(Raise hands)*
Praise Jesus the Saviour.
Praise the Lord! *(Raise hands)*
Praise Christ the Redeemer.
Praise the Lord! *(Raise hands)*
Live in peace.
Praise the Lord! *(Raise hands)*
Amen.

A prayer activity

*Just as we send 'thank you' messages for gifts,
write either individual messages/texts or a group
one to God. Thank God for Jesus and ask for help
in showing and sharing the excitement of knowing
Jesus with others. Read out the prayer/s. Display
them for the rest of the church.*

A children's prayer for faithfulness

Dear God,
Those two old people,
Anna and Simeon,
Were amazing.
They were so patient,
Waiting and worshipping,
Year after year.
Please help me to be
Patient and helpful,
Just like them.
Amen.

Year B   CHRISTMAS 2

Jeremiah 31.7–14, or Sirach 24.1–12; Psalm 147.12–20, or Wisdom of Solomon 10.15–21; Ephesians 1.3–14; **John 1.(1–9) 10–18** *The light shines in the darkness, and the darkness did not overcome it.*

A gathering prayer *based on John 1.1–18*

In the beginning;
A daughter of a voice glows softly:
Are you listening?
The Word, whispered, flickers and flares:
Are you listening?
The radiant rhyme of life is spoken:
Are you listening?
Rays of gospel start to speak.
God's laughter twinkles.
God's grace shouts glory.
All creative energy explodes into light.
In the beginning was the Word:
Are you listening now?

A prayer of approach

Almighty God,
You entered our world in Jesus,
and know the secrets of all hearts.
Enter our lives by your Spirit,
cleanse us by the flame of your love,
and turn us to respond to you,
that we may worship as you deserve,
both with our lips and with our lives;
through Jesus Christ our Lord.
Amen.

A prayer of confession

Before they were baptized by John,
the people confessed their sins.
We too come to God in confession.
Because of the pressure of our responsibilities, the business of the week and the turmoil of the week's news, we forget God.
In the rush of events, we neglect our neighbour, we turn in on ourselves and our own concerns and do not allow the love of God to direct our thinking and our actions.
Gracious God, we come seeking the forgiveness you have promised. Release us from all that prevents us from being more truly Christ's disciples. Set us on our feet again and renew us with the companionship of your Holy Spirit.
Amen.

A responsorial litany of thanks for light

Candles can be lit during this litany
For light to guide and light to reveal hidden things,
thanks be to God.
For light composed of many colours,
thanks be to God.

For bright light that throws strong shadows and gentle light that caresses,
thanks be to God.
For the inner light of people who cannot see light,
thanks be to God.
For the light that points us to greater light,
thanks be to God.
For Jesus, light of the world and light in all light, here portrayed before us,
thanks be to God.
Amen.

A prayer activity

Display pictures of different sources of light. Light a candle and stand or sit round it. Think together about people who need the light of Jesus. Write the names on slips of paper and put them round the candle. Close with this prayer:
Jesus, the light that shines in the darkness,
Shine in our lives and help us to see what we should do.
Shine in our hearts when we are lonely, sad, scared or hurting.
Shine through us into the lives of other people.
Light up the world with your glory, full of grace and truth.
In the name of Jesus, the true light,
Amen.

A prayer of intercession

God of light and of darkness, we pray for people who cannot see light:
for those blinded by the truth by prejudice and for those so beset by problems that they cannot see a way ahead;
that you will be light for all who cannot see light.

God of light and of darkness, we pray for people carrying heavy responsibilities:
for those who work to create peace, or to improve our health service, police forces or schools,
and for those who seek to bring Christ's truth to the caring of disadvantaged groups,
and to children and young people vulnerable to bad influences;
that you will be light for all who carry heavy responsibilities.

God of light and of darkness, we pray for your church throughout the world:
for the church where few people are interested in a truth outside themselves, or where they feel uncertain of Christ's truth;
for the church where the light of Christ seems not to shine as brightly as other lights;
that you will be light and truth renewing your church, through Jesus Christ, our Lord,
Amen.

Year B   EPIPHANY 1

Genesis 1.1–5; Psalm 29; Acts 19.1–7; **Mark 1.4–11**
I have baptized you with water; but he will baptize you with the Holy Spirit.

Call to worship *based on Psalm 29*

Lord, your glory and strength are all around us.
Glory to the Lord.
Lord, we come to worship you.
Glory to the Lord.
Your voice brought forth creation's splendour.
Glory to the Lord.
You speak to us in word and song,
through the lives of your people.
Glory to the Lord.
Your voice brings challenge and rebuke.
Glory to the Lord.
You, Lord, give us strength in times of need.
Glory to the Lord.
You, Lord, give us peace.
Glory to the Lord.

A prayer of confession

Lord, we have turned away from you.
In our church:
forgive us, Lord. We turn to you again.
In our work:
forgive us, Lord. We turn to you again.
In our homes and families:
forgive us, Lord. We turn to you again.
In our individual lives:
forgive us, Lord. We turn to you again.
Amen.

A prayer of thanksgiving

Let us give thanks to God for the wonder of creation.
Let us thank God for the variety of plants and animals
within this creation.
Let us thank God that the provision of his creation
enables all to be fed,
and let us thank God for his creating power,
which brings each new day and each new life to birth.
Lord, we thank you.

Let us thank God for Jesus, God's own Son,
for his revealing of your way of love,
for his death on the cross,
for his resurrection and the new life
we have with God through him.
Lord, we thank you.

Let us give thanks to God for the Church, the body
here on earth.
We thank God that the Church reveals God's love in
so many ways,
through its caring, through its speaking,
through its challenging of the ways of the world.
Lord, we thank you.

Gracious and loving God,
we offer you our thanks and praise
through Jesus Christ, your Son and our Lord.
Amen.

A prayer of adoration

Lord God, we need only to look around your creation
to catch a glimpse of your splendour; for within the
beauty of the flowers, the rivers, the mountains and
the ocean depths, your glory is reflected and for this
we praise you.

Gracious God, we praise you that through your son
Jesus, a new beginning with you is possible.
We praise you that Jesus came, revealing your love
and compassion for the whole of your creation.
We praise you for his obedience to you, and that he
lived in perfect union with you, setting an example for
us to follow.

Life-giving God, we praise you for your gift of the Holy
Spirit who comes into our lives, revealing your ways
and your truth to each one of us.
Lord God, gracious God, life-giving God,
reveal your glory.
Speak your word to us.
Draw us to new understandings of yourself as we
worship you.
Amen.

A prayer activity

*All stand in a circle holding hands. Ask the Holy Spirit
to come and be with you. All turn to your left and put
your hand on the shoulder of the person in front of
you. Ask God to be with that person. All turn to your
right and do the same. All turn to face outwards and
hold hands. Ask God to be with all our brothers and
sisters all over the world.*

A prayer for all ages

God, you know me and you love me.
Your love for me is wider than the widest ocean,
And deeper than the deepest sea.
It flows like a river through me,
And pours over me like rain.
You named me in your heart before the world began.
God, you know me and you love me.
Amen.

A reflective prayer

Listen to the voice of the Lord thunder.
Listen to the voice of the Lord flash.
Listen to the voice of the Lord
as it tears through the forest.
Listen to the voice of the Lord coming close,
giving you strength.
Listen to the voice of the Lord
as it whispers a blessing.
Listen, and say 'Glory!'
Amen.

Year B   EPIPHANY 2

1 Samuel 3.1–10 (11–20); Psalm 139.1–6, 13–18;
1 Corinthians 6.12–20; **John 1.43–51** *You will see
greater things than these.*

Call to worship

Lord God, as a new day begins,
we come to worship and praise you.
In answer to your call, we come.
Lord God, we come with thanks for all you have given
us this week.
In answer to your call, we come.
Lord God, we come with the wrongs we have done
this week.
In answer to your call, we come.
Lord God, we come to hear your words for us and our
generation.
In answer to your call, we come.
Lord God, through your Spirit unite us,
both young and not so young,
in joyful celebration, as we worship you.
In answer to your call, we come.

A prayer of confession

Lord, we ask you to show us the Father –
but we have failed to recognize you.
Lord, have mercy.
Lord, you have been with us all our lives –
yet still we do not know you.
Christ, have mercy.
Lord, though the world cannot receive you –
give us your spirit of truth to abide in us.
Lord, have mercy.
Amen.

A prayer of praise *based on John 1.43–51 and John 20*

All praise to you, O Christ, who took the doubts of
Nathanael, asking whether anything good could come
from Nazareth, and revealed yourself to him as Son
of God and King of Israel.
All praise to you, O Christ, who took the doubts of
Thomas who would not believe in your resurrection
until he had touched and seen, for you revealed
yourself to him, the living proof he asked.
With your apostles we acclaim you in faith as our
Lord and our God and our Saviour.
Amen.

A prayer activity

*Stick some large pieces of paper together to form a
graffiti board. Invite everyone to write on it the names
of groups of people they sometimes stereotype,
along with prayers for those groups. Pray both for
forgiveness for stereotyping people and wisdom not
to do it.*

A prayer of intercession

With confidence in Jesus,
who calls us to walk alongside him,
we bring our heartfelt needs before God.

We pray for all in this community of faith, that we may
always remain open and receptive to the call to trust
in God's will for us.
We pray to the Lord:
Lord, hear our prayer.

We pray that the knowledge of God's love will grow
strong in our hearts, leading us to use our lives, body
and soul, for the glory of God.
We pray to the Lord:
Lord, hear our prayer.

We pray for those who struggle to see God's
presence in the world and their own lives. May our
faith and generosity help them to recognize his loving
touch.
We pray to the Lord:
Lord, hear our prayer.

We pray for those in need, remembering in particular
the unemployed, the sick, the elderly and those who
have asked for our prayers. May we reach out to
them in gentle solidarity as Jesus reached out to us.
We pray to the Lord:
Lord, hear our prayer.
Amen.

A prayer for all ages

Put your hands behind your ears
Lord, open our ears to your voice when you call us to
come to you.
Point to your eyes
Lord, open our eyes to your presence when you invite
us to see you.
Cup hands around your mouth
Lord, open our lips to praise you,
Put your hands on your heart
and our hearts to welcome you.
Stamp your feet
Lord, quicken our feet to follow you,
Wave your hands
and our hands to do your will.
Point to your lips, then to your heart, then beckon
Lord, give us your word on our lips and your love in
our hearts as we call your people to come and see
Jesus.
All this we ask in his name.
Amen.

A sending out prayer *from 1 Corinthians 6*

Lord, as you have called us,
make us worthy of our calling.
Unite us with you, that we may be one with you
as temples of your holy spirit,
that your glory may be seen in us.
Amen.

Year B   EPIPHANY 3

Jonah 3.1–5, 10; Psalm 62.5–12; 1 Corinthians 7.29–31; **Mark 1.14–20** *The time is fulfilled, and the kingdom of God has come near.*

Call to worship

Jesus says, 'Follow me.'
Lord, here I am.
Leave what you know, leave your own expertise,
leave the people and the way you know.
Lord, here I am.
Learn a new way of living,
a new way of following, a new way of fishing.
Lord, here I am.
Put down your net, take up your cross.
Lord, here I am.
Know you are forgiven,
take up your bed and walk in my strength.
Lord, here I am.

A prayer of confession

Lord, you call us to repent.
But I said, 'What about him, Lord?'
'What is that to you? You are to follow me,'
says the Lord.
To whom else can we go?
You have the word of life.
Lord, you call us to repent.
For we imagined your kingdom was just for us.
Lord, you welcomed the repentant sinner with a fatted calf.
May we know we too are sinners, and may share your feast.
Lord, you call us to repent.
Your blood was shed for my sins.
Amen.

A prayer of adoration

Gracious God, we adore you.
We see your glory in the vastness and beauty of the universe, with its array of colours,
its beauty in the spiralling clouds of gas.
Gracious God, we adore you.
Lord Jesus Christ, we adore you,
for you came as one of us.
You did not seek power but came to serve.
You revealed to us that humanity and God may live in perfect harmony.
Lord Jesus Christ, we adore you.
Holy Spirit, we adore you.
You unite us with God.
You reveal to us the truth of God,
and bring God's power into our lives.
Holy Spirit, we adore you.
Gracious God, Lord Jesus Christ, Holy Spirit,
three in one, we adore you, now and for ever.
Amen.

A prayer activity

In a tray of sand, take turns to write or draw things you are sorry for. Then smooth the sand as a reminder that God hears our prayers and forgives us.

A prayer of intercession for all ages

Through the person of Jesus we are called to a new and deeper knowledge of God's love for us.
Strengthened by that knowledge, we dare to bring our needs and concerns before God.
We pray for the grace to respond to the promptings of the Spirit in our work for the good of others.
Let us pray to the Lord:
Lord, hear our prayer.

We pray that all Christian churches may be made strong in God's love and united in their common witness to the truth and power of God's Word.
Let us pray to the Lord:
Lord, hear our prayer.

We pray for those involved in education, particularly of the young, that their work may inspire young people to work for the good of others and not just for personal gain.
Let us pray to the Lord:
Lord, hear our prayer.

We pray for the various businesses and industries in our town/city. May they be successful, and their workers treated with fairness and justice.
Let us pray to the Lord:
Lord, hear our prayer.
Amen.

A prayer for the coming of the kingdom

Lord, let your kingdom come near.
Let us see your world through your eyes,
that we may perceive its goodness and promise,
its failure and frustration,
its needs and its gifts.
Lord, let your kingdom be upon us,
to rebuild your world,
and to rebuild our lives,
that your good news may be proclaimed
and your kingdom come on earth
as it is in heaven.
Amen.

A personal prayer for the week

Compassionate God,
We pray for all who need your touch and love in their lives.
Give them strength and courage.
We ask this through Jesus Christ our Lord,
who chose to reach out and heal.
Amen.

Year B   EPIPHANY 4

Deuteronomy 18.15–20; Psalm 111; 1 Corinthians
8.1–13; **Mark 1.21–28** *But Jesus rebuked him,
saying, 'Be silent and come out of him!'*

Call to worship

Healing God:
we come to praise you.
Life-giving God:
**we come to hear and receive your life-giving
word.**
Transforming God:
**we come to you in an awareness of the need for
transformation.**
As we gather to worship in God's name:
may the Lord be with us.
Amen.

A prayer of confession

Healing and forgiving God,
We confess to you before this congregation,
the times we have failed to recognize you in those
whom we meet.
We confess to you the times we have
walked away from those who need your healing
presence.
We confess to you the times we have hurt
and failed others.
Be gracious, be merciful and heal us,
in the name of Jesus Christ, your Son,
our Lord.
Amen.

A prayer of petition

Forgive us, O Lord, those times when we
have felt possessed by our possessions,
obsessed by our obsessions,
distressed by our shortcomings,
impressed by that which is worthless,
unable to let go.

Help me to remain silent and to trust,
as you bid these unclean spirits
to come out and let me live again.
Amen.

A prayer of thanksgiving and
intercession for all ages

Loving God, you are with us always.
Thank you that you never leave our side.
We praise you, O God, and we bless you.

Thank you for your promises made real for us
in Jesus.
We praise you, O God, and we bless you.

Thank you for being our comfort and strength when
life is hard or painful.
We praise you, O God, and we bless you.

Hear our prayer for all who are sick or sorrowful.
Today we remember …………
Help us to trust in your power to heal.
We praise you, O God, and we bless you.

Hear our prayer for all who have hard jobs to do and
difficult decisions to make …………
Help us to follow your wise advice.
We praise you, O God, and we bless you.

Hear our prayer for those we love,
and our thanks for all who love us.
Bless them and watch over them day and night.
We praise you, O God, and we bless you.
All this we pray in Jesus' name.
Amen.

A prayer activity

*Give out inflated balloons. Ask the children to write
or draw on their balloon something that needs Jesus'
help. Gather all the balloons together and pray for
those things. Then pop the balloons.*

A children's prayer for healing and
peace

*Practise the response. When a leader says 'Jesus',
the children reply, 'you bring us healing and peace'.
Invite older children to add situations they would like
to include:*
Jesus, **you bring us healing and peace.**
When we are ill,
Jesus, **you bring us healing and peace.**
When we are sad,
Jesus, **you bring us healing and peace.**
When we are lonely,
Jesus, **you bring us healing and peace.**
When other people hurt us,
Jesus, **you bring us healing and peace.**
When people argue,
Jesus, **you bring us healing and peace.**
When things go wrong,
Jesus, **you bring us healing and peace.**
Amen.

A prayer for silence

Lord, you told unclean spirits to be silent.
You instructed your followers to say nothing.
Your authority did not depend on words.
Let us enter your world with lips closed and hearts
open, so that your wondrous gift is given.
May 'poor talkative Christianity' be consigned to
history, for you gave us two ears and one mouth.
May we listen twice as much as we speak, and
ensure that listening be to our neighbour, but chiefly,
dear Lord, to you.
Amen.

Year B EPIPHANY 5

Isaiah 40.21–31; Psalm 147.1–11, 20c; 1 Corinthians 9.16–23; **Mark 1.29–39** *That evening at sundown, they brought to him all who were possessed with demons.*

Call to worship

We gather together here this day to get away from it all, but we never can.
As we quieten ourselves and ponder more deeply the wonderful works of God, we are invited to celebrate this world with him, concern ourselves with its issues and act with love, mercy and justice in our daily lives.
May we drink deeply from the well of life.
Refresh us today, O living Lord, and endue us with the power of your love to think and speak and walk justly in your name, through Jesus Christ our Saviour.

A prayer of approach *based on Psalm 147*

God of love and compassion,
we have come from different places to worship you.
Praise the Lord.
God of love and compassion,
we come to hear your word.
Praise the Lord.
God of love and compassion,
we come to make melody to you.
Praise the Lord.
God of love and compassion,
turn our thoughts to you in the knowledge of your steadfast love towards us.
**Great is our Lord, and abundant in power;
our Lord's understanding is beyond measure.
Amen.**

A prayer of confession

For our lack of consideration at home:
Lord, have mercy.
Lord, have mercy.
For our lack of respect and understanding for one another:
Christ, have mercy.
Christ, have mercy.
For our lack of patience and forgiveness:
Lord, have mercy.
Lord, have mercy.

Merciful God, we are sorry for our apathy, for our lack of action, for our ignorance, for our indifference.
Forgiving God, help us to be free from the feeling of being overwhelmed,
free to reflect, pray, focus and act in whatever way possible.
Help us not to deceive ourselves but always to grow towards truth and action.
Loving God, help us in our journey with you to be growing, imaginative, generous, letting-go people.
Amen.

A prayer activity

Talk about the things that other people do for us. Can the children tell the group about something special someone at home has done for them? Tie a length of gift ribbon around each child's wrist. Suggest they leave it there until they have gone home and said thank you to that person for what they have done.

A prayer of intercession for all ages

Thank you, God, for the diversity of families:
for members of our own family whom we see every day,
and for those whom we see less often.
In this quiet space we remember our own families…
Thank you, God, for the family of the Church.
We remember our Christian friends in neighbouring churches and those all over the world.
We thank you that we belong to such a big family, the family of all men, women and children.
We pray for all those who are finding life hard:
for those who suffer because of the break-up of their family,
for those who suffer because of illness within the family.
Help us to love our family and friends,
both near and far.
We ask this through Jesus Christ our Lord.
Amen.

A personal prayer for the week

God of love and compassion,
I pray for family life:
for all newly married couples, grant joy and a love that grows;
for families where there is suffering in body or mind, grant patience and endurance;
and especially for those who are suffering family break-up, grant strength, courage and hope.
Amen.

A sending out prayer

God of love and compassion,
you meet us in the messiness of our lives:
stay with us now.
God of love and compassion,
you share our pain and heal our weaknesses:
stay with us now.
God of love and compassion,
you meet us where we least expect to find you:
stay with us now.
Stay with us in our frailty and in our difficulties.
Stay with us on our journey.
**Take our hand and walk beside us,
live within us,
lead us to glory,
lead us home to you.
Amen.**

Year B EPIPHANY 6

2 Kings 5.1–14; Psalm 30; 1 Corinthians 9.24–27;
Mark 1.40–45 *Immediately the leprosy left him, and he was made clean.*

Call to worship

Holy Father, yours is the kingdom:
a kingdom of love, justice and peace.
Holy Christ, yours is the power:
the power to choose to forgive and heal us.
Holy Spirit, yours is the glory:
the glory to renew and recreate us.
**Holy Father, Holy Christ, Holy Spirit,
we come to worship you.**

A prayer of confession

Heavenly Father,
we think of the times we have chosen not to love
those who are different from us.
Father, forgive us.
Heavenly Father,
we think of the times we have failed to touch people
in their need.
Father, forgive us.
Heavenly Father,
we think of the times we have not listened to you
and gone our own way.
Father, forgive us.
Transform our lives so that we may bring your healing
and loving presence to all we meet;
we ask this through your Son
who touched and healed.
Amen.

A prayer of asking

O loving and compassionate God,
when our hearts feel unclean,
when we want to hide ourselves away,
when we hate what we look like and the air is thick
with self-loathing,
then, Lord, in your mercy, choose to cleanse us.
Break through our doubts and our failure to love
ourselves.
Restore our self-respect.
Just as Jesus looked into the face of the leper and
saw him as a needy child of God,
look deeply into our hearts and bring all the love we
hold inside to transform our outward appearance.
And give us companions who will affirm and
challenge us on that journey from hatred to love.
Amen.

A prayer of thanksgiving

Thank you, Lord, for the strength you give us:
strength of body,
strength of mind or strength of spirit.
May we so train these gifts within us that we run the
race that is set before us, exercising all necessary
self-control in order to attain it.

Help us not to run after worthless goals,
but help us to temper our energies to serve our
hearts' desire: you, our living Lord and master.
We praise your holy name
through Jesus Christ, our Lord,
in the power of the Holy Spirit.
Amen.

A prayer of intercession for all ages

Jesus, you were not afraid to touch the leper.
Give us courage to reach out in love to people in all
kinds of need.
We reach out in love to people all over the world,
especially the poor, the broken-hearted, the lonely
and those who feel unloved.
We reach out in love.
You hold them in your heart.

We reach out in love to the people who live around
us, especially those without friends or family.
We reach out in love.
You hold them in your heart.

We reach out in love to people who are ill or in any
kind of distress, especially anyone with problems that
others find difficult to deal with.
We reach out to the mentally ill, people who look
different, and those who are dying.
We reach out in love.
You hold them in your heart.

We reach out in love to those who have died
and to the people who love them.
We reach out in love.
You hold them in your heart.

When we call, we know you listen.
You hold us in your heart.
Amen.

A prayer activity

*Give everyone one piece of paper chain. Ask them
to write on it an issue of injustice that we need to
speak up about. Link the chain around a candle and
pray for courage and guidance to take action. Then,
symbolically break the chain.*

A prayer of inclusion

In the times when we exclude others,
Lord, remind us you are there.
In the times when we feel excluded,
Lord, remind us you are there.
In the times when we judge others,
Lord, remind us you are there.
In the times when we are judged by others,
Lord, remind us you are there.
Amen.

Year B EPIPHANY 7

Isaiah 43.18–25; Psalm 41; 2 Corinthians 1.18–22;
Mark 2.1–12 *Then some people came, bringing to him a paralysed man, carried by four of them.*

Call to worship

Invite people to stand and to punch the air as they say, 'Yes!'
YES! Our God is faithful.
YES! God's love for us is eternal.
YES! The Son of God, Jesus Christ our
Lord, expressed God's love in all he said and did.
YES! We stand firm in him.
YES! He has chosen us for his own and put his Spirit in our hearts, assuring us that all his promises will be fulfilled.
YES! AMEN!

A prayer of confession

Lord, you have formed us for yourself
so that we may proclaim your praise,
but we are forgetful.
You demolish barriers, and open up amazing new horizons so that we may step out in faith,
but we are hesitant.
You are always creating infinitely fresh possibilities, brimming with sparkling promise,
but we are nervous, harking back to how things used to be, suspicious of change.
You establish safe routes through impenetrable wilderness,
but we are not adventurous enough to set out.
You refresh parched wasteland with springs of water,
but we are reluctant to get our feet wet.
Forgive us our neglect, our forgetful, casual worship.
Forgive us for trying to lock you up in church
and for not acknowledging you in our homes, community, schools, hospitals and workplaces.
Forgive us our lack of vision, our lack of courage.
Create in us a new heart, O God, and fill us with your irrepressible Spirit.
Amen.

A prayer of thanksgiving for all ages

Lord, we thank you for new beginnings,
for blotting out our sins,
for washing our mistakes away.
You transform our desert hearts into flowering oases.
We give you thanks.
Lord, we give you thanks and praise.

Lord, we thank you for health and healing,
for always knowing what is needed most,
for listening, whether or not we bother to address you.
You respond to what we need,
not what we think we need.
We give you thanks.
Lord, we give you thanks and praise.

Lord, we thank you for our friends,
friends to pray for and friends who pray for us,
for the opportunity to find you through each other.
Your presence among us makes a difference to us all.
We give you thanks.
Lord, we give you thanks and praise.

Lord, we thank you for grace and forgiveness,
for drawing us to you, for touching our hearts.
You are the water that springs in the wilderness,
flooding our lives with the promise of peace.
We give you thanks.
Lord, we give you thanks and praise.
Amen.

A prayer activity

Ask the children to lie down very still on the floor. Say a prayer for people who are ill or who are not able to move much and do all the things the children can. The children may want to suggest people to pray for. Then the children jump up and shake their arms and legs. Thank God together for all the things we can do, and for the fact that we are all loved and forgiven by God.

A prayer of intercession

Jesus, the friends carried the paralysed man to you because they knew you would make him whole.
We carry people to you in prayer and we ask you to make them whole.
We remember people who are trapped by hunger and poverty.
We carry them to you.
Make them whole in your love.
We remember people who are broken by disease, accident, or mental illness.
We carry them to you.
Make them whole in your love.
We remember people who are dying.
We carry them to you.
Make them whole in your love.
We remember each other.
There are many things in our lives that hold us back.
We carry ourselves to you.
Make us whole in your love.
Amen.

A prayer of petition

God of friendship, grant us your healing power in our broken world.
Strengthen our goodness in building your kingdom of love and forgiveness.
Challenge us to respond as Christ to those in need, even when it may cause us to turn the world upside down.
Amen.

Year B   EPIPHANY 8

Hosea 2.14–20; Psalm 103.1–13, 22; 2 Corinthians 3.1–6; **Mark 2.13–22** *Jesus said, 'I did not come to call the virtuous but sinners.'*

Call to worship *based on Psalm 103*

Bless the Lord, O my soul, and all that is within me bless his holy name.
Bless the Lord, O my soul, and do not forget all his benefits,
who forgives all your iniquity, who heals all your diseases.
Bless the Lord, O my soul, and do not forget all his benefits,
who redeems your life from the pit, who crowns you with steadfast love and mercy.
Bless the Lord, O my soul, and do not forget all his benefits,
who satisfies you with good as long as you live so that your youth is renewed like the eagle's.
Bless the Lord, O my soul, and all that is within me bless his holy name.

A personal prayer

Call us, Lord, as you called Levi.
Call us from our custom houses of complacency.
Call us from our seats of self-importance.
Call us from lives that are destructive.
Call us to follow your way of generosity, repentance and healing, that we may take our place at your table and enjoy the feast of the kingdom with all your people.
Amen.

A prayer of thanksgiving

We praise you, Lord, for calling sinners to your table.
We praise you for calling us.
We praise you for challenging the prejudices of your day.
We praise you for challenging us.
We praise you for the truths you shared with those who followed you.
We praise you for the truth you share with us.
We praise you for all you are.
We praise you.
Amen.

A prayer of intercession

We take a moment in silence to pray for those excluded from the tables of the world, because they do not come up to other people's expectations because they are a different colour, because they believe different things…

We pray for those we exclude from our tables… family we have fallen out with, people who can't invite us back…

We pray for those have no home, no table and no food to share…

We pray that we may welcome as we have been welcomed, forgive as we have been forgiven, and feed others as we have been fed, in Jesus' name.
Amen.

A prayer for all ages

Jesus said to Levi,
Follow me, follow me.
Give up all that's bad and
Follow me, follow me.
Come and eat at my table and
Follow me, follow me.

Jesus says to us,
Follow me, follow me.
Bring along your friends and
Follow me, follow me.
Let everyone together
Follow me, follow me.
And be known as my disciples.
Alleluia! Follow me.

A prayer activity

On a large sheet of paper, draw a table and chairs and ask the children to write near each place the names of those they want to pray for and invite to their meal. Then ask them to draw the food they would like to serve on the table and then say this prayer together:
Dear Jesus, thank you that we have friends and family and food to enjoy together. We pray for those who have no friends, no family, no homes and no food. Help us never to take the good things we have for granted, but to be generous and to share. Thank you, Jesus, for everything. Amen.

A sending out prayer

May God surprise you, encourage you, and strengthen you as you go from this place to your homes, your school and your work.
Amen.

If Easter falls late, Proper 4 on page 91 may be used as Epiphany 9.

Year B LAST AFTER EPIPHANY/ TRANSFIGURATION

2 Kings 2.1–12; Psalm 50.1–6; 2 Corinthians 4.3–6;
Mark 9.2–9 *Rabbi, it is good for us to be here; let us make three dwellings.*

Call to worship

Rise and shine!
Darkness flees from the earth.
Light dawns.
The king is coming!
The God of all creation calls us to worship.
Church bells ring out.
Birds sing.
Rise and shine!
Sunlight, crisp air, rain, frost and snow declare:
The king is coming!
Green shoots burst through frozen earth.
Crocuses, golden and royal purple, carpet the way.
Rise and shine and give God the glory.
The king is coming here today!

A prayer of confession

Loving God, you have brought us
out of darkness
and into your glorious light.
Forgive us for the times
when we have continued to live
as though we were still in darkness.
Show us the way to life eternal,
that we may share your light for all eternity.
Amen.

A prayer of adoration for all ages

Day and night, dark and light,
the glory of God shines out.
Sunshine and rain, joy and pain,
the love of God breaks through.
Glistening evergreens brave the winter chill,
bare branches stir in longing for spring,
creation proclaims the care and provision of God.
Mountain peaks, rolling hills, craggy rocks,
crashing seas, rushing rivers, surging streams,
marshlands, peat bogs, heaths and moors,
fields and downs, hamlets, villages, towns and cities
and all who live there, call with one voice:
**God made us and we are in God's good
and generous hand,
great is the Lord and worthy of praise.
Amen.**

A prayer activity

Display different images of Jesus. Explain to the children that we know Jesus did and said many things during his life on earth. Because we know that he is the Son of God, we know that all he did and said leads us to God. Ask the children to concentrate on the image of Jesus they like best and wonder about God's presence in their lives.

A prayer of petition

Lord, be with us during times of change:
times when we start new ventures; take on new responsibilities, as Elisha did; times when we feel ourselves lurching forwards.
Be with us, Lord,
guide us, lead us, comfort and inspire us.

Lord, be with us during times of loss:
times when we have to say goodbye to people we love and respect, as Elisha did; times when we feel our road ahead is lonely.
Be with us, Lord,
guide us, lead us, comfort and inspire us.

Lord, be with us during times of confusion:
times when we say the first thing that comes to mind, and feel foolish, as Peter did; times when we fear we won't be able to get it right.
Be with us, Lord,
guide us, lead us, comfort and inspire us.

Lord, be with us during times of revelation:
times when we glimpse your kingdom here on earth, as the disciples did.
Show us how to do our bit in making it happen.
Be with us, Lord,
**guide us, lead us, comfort and inspire us.
Amen.**

Prayer of praise and thanksgiving

When we enjoy being alive
and everything is going well,
Jesus in heaven, we thank and praise you.
When everything is going wrong,
Jesus who came to earth, you know how we feel.
When we get through a tough patch
and know it's OK now,
Jesus in heaven, we thank and praise you.
When we're in a tough patch
and it's hard to believe,
**Jesus who came to earth, you know how we feel.
Amen.**

A personal prayer

Lord God,
You chose to reveal your glory to me
through the life and death of your Son, Jesus.
Help me to live my life in the light of that glory.
Lord, let my life reflect you in everything I do.
Amen.

Year B   LENT 1

Genesis 9.8–17; Psalm 25.1–10; 1 Peter 3.18–22;
Mark 1.9–15 *The Spirit drove Jesus into the wilderness and he remained there for 40 days tempted by Satan.*

Call to worship

Spirit of God, moving over the deep,
bringing order out of chaos in the beginning,
bring us your peace.
Come, Holy Spirit.

Lowly dove, winging your way over the waters of the flood, bringing signs of a new beginning for the world,
bring us your hope.
Come, Holy Spirit.

Spirit, descending as a dove over the waters of the Jordan, bringing the approval of God at the beginning of Jesus' ministry,
bring us your blessing.
Come, Holy Spirit.

A prayer of confession

Living, loving God,
you know our weaknesses and our frailties, you know the many times we stumble and fall and fail you.
Forgive us the times when we have gone our own way. Help us to know the strengthening and leading of your Spirit, that we may be led to serve and worship you in spirit and in truth,
for the sake of your Son, Jesus Christ.
Amen.

A prayer of intercession

We pray for those who feel that all that was precious to them has been washed away:
Lord, remember them.

For those who feel that they are lost in a wilderness, beset by temptation:
Lord, remember them.

For those who have never heard your voice speaking to them, for those who feel in need of cleansing:
Lord, remember them.

For those who need to know what way they should go next, for those who feel they have no more strength to go on:
Lord, remember them.

May they hear your good news.
May they know that you are near at hand.
May they know your Spirit descending on them,
through Jesus Christ.
Amen.

A personal prayer

Lord Jesus Christ,
in the inhospitality of the desert, you were tested and challenged to reveal who you were.
In spite of the pressure you did not give in to temptation.

In the inhospitable place of our lives, help us to resist the temptations we encounter,
when we want to find comfort in possessions,
when we want to find self-worth through domination,
when we want to deny that we follow Jesus.

In the comfort zone of the church, help us to resist the temptations we encounter,
when we take refuge in tradition,
when we allow finance to limit our vision,
when we accept others only if they conform.

Help us to turn once again to you.
Give us strength when our commitment is weak.
Enable us to place our trust in you.
Amen.

A prayer for all ages *based on Genesis 9.8–17*

Saving God,
Thank you for your promise to your people
so long ago.
Help us to live in a way that pleases you,
reflecting your goodness and love for all.
You created all things and still sustain us
in love today.
Help us to remember that we are not alone,
but can count on your help.
Help us to make a good impression on our world and on the people we meet. That all may come to know your love, your goodness and your promise.
Amen.

A prayer activity

Make lots of simple paper dove shapes, large enough to write on them, across the wings, the name of someone the children would like to pray for. Go to a high point of the building or stand on a chair and release the doves as an act of prayer. Then pray together:

We are all God's children.
We are loved.
When we are happy, when we are sad.
When we are scared and when we are brave.
When we are mean and when we are kind.
We are loved.
Thank you, God.
Amen.

A benediction

May you know God breathing his peace over the troubled depths of your soul.
May you know that Jesus is with you on your journey in the week to come.
May you know the Holy Spirit strengthening and sustaining you, this day and for ever more.
Amen.

Year B   LENT 2

Genesis 17.1–7, 15–16; Psalm 22.23–31; Romans 4.13–25; Mark 9.2–9 or **Mark 8.31–38** *Jesus said, 'Whoever wants to be a follower of mine must renounce self; take up his cross and follow me.'*

Call to worship

Jesus said, 'Those who would come after me, must deny themselves, take up their cross and follow me.'

Lead us, Lord Jesus.
Help us to follow you.

You denied yourself.
Help us to follow you.

You took up the cross.
Help us to follow you.

A prayer of confession

When we find it easier to walk the way of the world and not the way of the cross.
Forgive us, Lord, and set our minds on you.

When we place self before others and seek reassurance in our own importance.
Forgive us, Lord, and set our minds on you.

When we turn our backs on God because we fear the consequences of looking to the future and our vision is narrowed by what we think we might achieve.
Forgive us, Lord, and set our minds on you.

When we give up our lives for the sake of a comfortable existence.
Forgive us, Lord, and set our minds on you.

When the cross is rough and heavy and our shoulders ache and we feel unable to carry on.
**Forgive us, Lord, and set our minds on you.
Amen.**

A prayer of intercession

We have so much, that we constantly throw away, wasting the earth's resources and denying others what they really need.
We pray for the earth that we have plundered and the people we have denied.
Help us to live in harmony with the earth and in co-operation with one another.

We have so much that we make ourselves immune to others' pain, taking out our cheque books, not rolling up our sleeves.
We pray for those who suffer the pain of hunger, disease or poverty.
Help us to challenge injustice and be willing to share from our abundance.

We have so much freedom to believe and to express ourselves.
We pray for those who long to be free, to determine their own future, free of prejudice and discrimination.
**Help us to feel compassion and to pick up our cross and follow you.
Amen.**

A people prayer

God, the creator of the rich tapestry of humankind,
we give you thanks for our heritage:
for our ancestors, known and unknown,
for our ever-evolving culture,
shaped deep in the past, yet flowering today.
We thank you for our Judaeo-Christian heritage,
for the tales of the patriarchs,
for the opportunity to rejoice in your gifts,
and for your love, so deep that you sent your Son to die for us.
Make us faithful, Lord,
responsive to our calling
and eager to hear your voice.
Through Jesus Christ our Lord.
Amen.

A prayer for all ages

God who calls us to a new way of living,
Of loving,
Of sharing,
Different and special.
Name us as your children.
Enable us to
Welcome others and
Send us out to live in your name.
Amen.

A prayer activity

Hold up a large cross. Remind the group that Jesus loved each of us so much that he suffered a great deal and finally died on the cross so that we could be forgiven. Allow time for children to pray silently or out loud to Jesus to say thank you for the cross.

A sending out prayer

Go and continue on your life's journey,
knowing that God is with you each step of the way.
And may the God of peace bring you every blessing,
with which to serve him and make his will known
through Jesus Christ,
to whom be all glory and honour,
now and for ever more.
Amen.

Year B   LENT 3

Exodus 20.1–17; Psalm 19; 1 Corinthians 1.18–25;
John 2.13–22 *Stop making my Father's house a marketplace.*

A prayer of approach

When we stand in awe of the magnificence of the Temple:
Jesus calls us to look for the kingdom hidden among us.
When we allow corruption and injustice to go unchallenged:
Jesus prompts us to ask the difficult questions. We draw near, hesitant, afraid, searching, to worship the one who calls us to a new way of living for ourselves and the world.
Amen.

A prayer of confession

Our merciful and loving God,
we have wandered from your way, following our own ways. We are truly sorry for our failure and humbly claim your promise to forgive. Help us to live lives worthy of your calling – to be fit temples within which you may abide.
For the sake of your Son Jesus Christ.
Amen.

A prayer of intercession

Where earth is polluted and plundered;
where God's creation is driven to extinction;
where habitats are destroyed:
let tears fall as we feel the pain of your creation,
and make us holy as we tread the earth.

Where people are hungry or cold;
where children die of treatable diseases;
where women are trafficked and abused:
let tears fall as we feel the pain of injustice,
and make us holy as we encounter the lives of others.

Where war denies the right to life;
where refugees are driven from homelands;
where people are scarred physically and mentally:
let tears fall as we feel the pain of conflict,
and make us holy as we are challenged to live your shalom.
Amen.

A quiet prayer

In the noise of the Temple,
Jesus made a holy place.
In the pushing and the shoving,
Jesus made a holy place.
In the busy times at school,
Jesus, make a holy place.
In the bustle of my home,
Jesus, make a holy place.
In the quiet of my heart,
Jesus, make a holy place.
Amen.

A prayer for all ages

In many faiths, prayer involves the whole body, and cleansing is important before prayer:
Some people pray in a temple or church. *(Make roof shape with arms)*
Some people kneel to pray. *(Kneel)*
Some people bow to pray. *(Bow down)*
Some people stand to pray. *(Stand)*
Some people take off their shoes to pray. *(Take off or point to shoes)*
Some people wash their hands or feet to pray. *(Mime washing hands)*
Some people sit to pray. *(Sit)*
Some people close their eyes to pray. *(Close eyes)*
Some people put their hands together to pray. *(Put hands together)*
Whatever our actions, Lord,
we give ourselves to you.
Thank you for making our whole body holy,
a living temple,
and for loving each one of us.
Amen.

A prayer of response

Jesus, you spoke words that changed attitudes.
May we be strong for what is right.
You spoke words that made the powerful worry.
May we be strong for what is right.
You did things that made people fear.
You showed your anger, which made evil run away.
May we be strong for what is right.
You did all this in your father's temple.
May we be strong for what is right.
Amen.

A prayer activity

Ask everyone to write on a piece of paper a situation they care passionately about – maybe bullying, or animal cruelty. Then together rip the papers to shreds as an indication of anger about such situations. Put the pieces in a basket and pray: 'Your kingdom come, your will be done'.

A sending out prayer

As we leave this place,
we turn ourselves to you.
As we leave this place,
we turn over to a new beginning.
As we leave this place,
may we live as you call us,
holy people, a living temple.
Amen.

Year B   LENT 4

Numbers 21.4–9; Psalm 107.1–3, 17–22; Ephesians 2.1–10; **John 3.14–21** *God so loved the world that he gave his only Son, so that whoever believes in him may not perish but have eternal life.*

A prayer of approach

Spirit of life, creator of all,
with heart and voice, with love and joy,
we offer you our worship and praise.
Truly you have been a good God to us.
You have revealed yourself in Jesus Christ and
fulfilled your promises by the Holy Spirit.
You have accompanied us on each step of
our journey.
Praise be to you, O Lord our God.
Amen.

A prayer of confession

I'm sorry, God, for the times when I have thought
dark things.
I'm sorry, God, for the times when I have done
dark things.
I'm sorry, God, for the times when I have ignored
your light.
I'm sorry, God, for the times when I have not shared
your light with others.
Thank you, God, that your light shines in
my darkness.
Thank you, God, that you forgive me.
Amen.

A prayer of intercession *based on Numbers 21.4–9 and John 3.16*

God who journeys with us, we pause on our journey
of life to think about those whose journeys are painful
and difficult…
…people who don't have enough food or access to
clean water:
for God so loved the world;
…people who are ill:
for God so loved the world;
…people who mourn the loss of loved ones:
for God so loved the world;
…people who experience the darkness of depression:
for God so loved the world;
…people who suffer from low self-image and worth.
For God so loved the world,
that he sent his only Son
so that none should perish
but that all may know God
and all may have life.
Amen.

A prayer of thanksgiving

For you so loved the world,
and we thank you that that includes us.
That you gave your only son,
and we thank you that you gave him for us.
You invite us all to believe in him,
and we thank you that that invitation is for us.
You give eternal life,
and we thank you that that is given to us.
Amen.

A prayer for all ages together

When we don't know what to do,
Jesus, be the light in our world.

When we are frightened or worried,
Jesus, be the light in our world.

When we are struggling in the dark,
Jesus, be the light in our world.

When we fall out with our friends,
Jesus, be the light in our world.
Amen.

A prayer activity

You will need four candles.
Light the first candle, and say:
When we are in the darkness,
it is difficult to find our way.
We can feel very alone.

Light the second candle, and say:
When we can see a little light,
it can give us courage
to face the choices that lie ahead.

Light the third candle, and say:
As the light becomes brighter,
we feel safer and can see further.
Making choices is easier.

Light the final candle, and say:
It is bright and warm.
Let us be like these candles, growing brighter with
your love and teaching, Jesus.
Amen.

A sending out prayer

Go from this place in peace.
Go from this place with love.
As you have received from God,
so give and be to others,
in Jesus' name.
Amen.

Year B   LENT 5

Jeremiah 31.31–34; Psalm 51.1–12, or Psalm
119.9–16; Hebrews 5.5–10; **John 12.20–33** *Unless a
grain of wheat falls into the earth and dies, it remains
a single grain: but if it dies, it bears much fruit.*

Call to worship

Night has gone, day has broken.
Thanks be to God.
We are loved as the people we are.
Thanks be to God.
With hearts aflame with love,
We praise the Lord.

A prayer of confession

Lord our God,
you know who we are and how we are.
Our strengths and our weaknesses are known to you.
Forgive our failure to hear and respond.
Forgive our unwillingness to trust your promises.
Let us know the healing touch of your forgiveness,
through Jesus Christ our Lord.
Amen.

A prayer of petition

Jesus said:
'Unless a grain of wheat falls into the earth and dies,
it remains a single grain.'
Help us, Lord, to understand this saying
and to be one of those who bear much fruit in your
name.
Jesus said:
'Those who love their life, lose it.'
Help us, Lord, to understand this saying
and to be willing to give up all we have in your
service.
Jesus said: 'When I am lifted up from the earth, I will
draw all people to myself.'
Help us, Lord, to understand this saying
and to be part of your mission to bring good news
to our neighbours and to all humankind.
Amen.

A prayer of intercession

Wherever we find devastation and hopelessness:
help us to plant seeds;
make us nurturers of fertile ground.
Wherever we meet fear and anxiety:
help us to plant seeds;
make us nurturers of fertile ground.
When we find people who want to give up:
help us to plant seeds;
make us nurturers of fertile ground.
When people want to learn;
when people don't want to learn:
help us to plant seeds;
make us nurturers of fertile ground.

Make us workers with you, Lord,
in your project of creation:
help us to plant seeds;
make us nurturers of fertile ground.
Amen.

A prayer of thanksgiving for all ages

Dear God,
Jesus had to go down so that he could rise up for
everyone to see.
Thank you that Jesus went down for me.
Jesus had to go into the darkness so that he could
shine the light.
Thank you that Jesus went into darkness for me.
Jesus had to suffer so that he could free the world
from suffering.
Thank you that Jesus suffered for me.
Jesus had to give up everything so that he could give
people life.
Thank you that Jesus gave up everything for me.
Jesus had to die so that he could come alive again.
Thank you that Jesus died for me.
Amen.

A prayer activity

*Place a large bowl or pot of earth on a table and give
each person a seed. Allow time for everyone to plant
their seed and remember to tend them so that the
promise of bearing much fruit can be seen. Say:*
You hold in your hand a seed,
small and brittle, new life that can only be realized
when that seed is buried in the dark earth,
tended by water and sun.
Our lives are like that seed,
filled with potential,
yet buried in darkness,
while we wonder if new growth will come.

Invite the group to plant their seeds
Tended by the light of Christ,
and the water of your word,
bring forth new life,
and draw us closer still to you.
Amen.

A sending out prayer

May God bless you with rain,
may God bless you with sunshine.
May God bless you with food,
may God bless you with shelter.
And until we meet again,
may you grow in God's love
and plant seeds of God's love,
wherever you may be.
Amen.

Year B LENT 6/PALM SUNDAY

Palms: Psalm 118.1–2, 19–29; John 12.12–16, or
Mark 11.1–11 *Blessed is he who comes in the name
of the Lord. Passion*: Isaiah 50.4–9a; Psalm 31.9–16;
Philippians 2.5–11; Mark 14.1–15.47, or Mark 15.1–
39 (40–47)

Call to worship

Lord Jesus Christ,
approach and enter the city of our hearts.
Lord Jesus Christ,
correct our priorities and still the clamour.
Lord Jesus Christ,
find your home in us and give us peace.

A prayer of commitment

As the crowds gathered to welcome and celebrate
the coming kingdom of freedom, peace and justice,
so we lay 'our cloaks' under his feet as signs of our
commitment to the donkey-riding king, Jesus Christ
our Lord.
His vision is our vision.
His kingdom is our kingdom.
His call is our call.
His journey is our journey.
His life is our life.
Hosanna!
Blessed is he who comes in the name of the Lord.
Amen.

A prayer of intercession

Almighty and everlasting God,
We pray for the rootless in our society:
those who know nothing of love and security, those
who have no one to love, no place to call their own.
Lord, hear our prayer.

We pray for those who live in cities:
those who came with eager anticipation,
those who enter seeking refuge;
the many who look at shop windows showing goods
they cannot afford,
and those who can easily afford them.
Lord, hear our prayer.

We pray for those who make their living in the city:
those elected to positions of civic leadership,
all who pay their council tax,
and those with the responsibility of spending it.
Lord, hear our prayer.

Lord Jesus Christ,
you entered the city of Jerusalem
in all its rich diversity
to celebrate the glory of God,
to conquer by love the forces that demean
humankind.
Enter the cities of our land, through your Church.
Enter the cities of our heart, through your Spirit.
Hear our prayers,
and by your power transform all life.
For Jesus' sake.
Amen.

A prayer for all ages

Lord Jesus, traveller to Jerusalem,
thank you for the life we have,
for those who share it with us,
who love us and allow us to love them.
When life presents each of us with challenges
help us to decide which ones are important.
Give us wisdom in reacting to them:
when we are afraid, uphold us,
when we need courage, supply it.
Thank you for those around us
who share, encourage and support.
As they are to us,
so may we be to other people.
So bless us all, in Jesus' name.
Amen.

A prayer of confession

Forgive us, O God. Our cloaks of faith are thin
with excuse, frayed with neglect, crumpled with
forgetfulness and torn with abuse.
Lord, forgive us.
Lord, save us.
Lord, hear us.
Hosanna!
Blessed is he who comes in the name of the Lord.
Amen.

A prayer activity

*Give everyone a paper palm branch and encourage
them to wave them as you say the following prayer:*
Lord Jesus, you are a special friend.
Hosanna!
Lord Jesus, you are our King.
Hosanna!
Lord Jesus, we love you.
Hosanna!
Praise the name of Jesus.
Hosanna!

A sending out prayer

May the blessing of God,
who resides in our hopes and our dreams,
grant us peace.
May the blessing of Jesus,
who rides to wild acclaim and waving palm branches,
grant us peace.
May the blessing of the Spirit,
who holds us through fears and nightmares,
grant us peace, and the hopes and dreams
of the dawning of an Easter Morning.
Amen.

Year B   EASTER DAY

Isaiah 25.6–9, or Acts 10.34–43; Psalm 118.1–2, 14–24; 1 Corinthians 15.1–11, or Acts 10.34–43; John 20.1–18, or **Mark 16.1–8** *Jesus of Nazareth who was crucified has been raised. He is not here. Look, there is the place they laid him.*

Call to worship

Gathered now on this Easter morning, we join our voices with the whole Church, across the world and across time, as we proclaim:
Christ is risen!
He is risen indeed.
Alleluia!

A prayer of approach

Today, this day of celebration, we come to this place, scarcely believing the news – he is risen!
Today in this place,
may we meet the risen Jesus.

We come to this place, unprepared to meet you – the one who is risen.
Today in this place,
may we meet the risen Jesus.

We come with all our burdens to give to the one who is risen, looking for acceptance.
Today in this place,
may we meet the risen Jesus.

Today, as we come to worship Jesus who is risen, may we all meet him and know the joy of life with him.
Amen.

A prayer of intercession for all ages

Dear Jesus,
We thank you that you are our friend who is alive and who we can talk to. Please be with everybody today in all the churches around the world, as they celebrate that you are alive.
Please be with them,
as you are with us.

Please be with all people who are scared, or who are sick or weak, especially those who don't have any friends or family to help them.
Please be with them,
as you are with us.

Please be with all people who feel that they are no good, especially those who don't know that you love them and that you want to be their friend.
Please be with them,
as you are with us.
Amen.

A prayer at the empty tomb

Lord Jesus Christ, risen Lord.
Lord of the morning,
of this day, of all our days.
In our hearts we wonder and stare with the disciples who discovered the empty tomb.
In our hearts we run to you again, anxious to meet you here, on home ground, in the people and places we love, as well as in people we have yet to meet.
Give us courage to risk everything for you, as you have given all of yourself for us.
Amen.

A prayer for all ages

Lord Jesus Christ, thank you for your promise to be with us always, even until the end of time.
Help us to remember your promise when we are fearful or unsure about whether we are brave enough to be your disciples.
Help us always to remember that you rose from the tomb, and that the first people to know were ordinary people like us, who didn't feel very brave.
Give us courage to speak and act faithfully, lovingly and fairly,
in the places where we live and learn and work, this Easter week and always.
Amen.

A prayer of confession

Lord, you are risen, yet we doubt you.
Lord, have mercy.
Christ, you appear to us, but we fail to notice.
Christ, have mercy.
Most glorious Lord of life, have mercy on us.
Have mercy on us.
Amen.

A prayer activity

Sit around a large candle. Play gentle music. Give everyone a smooth pebble as a reminder of the stone in front of the tomb. Be quiet and still with God. Then ask the group to write a couple of words in felt tip on their pebbles as a topic of prayer. Say the prayers in turn, ending each one as below:
The stone is rolled away.
Each person puts their pebble beside the candle.
Jesus, you are alive today.

A sending out prayer

Let us go out with joy, and with courage, to love and serve the risen Lord.
The Lord is risen.
He is risen indeed.
Alleluia!

Year B EASTER 2

Acts 4.32–35; Psalm 133; 1 John 1.1–2.2;
John 20.19–31 *Jesus stood among his disciples and said, 'Peace be with you.'*

A gathering prayer

We gather as the disciples did.
Come, risen Lord, and stand among us.
We open the doors of our hearts to you.
Come, risen Lord, and stand among us.
Grant us your peace, and breathe upon us.
Come, risen Lord, and stand among us.
Amen.

A prayer for peace

Jesus came and stood among the disciples,
saying, 'Peace be with you.'
Lord, where there are families in distress,
help us walk beside them, saying, 'Peace be with you.'
Lord, in the playground or park,
where children fight or disagree,
put us among them to say, 'Peace be with you.'
Lord, where there is stress in the workplace
and tension between colleagues,
make us present to say, 'Peace be with you.'
Give us your peace, Lord,
and make us peacemakers.
Amen.

A prayer of intercession

We experience this world through five senses.
We see how people suffer:
help us to see with your eyes, compassionate God,
so that we will know how to help.
Lord, keep us watchful.

We hear the awful sounds of warfare:
help those caught up in it to hear your still, small voice.
Lord, help us listen.

We touch what is pleasing to us:
help us to touch those in need, loving Lord, the
outcast, the stranger, the sick and the bereaved.
Lord, make us gentle.

We smell the pollution we have inflicted on your
world: help us to remedy this,
so that we may smell again the freshness of creation.
Lord, make us careful.

We taste the bitterness of doubt and disappointment:
pour your blessing of belief on an unbelieving world,
so we may taste your victory!
Lord, make us hopeful.
Amen.

A prayer for all ages

Lord Jesus Christ,
Thank you that you greet us today with your gift of
peace and with the promise of your Holy Spirit.
Help us to be as honest and brave as Thomas,
especially at times when we find it hard to know that
you are with us.
Thank you for the promise of your blessing at those
times, and may we learn to recognize the signs of
your presence all around us each day.
Amen.

A prayer of confession *based on Psalm 133 and today's Gospel*

O God of peace and unity, we confess that in our
words, our ways, our priorities, we have sometimes
denied or restricted our risen Lord's giving of himself.
How good and how lovely it is to live together in unity.

Forgive us, we pray, and make us yet a people known
for the generosity of their forgiveness.
How good and how lovely it is to live together in unity.
Amen.

A prayer activity

*Reflect on Jesus' words 'Peace be with you' and use
them as a prayerful greeting to each other. You could
shake hands and say them, write them on paper
darts and throw them at each other or hold hands in a
circle and say them together.*
*See how many creative ways of saying them the
group can invent.*
To close say together:
**Jesus, bringer of peace, help us to know your
peace. And to share your peace with others.
Alleluia!**
Amen.

A sending out prayer

May the peace of Christ be with you
as you leave this place.
May the peace of Christ be with us
in our homes and our communities.
May the peace of Christ be with everyone
in their dealings with others.
Amen.

Year B EASTER 3

Acts 3.12–19; Psalm 4; 1 John 3.1–7;
Luke 24.36b–48 *Jesus said, 'You are witnesses of these things.'*

Call to worship

Spoken by three people from different parts of the church:
In times of surprise and joy, the peace of Christ be with you.
In times of fear and despair, the peace of Christ be with you.
In times of challenge and new beginnings, the peace of Christ be with you.

A prayer of intercession

We pray for those who need to hear the good news.
For those who live in poverty.
Lord of the resurrection,
send us out.
We pray for the sick, the war-worn,
the weary and the dying.
Lord of the resurrection,
send us out.
We pray for children, delight of the world today,
hope of the world tomorrow.
Lord of the resurrection,
send us out.
We pray for older people,
guardians of the faith, custodians of wisdom.
Lord of the resurrection,
send us out.
We pray for community workers,
those who share values, culture and care.
Lord of the resurrection,
send us out.
We pray for travellers,
those who share and learn across the world.
Lord of the resurrection,
send us out.
Lord, make us your witnesses.
Lord of the resurrection,
send us out.
Amen.

A prayer for children

We witness with our minds, *(Fingertips on temple)*
and with our hearts, *(Hand on heart)*
with our mouths, *(Touch lips)*
and with our hands, *(Hold out hands, palms upwards)*
that Jesus Christ is the risen Lord!
Amen.

A prayer of confession

Forgive us, God, when we become set in our ways,
refusing to change, believing that what we have
always known is the only truth.
Living God, **forgive us and startle us into new life.**

Forgive us when we set up barriers, not recognizing
your voice or presence in other cultures or faiths, or
in neighbours who are different from us.
Living God, **forgive us and startle us into new life.**

Forgive us when we have been so preoccupied with
maintaining structures and customs that we have
missed the moment of revelation, and been too busy
for new insights.
Living God, **forgive us and startle us into new life.**
Amen.

A prayer of thanksgiving

Thank you, Lord, for the resurrection.
Thank you, Jesus, for being so real.
Thank you for showing yourself to your people.
Thank you, Jesus, for being so real.
You bear the wounds the world inflicted.
To your resurrection, we bear witness.
You bring repentance, and forgiveness.
To your resurrection, we bear witness.
We thank you for your grace upon us.
Let the light of your face shine on us!
Amen.

A prayer for all ages

Your friends were frightened and upset.
They didn't know what was going to happen next.
You came to them, to show them you were there
for them.
Loving Jesus, **be there for us.**
Your friends were mixed up,
and not sure what to think.
You showed them your hands and feet,
and shared a meal with them.
Loving Jesus, **share with us.**
Your friends were happy,
but didn't know what to do.
You talked to them and taught them,
and told them the story of God's love.
Loving Jesus, **tell us the story too.**
Amen.

A prayer activity

*In advance, make picture frames from card. Provide
gold/silver paper, sequins, etc. Ask the children
to decorate the frames as if they were framing
something that was too good to be true. Then give
each child a piece of paper saying, 'Jesus is alive and
he loves me' to put in the frame. The message may
seem too good to be true but it is the truth: he loves
each one of us.*

A sending out prayer

Refreshed by this time in your house, Lord,
we go out to witness in your world.
Help us to live the truths that we have learned,
so all may see your presence in our lives.
Amen.

Year B   EASTER 4

Acts 4.5–12; Psalm 23; 1 John 3.16–24;
John 10.11–18 *Jesus said, 'I am the good shepherd.*
I lay down my life for the sheep.'

Call to worship

In God we find our soul's restoration:
he leads his flock as the good shepherd, our Lord.
In God we learn to fear no evil:
he leads his flock as the good shepherd, our Lord.
In God we are granted goodness and love:
he leads his flock as the good shepherd, our Lord.
May each of us sense the guidance of God and the
blessings he pours upon his people.

A prayer of intercession *based on Psalm 23*

Lord our shepherd,
you lead us with tender, loving care.
We pray for those who wander, trying to discern their
way in difficult times:
for the unemployed, those seeking work and new
direction.
Lord our shepherd, **guide us.**
We pray for those who are passing through dark
valleys: the sick, the depressed, the hungry.
Lord our shepherd, **guide us.**
We pray for those who are anointed with the task of
leadership: leaders of nations, of local and religious
communities.
We pray for those who must negotiate to bring an end
to enmity and violence.
Lord our shepherd, **guide us.**
We pray for ourselves, that we may set a table of
hospitality before all who need our help,
that our overflowing cup will be shared with others.
Lord our shepherd, **guide us.**
We pray for the dying,
that they will come to dwell in your house
and know your comfort in their final days.
Lord our shepherd, **guide us.**
All this we ask in the name of the Good Shepherd,
Jesus, our master and our friend.
Amen.

A prayer for all ages *based on Psalm 23*

You, Lord, are our good shepherd:
you give us all we need.
You make us lie down in green pastures:
lead us by quiet waters.
You guide us in paths of righteousness:
may we go in your name.
Sometimes we must walk through dark valleys:
please help us to not be afraid.
You are with us to guide and to comfort:
we will not be afraid!
You provide so much for us:
make us grateful.
Your goodness and love will follow us all the days of
our lives:
we will dwell in your house for ever!
Amen.

A prayer of confession

Far we wander, frequently we stray,
in mind and word and deed.
Please look on us with goodness and mercy, Lord,
when we have wronged you,
and where we have injured others on the way.
It is never your desire that any be hurt or harmed,
always your will that blessings will overflow.
Yet, where our actions hinder such blessing,
for ourselves and for our neighbour,
rescue us with your eternal staff
and lead us back to your path of righteousness.
Amen.

A children's prayer

He looks after his sheep.
His name is Jesus.
He makes sick people well.
His name is Jesus.
He lets prisoners go free.
His name is Jesus.
He came back from death.
His name is Jesus.
He is always with us.
His name is Jesus.

A prayer activity

*Draw a sheep pen on a large piece of paper. Remind
the children that the shepherd cares for his sheep
and leads them away from the wolf. Jesus, the good
shepherd, loves us, and helps us with things we are
worried or frightened about. Talk together about their
worries and ask them to write or draw them on a
sheep outline. Ask the children to hold these sheep
as you pray:*
**Jesus, the good shepherd, there are so many
things we are worried about. We bring them to
you now. Please guide us to safe places and help
us to listen to your voice.**
Each child puts their sheep in the pen.

A sending out prayer

In the name of the Good Shepherd,
who sacrificed his all for his flock,
go onward from this place.
In the name of the Good Shepherd,
who calls us to sacrifice for his flock,
go onward from this place.
And as he drives us on,
may we know his presence with us,
night and day, now and always.
Amen.

Year B   EASTER 5

Acts 8.26–40; Psalm 22.25–31; 1 John 4.7–21;
John 15.1–8 *Jesus said, 'I am the vine, you are the branches. Those who abide in me and I in them bear much fruit.'*

Call to worship

God is the Creator.
We are the created.
Let us abide in the Creator.

Jesus is the Vine.
We are the branches.
Let us abide in the Vine.

The Spirit can live in us.
We can live in the Spirit.
Let us abide in the Spirit.

Our God is a Trinitarian God,
abiding in relationship.
We too, shall abide in the Trinity.

A prayer of confession

God, forgive us when we isolate ourselves from you and one another. Withering away through our clinging to dead tradition, or stunted because we are afraid of new growth.
Give us the joy that comes from knowing the words of Christ dwelling in us and shaping our lives.
Give us the joy that comes from a delight in diversity and the recognition of the gifts of others.
Give us the joy that bears fruit in love and community, so that the world may see us as disciples of Christ.
Amen.

A prayer of intercession

My Father is glorified in this, that you bear much fruit and become my disciples.
Father, we thank you for this community and our friends; help us to work together so that all flourish together and your name is made known.
Lord, you are the vine,
and we are the branches.

We pray for all who support others:
the leaders of nations and communities,
those who care and those who educate,
those who serve and those who construct,
those who farm and trade.
Lord, you are the vine,
and we are the branches.

We pray for those who may feel like the pruned branches:
those who feel unwanted and unloved,
those who feel themselves to be a burden,
those who feel bullied or left out.
Lord, you are the vine,
and we are the branches.

We pray for new shoots,
released into life through the pruning of old branches:
for babies and children,
for those moving to new lives and new ventures,
those passing on from the journey of this life to new life eternal.
Lord, you are the vine,
and we are the branches.
Hear our prayer, draw near and help us.
Amen.

A pruning prayer

For the times when I've not been fruitful,
Lord, cut away the dead wood.
For the times when I've not helped others to grow,
Lord, cut away the dead wood.
For the times when I've clung on to my weakness,
Lord, cut away the dead wood.
For the times I've separated myself from you,
Lord, cut away the dead wood.
Amen.

A prayer activity

Draw a large plug with three pins, marked, Thank You, Sorry and Please. Ask the children to write or draw something they want to say thank you or sorry for, or someone or something they want to pray for. Remind the children that prayer is one way of keeping plugged in and connected to God.

A prayer for all ages together

You are the vine.
We are the branches.
Keep us connected to you.
We want to hear what God is saying.
Like a phone connected to a phone line,
keep us connected to you.
We want to have power to do good for God.
Like a vacuum cleaner connected to a socket,
keep us connected to you.
We want our lives to be beautiful for God.
Like a flower connected to its stem,
keep us connected to you.
We want love, peace, joy and patience to grow in us.
Like grapes growing on a vine,
keep us connected to you.
You are the vine.
We are the branches.
Keep us connected to you.
Amen.

A sending out prayer

God abides in us and we abide in God. So as we go forth from this place, may our God of goodness and nurture, Father, Son and Holy Spirit, stay with us and we stay with him, now and always.
Amen.

Year B EASTER 6

Acts 10.44–48; Psalm 98; 1 John 5.1–6;
John 15.9–17 *Jesus said, 'As the Father has loved me, so I have loved you: abide in my love.'*

Call to worship

In love we were made, by love we are redeemed.
And love at last shall bring us home.
In gratitude for all that we have and all that we are,
we come to give thanks to our loving God,
and to praise God's holy name.

A prayer of praise

Lord, you are the friend of the poor and impoverished.
We praise you for sharing your riches.
You are the friend of the lost and forsaken.
We praise you for guiding us home.
You are the friend of the outcast and stranger.
We praise you for including us in.
Friend of the friendless, companion to the lonely, host to all humanity.
We praise your holy name!
Amen.

A prayer of confession

Jesus taught us to love one another,
but often we argue, and hurt one another.
God of all goodness,
we are sorry.

Jesus taught us to love one another,
but often we think of ourselves,
and ignore each other.
God of all goodness,
we are sorry.

Jesus taught us to love one another,
but often we forget what he taught,
and forget one another's needs.
God of all goodness,
we are sorry.
Silence

God of all goodness,
help us to love one another,
as Jesus loves us;
and when we don't,
let us remember that you still love us and forgive us,
so we can pick ourselves up
and start again.
Amen.

A prayer of intercession

O God, our maker, you are worthy of praise and glory from all that dwell in heaven and on earth.
You alone called everything into being.
We pray for your Church, that your children may be one.
We pray for ....

Alert us to the needs of others and equip us with the skills to share each other's burdens as well as joys.
We pray for ....

Inspire the leaders of our world.
Guide them – and us too – in the ways of justice and of peace.
We pray for ....

Inspire us in our relationships with our families and friends.
We pray for ....

Give us the skills to care for the sick, the sad, the troubled and the lonely.
We pray for ....

Heavenly Father, we ask this, and all that we cannot put into words, in the name of our Lord and Saviour, your Son, Jesus Christ.
Amen.

A prayer for all ages

Make me a true friend, O God.
Make me a faithful friend.

Give me a patient heart, so that I may listen.
Give me a loving heart, so that I may hear.
Make me a true friend, O God.
Make me a faithful friend.

Give me a strong heart – take away my fear.
Give me a courageous heart – make me daring in your name.
Make me a true friend, O God.
Make me a faithful friend.

Give me a quiet heart – to act for others setting self aside.
Give me a peaceful heart – to act out your love in all creation.
Make me a true friend, O God.
Make me a faithful friend.
Amen.

A prayer activity

Ask the group to create the word 'Love' on the floor, using their bodies to form the shapes of the letters. As each person joins the emerging shape, ask them to say out loud:
I'll work to build your love, Lord.

A sending out prayer

Go! You are friends of the most high!
Go and praise the maker of heaven and earth – our God, our Friend.
In the name of the most high!
Amen.

Year B   EASTER 7

Acts 1.15–17, 21–26; Psalm 1; 1 John 5.9–13;
John 17.6–19 *Jesus prayed, 'Protect them in your name … so that they may be one as we are one.'*

Call to worship

You could ask people to turn to face the relevant direction as these words are said:
I look to the East where the sun breaks the dawn,
Christ is there.
I look to the West where the sun slips from sight,
Christ is there.
I look to the North where the winter sun is scarce,
Christ is there.
I look to the South where the summer sun blazes warm,
Christ is there.
I look to the past where memories remind us of times gone by,
Christ is there.
I look to the future where dreams are dreamed and hope burns bright,
Christ is there.
I look at the faces revealed around me and the self buried within me,
Christ is here.

A prayer of approach

Jesus, we come before you with open eyes so that we may see the glory of your resurrection.
With open hearts so that we may know your presence with us.
With open ears so that we may hear your word.
With open minds so that we may learn your will,
and with open hands so that we may do the work to which you call us.
Amen.

A prayer of confession

God, forgive us when we deny your presence in the world you have created.
Forgive us when we deny your presence in those who we perceive to be different from us.
Forgive us when we deny your presence in those whom we know and love.
Forgive us when we prefer the safety of the familiar and help us to embrace the adventure of faith.
Amen.

A prayer of thanksgiving and intercession

To be read by two voices
1: When the world forgets to say thank you:
2: Let us give thanks for the good things we have and the freedoms we enjoy.
1: When the world forgets to say thank you:
2: Let us give thanks for the time we have left to save this world from itself.
1: When the world forgets to say please:
2: We pray for this planet, now at the mercy of the lives we lead.

1: When the world forgets to say please:
2: We pray for peoples and cultures at the mercy of those in power.
1: When the world forgets to say please:
2: We pray for those who live only for themselves:
Amen.

A caim prayer for all ages together

Christ, encircle us.
Keep out all that would hurt us.
Keep your creation safe.
Christ, encircle us.
Keep us from hurting those around us.
Keep everyone safe.
Christ, encircle us.
Keep us from hurting ourselves.
Keep us safe.
Christ, encircle us.
Enfold your arms around us,
and give us faith to go out and live.
Amen.

A prayer for unity

Gracious God,
Though you have cast us all from the one mould that is your love, we are a wealth of different shapes and sizes; a vast army of pilgrim people you cherish as sons and daughters.
Unite us as one family, one humanity,
that clamours not for security, but for peace.
May we never stand alone
when we could stand together;
and never isolate, when we could include.
That all may recognize in all your image and your likeness, revealed most fully in Jesus Christ,
our Saviour.
Amen.

A prayer activity

Give each child a blank cardboard shield with a large circle in the centre. Ask them to illustrate the shield with all the things they need in life to keep them safe, but to keep the centre blank. Read John 17.14–15. Remind the children that though the disciples were enthusiastic to do Jesus' work and pass on his message, it wasn't easy and Jesus prayed to God to keep them safe. Get the children to write 'God' in the centre of their shields and the words 'Holy Father protect them' round the edge of it.

A sending out prayer

As we leave this place, Jesus goes with us.
He loves us, he looks after us,
he protects us, he holds us.
As we leave this place, Jesus goes with us.
Amen.

Year B   PENTECOST

Acts 2.1–21, or Ezekiel 37.1–14; Psalm 104.24–34,
35b; Romans 8.22–27, or Acts 2.1–21;
John 15.26–27, 16.4b–15 *Jesus said, 'When the
Spirit of truth comes, he will guide you into all truth.'*

A prayer of approach

Spirit of God, come as flame, and fill our hearts with
the fire of your love.
Come, Holy Spirit, come.
Spirit of God, come as wind, and refresh our senses
with the breath of new life.
Come, Holy Spirit, come.
Spirit of God, come in words of power, and enlighten
our minds with your truth.
Come, Holy Spirit, come.

A prayer of intercession

The Holy Spirit comes to set us free.
Let us pray for those who long for freedom
from oppression and tyranny.
We pray to the Lord.
Let us pray for those who long for freedom
from war and conflict, from poverty and want.
We pray to the Lord.
Let us pray for those who long for freedom
from injustice and ill-treatment, from abuse and
neglect.
We pray to the Lord.
Let us pray for those who long for freedom
from insecurity and addiction, from fear and doubt.
We pray to the Lord.
Amen.

A prayer for all ages

Spirit of the four winds,
we thank you for the wind of the South
that fills us with the warmth of your comfort
and encourages us to welcome others.
Fill us with your breath of life.

Spirit of the four winds,
we thank you for the wind of the West
that brings rain to refresh and cleanse
and helps us reflect on the endings of life.
Fill us with your breath of life.

Spirit of the four winds,
we thank you for the wind of the North
that blows the cobwebs of laziness away
and stirs us up with courage to try new things.
Fill us with your breath of life.

Spirit of the four winds,
we thank you for the wind of the East
that brings birth and light and peace
and fills us with hope and dreams for tomorrow.
Fill us with your breath of life.
Amen.

A prayer of confession

God of flame, your life has flowed through our history,
leaping from one generation to another,
releasing captives, affirming the poor, welcoming
outcasts.
Upon this day you spoke with the accent of all people
in displaying your love for all life.
We confess to you and each other
our drabness and uniformity,
our desire to control rather than share life;
to reproduce the past rather than explore the future.
We confess the narrowness of our vision,
and our choosing of the most comfortable path.
God of flame and colour, dance around us, enchant
us; quicken us and, above all, forgive us
for painting your gospel in the dowdy colours of our
limiting culture.
In the name of Christ, release us from the prisons of
our own making.
Amen.

A prayer for Pentecost

Lord, open our hearts, that we may be truly alive to all
the sounds and colours of your Spirit among us:
the trickles and the waterfalls,
the flickers and the fireworks,
in the ordinary, in the mundane, in the unknown;
in stirrings that echo in our hearts
and excite us, dare us, free us.
Overturn our expectations, and explode our
complacencies, that this Pentecost will be as the
first – a new beginning,
overflowing with possibility and passion
and all that brings life and healing and you,
afresh in our midst.
Amen.

A prayer activity

*Ask the children to imagine that they are like
drainpipes, as they stand with their arms outstretched
with one hand pointing towards God and the other
hand pointing towards the people they are praying
for. Ask them to imagine they are channelling the
Holy Spirit through them like a drainpipe channelling
water. Pray for the Spirit of God to flow down them
and to fill the person they are praying for.*

A sending out prayer

As we leave this place, **come Holy Spirit.**
Like fire and wind, **come Holy Spirit.**
As we leave this place, **come Holy Spirit.**
Like a whispering breath, **come Holy Spirit.**
Go with us as we leave, **come Holy Spirit.**

Year B TRINITY SUNDAY

Isaiah 6.1–8; Psalm 29; Romans 8.12–17;
John 3.1–17 *Jesus said, 'No one can enter the kingdom of God without being born of water and spirit.'*

Call to worship

Come gather before God who spans the heavens.
Come gather before God who fashions each human cell.
Come gather before Christ known across the centuries and nations.
Come gather before Christ who encounters each one of us.
Come gather before the Spirit who dances through time and space.
Come gather before the Spirit who weaves our lives together.

A prayer of confession

When we have forgotten
that you are the Father of all,
the Beginning of everything:
Lord, have mercy. **Christ, have mercy.**

When we have not recognized you
in our sisters and brothers in Jesus;
when we forget that we are Christ's body:
Lord, have mercy. **Christ, have mercy.**

When we have forgotten that you live inside us,
that we are home to the Holy Spirit:
Lord, have mercy. **Christ, have mercy.**

When we have forgotten
that Love is the most important thing in the world,
and that you show us the wonder of Love
as Father, as Son and as Spirit:
Lord, have mercy. **Christ, have mercy.**
Silence

You are the singer who tells that all is well.
You are the song of forgiveness.
You are the music which reassures us.
Holy Trinity of Love,
we rest in you.
Amen.

A prayer of intercession

God our maker, you so love the world,
that you entrust us with its safe-keeping,
to cultivate, nurture and tend the garden;
to relax and enjoy the produce of its bounty;
and make our own contribution.
Grant us wisdom and understanding.

God our Saviour, you so love the world,
that you bequeath us your ministry,
to spread the good news, to care as neighbours;
to speak out against what is not right;
and herald the coming of your kingdom.
Grant us wisdom and mercy.

God the Holy Spirit, you so love the world,
that you fill us with your power
to make a difference and bring about change;
to draw others to a deeper knowledge of you
and leave a better legacy for generations to come.
Grant us wisdom and grace.

We ask in your name: Father, Son and Holy Spirit,
Holy Trinity of God.
Amen.

A prayer for all ages together

God, you are our father, and made us to be your children.
We praise you for giving us life,
and ask you to fill us with your love.

Jesus, you are God's son, and call us to be your sisters and brothers.
We praise you for showing us your care,
and ask you to fill us with your love.

Holy Spirit, you come to be our helper and guide.
We praise you for being with us always,
and ask you to fill us with your love.
Amen.

A prayer activity

Plait strands of wool in three colours to show how three can be one. Then sing this song to celebrate that God is 'three in one', to the tune, 'Twinkle, twinkle little star'.
God is Father,
God is Son,
God is Spirit,
Three in One.
Keep us safely day by day,
Keep our feet right on the way.
Show us how to do what's right,
Fill our lives with heavenly light.

Children's prayer of thanks to the Trinity

Thank you, Father, that you care for us.
Mime cradling a baby in your arms
Thank you, Jesus, that you are our friend.
Hold hands with the person next to you
Thank you, Holy Spirit, that you live with us.
Point to self and raise arms upwards to God
Thank you, God.
Amen.

A sending out prayer

May the blessing of the God who danced at the dawning of creation,
dance with us.
May the blessing of the Son who challenges us to dance the pain of the world's suffering,
dance with us.
And may the blessing of the Spirit who invites us to dance with her in the dance of celebration,
dance with us from now into eternity.
Amen.

Year B   PROPER 4

Deuteronomy 5.12–15; Psalm 81.1–10; 2 Corinthians 4.5–12; **Mark 2.23–3.6** *Jesus said, 'The Sabbath was made for man, not man for the Sabbath; so the Son of Man is lord even on the Sabbath.'*

Call to worship

Lord of the Sabbath,
we come to you this morning with our praise,
for you are our God.
We come with our worries,
for you are our God.
We bring those on our hearts,
for you are our God.
We bring the concerns of the world,
for you are our God.
We know that you welcome us,
for you are our God.
We know that you love us,
for you are our God.
Lord of the Sabbath,
we come to you this morning rejoicing,
for you are our God.

A prayer of confession

When we put convention before compassion,
Lord of the Sabbath, forgive us.
When we put tradition before truth,
Lord of the Sabbath, forgive us.
When we put laws before love,
Lord of the Sabbath, forgive us.
When we put ourselves before others,
Lord of the Sabbath, forgive us.
Amen.

A prayer of intercession

Jesus said, 'Stretch out your arm.'
We pray for those who are hungry in our world today
who stretch out their arms for food.
We pray for those in the midst of violence
who stretch out their arms for peace.
We pray for those who have lost their way
who stretch out their arms for a new beginning.
We pray for those who are ill
who stretch out their arms for healing.
We pray for those who are lonely
who stretch out their arms for companionship.
We pray for those who grieve
who stretch out their arms for comfort.
We pray for ourselves, that we stretch out our arms
to receive your spirit, and go from this place with the
confidence to stretch out our arms to others in your
name: Jesus, Friend and Saviour.
Amen.

A children's prayer

It's Sunday, your special day.
Your extra special day, because every day is special
in its own way.
We go to church and the minister lays a hand on
my head and says, 'May Christ bless you today and
always.'
And I know you love me.
I know you love me every day.
But Sundays are special.
I feel special and I love you.
I love lots of things and lots of people:
Mum, Dad, my hamster…
But I love you best on Sundays.
Amen.

A prayer for all ages

Lord, you did good things like make people better,
but the religious people grumbled at you and your
disciples. Help us not to be like them, but to be like
you: to be kind and to notice people when they are
sad or unhappy.
Lord, make us Sabbath people, people that know you
are Lord of everything. People who don't get bogged
down by our own petty rules. People who praise you
because you love us more than we can understand,
more than we deserve.
Lord, make us like you, please.
Amen.

A prayer activity

*Beforehand, draw ears of corn on card, with husks
big enough to write names on. Cut them out and
give one to every child. Ask the children to write the
names of the people they want to pray for on the ears
of corn. Ask each child in turn to read out the names
they have written and then say this prayer together:*
**Loving Jesus, we ask you to bless those we have
named. Shine your love on them like the sun
shining on fields of corn in the summer. Help
them to grow strong and enjoy life with all its ups
and downs. Thank you.**
Amen.

A sending out prayer

As you have been blessed, go and bless others,
this Sabbath day and every day.
Amen.

Year B PROPER 5

Genesis 3.8–15; Psalm 130; 2 Corinthians 4.13–5.1;
Mark 3.20–35 *Jesus said, 'Whoever does the will of God is my brother and sister and mother.'*

Call to worship

I wait for the Lord, my soul waits, and in his word
I hope.
**Lord, hear my voice! Let your ears be attentive
to the voice of my supplications!**
Jesus went home; and the crowd came together
again, so that they could not even eat.
**We too gather as the crowd did, waiting excitedly
to meet with God.**

A prayer of approach

Lord, you tell us that anyone who does your will
is part of your family.
Help us to put aside our differences
and be united in you,
ready to worship in spirit and in truth.
Amen.

A prayer of confession

We don't always put other people before ourselves.
Forgive us, Lord.
We don't always go the first mile, never mind the
extra one.
Forgive us, Lord.
We don't always give each other the space we need.
Forgive us, Lord.
We don't always hear what you are telling us.
Forgive us, Lord.
**Help us to see the good in everyone and to share
your love as freely as it is given to us.
Amen.**

A prayer of thanksgiving

Thank you, Lord, that we are family.
Thank you that we are all part
of a wonderful jigsaw, all shapes and sizes
brought together to be made whole.
Amen.

A prayer of intercession

Lord of the world, our Father, our Mother, our Saviour
and Friend: we pray for your children.
For families divided by war, poverty,
hunger or natural disaster:
for they are our brothers and sisters.

For families divided by acrimony and
misunderstanding:
for they are our brothers and sisters.

For families divided by economic circumstances:
for they are our brothers and sisters.

For agencies that support family life:
for they are our brothers and sisters.

For Christian people trying to do the will of God in
many different ways:
for they are our brothers and sisters.

We give thanks for our own families,
for parents who raised and taught us,
for children who delight and challenge us,
for those who depend on us:
for they are our brothers and sisters.

We give thanks for Jesus our Saviour,
and we pray in his name:
**for we are his brothers and sisters.
Amen.**

A prayer for all ages

*Pre-arrange for several people to call out names and
relationships of members of their family when asked*
Thank you, God, for my family, *(Cross arms over chest)*
for those I love, *(Big smile)*
and those it's hard to love sometimes. *(Frown)*
For: *(The names and relationships are called out)*
Thank you, God, that you love everyone. *(Shout
'Hurrah')*
Amen.

A prayer activity

*Thank God for the families we are part of. Invite
people to make paper-chain families by folding the
paper in a concertina and cutting out people shapes,
joined at the hands. Ask everyone to sit quietly and
hold their paper-chain families, and think about each
person in the family, in turn. Ask them to think of
one thing to thank God for about that person, and
one thing to ask God for on their behalf. Allow time
for everyone to work through their families in silent
prayer before saying, all together:*
**Thank you, God, that we can all be part of your
family.**

A sending out prayer

You never turned anyone away who needed you,
Lord. Help me not to exclude people,
but to be willing to welcome everybody into my life,
in your name.
Amen.

Year B PROPER 6

Sunday between June 12 and June 18 inclusive (if after Trinity Sunday)

Ezekiel 17.22–24; Psalm 92.1–4, 12–15;
2 Corinthians 5.6–10 (11–13),14–17; **Mark 4.26–34**
*A man scatters seeds on the ground … it sprouts and
grows. How he does not know.*

Call to worship

God has planted us like trees to flourish and grow.
Give thanks to the Lord.
Our soil is God's garden.
Give thanks to the Lord.
Daily we grow towards the light.
Give thanks to the Lord.
We give coolness, shade and beauty to God's garden.
Give thanks to the Lord.
God makes us blossom in our youth.
Give thanks to the Lord.
God makes us produce fruit in our maturity.
Give thanks to the Lord.
God renews our life, season by season.
Give thanks to the Lord.

A prayer of confession

Lord, we come to you with open hearts
and confess that often we're not as tuned in to
you as we should be.
We are too caught up in our own business
and only listen to you with half an ear.
We know that we miss so much.
Forgive us, Lord, and help us to settle,
focusing on you and the unfolding possibilities
of your kingdom.
Amen.

A prayer of intercession

Lord, we thank you for your ongoing love for us.
Like trees stretching up to the sun
we want to grow upwards towards you.
We bring the people of your world before you
and pray for those who do not find their security in you.
We ask that the gifts of your creation
will be spread more fairly,
and that those who have nothing
might receive enough to start them off.
We pray for those who waste wealth,
that they will see their mistakes.
We pray that your people will hear your word
and that, understanding it,
they may grow ever closer to you.
Amen.

A prayer of petition

*Invite people to hold a tiny seed in the palm of their
hand as this prayer is said:*
Just a tiny seed, Lord, but with such a hope of life;
energy and possibility crammed into a tiny shell,
waiting for warmth and moisture to unlock all its
potential.

God our creator,
bestower of our life, giver of our gifts,
plant us in the warm earth of your love;
shower us with grace,
so that we are awake to the possibilities of change
and alive to our potential to work for your kingdom.
Amen.

A prayer for all ages

From a little acorn grows a mighty oak.
From a tiny seed grows a beautiful flower.
From a tiny seed our food can grow,
and from the seed of your Spirit I can grow.
Thank you, God.
Amen.

A prayer activity

*Invite each child to plant a small flower into a pot or
hanging basket and, if they feel comfortable, to say a
small prayer as they plant it. For example:*
Dear Jesus, help me be kind to my brother this week.
Amen.
*When everyone has planted a flower say together, or
ask for a volunteer to lead the following prayer:*
Dear Jesus,
We have planted this tiny garden together.
We hope it will grow beautiful flowers.
We hope the flowers, colours and scents
will cheer people up.
Help us to plant seeds of your love
in the hearts of our friends and family,
because we know that your kingdom
is always growing and we can help it spread.
Amen.

A prayer for stillness

Just as the seed grows silently, slowly,
so, God, the life of your Spirit grows in us unseen.
Teach us to know your Spirit.
Teach us to make time in our lives to be with you
in stillness, in silence,
letting your peace settle,
letting our love for you grow,
letting what is bitter in our lives be ripened into good,
sweet fruit.
Amen.

A sending out prayer

Caring God,
just as we look after plants to give them what they
need to grow,
give us what we need so that we can become the
people we are meant to be
and welcome others to your kingdom.
Amen.

Year B   PROPER 7

Sunday between June 19 and June 25 inclusive (if after Trinity Sunday)

Job 38.1–11; Psalm 107.1–3, 23–32; 2 Corinthians 6.1–13; **Mark 4.35–41** *Who can this be? Even the wind and sea obey him!*

Call to worship

God is here.
The Spirit is with us.
In strength of faith.
In seas of doubt.
The Spirit is with us.
In brightness of hope.
In heaviness of despair.
The Spirit is with us.
In safety and certainty.
In distrust and danger.
The Spirit is with us.
In songs of wonder.
In dumb astonishment.
The Spirit is with us.
Let God move among us.
In all things we are God's people.

A prayer of confession

Lord, I confess that you don't always have the effect on me that you had on the waves.
I flap around in the deep waters, thinking I'm going to sink any minute and actually making things worse. You were even able to sleep through a storm because you knew you were safe
in your Father's hands.
Forgive me, Lord, that I just don't seem to have got the hang of that yet.
Amen.

A prayer of praise

God our creator, who laid the foundations of the earth, who made the ocean. You have the four corners of the earth in your hand and the wind and the sea obey you.
We stand in awe of your power and your beauty.
As the morning stars sang together at creation, so we sing our praises to you. As the heavenly beings shouted for joy, we shout for joy to you. Saviour God, we praise you in song and in shouting, and we praise you in peace and in stillness.
We quieten our hearts and listen for you speaking to us in a sound of sheer silence. Let that silence give us steadiness and calm in even the fiercest of storms. And may it lead us always to serve you with thanks and praise.
Amen.

A prayer of intercession

We pray today for all who face storms in their lives …
**Lord, meet them in their need
and give them strength.**

For those affected by war or natural disaster …
For those who have no shelter or food …
**Lord, meet them in their need
and give them strength.**
For those who have no money …
**Lord, meet them in their need
and give them strength.**
For those who are ill …
**Lord, meet them in their need
and give them strength.**
For those who have lost a loved one …
**Lord, meet them in their need
and give them strength.**
And, for us all.
**Lord, meet us in our need
and give us strength.
Amen.**

A prayer for all ages

When our lives skim through the water,
dancing in the waves,
Lord Jesus, **hold your peace in our hearts.**
When our lives are tossed in a choppy sea
and we feel unsure,
Lord Jesus, **hold your peace in our hearts.**
When our lives are blown off course
and we lose sight of you,
Lord Jesus, **hold your peace in our hearts.**
When our lives are thrown in the ruthless waves
and we are hurt and afraid,
Lord Jesus, **hold your peace in our hearts.**
When our lives are torn by the wind and deafened by thunder and we are blinded by tears,
Lord Jesus, **hold your peace in our hearts.**
When our lives are fulfilled and the harbour is near and our future with you is certain,
Lord Jesus, **hold your peace in our hearts.**
Amen.

A prayer activity

Give everyone a paper boat on which they can write something they want Jesus to help them with. Drape a large piece of blue paper or fabric on the floor. Let them come up one by one, read out their prayers and stick their prayer boat on the sea. At the end pray together:
Dear Jesus, who calmed the wind and waves, hold us in your heart with love as we learn to trust you.
Amen.

A sending out prayer

Now may he who laid the foundations of the earth, who stills the storm, and hushes the waves of the sea, speak his peace to you, as you go on your journey.
May you have grace to perceive the one whom even the wind and the sea obey, and strength to persevere in walking in his way, now and always.
Amen.

Year B   PROPER 8

Sunday between June 26 and July 2 inclusive

Wisdom of Solomon 1.13–15, 2.23–24, or
Lamentations 3.22–33; Psalm 30; 2 Corinthians
8.7–15; **Mark 5.21–43** *Jesus said to the woman,
'Daughter, your faith has made you well; go in peace.'*

Call to worship

So let us come to the Lord like Jairus,
seeking God's healing and love for others.
Let us come before God like the woman in the crowd,
seeking healing for ourselves and knowing that God
is always waiting to be gracious to us.
**The Lord's compassions are new every morning;
great is your faithfulness.**

A prayer of confession

Lord, we confess that we don't always think things
through. We rush into situations where perhaps we
ought not to go. Or we hang about outside when we
should be in there.
We are not always sensitive to others' needs.
Lord, forgive us, and teach us to listen,
not only with our ears, but with our whole being.
Amen.

A prayer of thanksgiving

For your caring ways,
Lord, we thank you.
For your gentle touch,
Lord, we thank you.
For your healing powers,
Lord, we thank you.
Just for being you,
Lord, we thank you.
Amen.

A prayer of intercession

We pray for the communities around us.
May the touch of Jesus' garment be known among us
– bringing respect, justice and peace.
Lord Jesus Christ, lover of all.

We pray for the sick and needy, the lonely and
bereaved.
May they reach out towards Jesus, and find
wholeness of life.
Lord Jesus Christ, lover of all.

We pray for your Church, which tries to be the hem
of your garment, spread wide in the world. Help us to
make you available, and to be a channel of your love
and healing.
Lord Jesus Christ, lover of all.

Let us bring our own prayers, as we come to touch
the hem of Jesus' garment.
May healing come to the people, places, situations
and communities for which we pray, and may we be
channels of your loving touch.
Lord Jesus Christ, lover of all.
Amen.

A prayer for all ages

Loving God,
You made us to be awesome and amazing.
When troubles come,
it is easy to forget how awesome and amazing
you made each one of your children.
When pain or sadness comes to us
it is easy just to give up,
to believe that maybe you don't care,
that maybe you have no power to help.
When other people hurt or grieve
it is easy to step away
so that we won't have to carry any of the weight of
what they are going through.
Give us the imagination to understand how they
must be feeling and the strength to bear each other's
burdens.
Help us to look for you at work around us,
to see the signs that you are here, with us;
our King and God, and loving Father,
bearing our pain and sadness,
giving joy, peace and new life.
Amen.

A prayer activity

*Talk about the different things our hands can do:
touching, holding, waving, clapping, talking (sign
language), helping, carrying, pushing or pulling. Ask
everyone to hold out their hands in front of them and
clap them together once whenever you say the word
'hands'. Then pray:*
Thank you, God, for hands.
Hands to hold, hands to wave,
hands that talk, hands that touch.
We are sorry when our hands hit.
We are sorry when our hands hurt.
Please give us helping hands.
Amen.

A sending out prayer

Lord, source of abundant life.
Send us out, made whole by your love.
Healed by your wounds.
Fed by your gifts.
To praise, love and serve you in all that lies beyond
the doors of this building.
We ask this through Jesus Christ,
whose coming is certain and whose day draws near.
Amen.

Year B   PROPER 9

Sunday between July 3 and July 9 inclusive

Ezekiel 2.1–5; Psalm 123; 2 Corinthians 12.2–10;
Mark 6.1–13 *Jesus summoned the twelve and sent them out two by two.*

Call to worship

God says,
you are never too young, never too old,
to be part of my work.
Come near,
all who are weak,
all who are afraid,
all who know their need of me.
Lord, meet us where we are,
meet us in our need.
We give our lives to you.

A prayer of confession

Loving God, as we meet to worship, we recognize
that we're not always what we want to be.
Sometimes we judge others, put them in boxes
and don't allow them space to be who they are.
Sometimes we seek meaning for our lives in things
that are fleeting and shallow.
Sometimes we're full of our success and
achievements and are insensitive to those who are
struggling.
Sometimes we're full of our own failures and
limitations and are insensitive to those who are
celebrating.
Sometimes we seek the big spiritual experience,
forgetting that you are there with us in the mundane,
the difficult, and the boring.
Sometimes we forget that you are a God of both the
extraordinary and the ordinary.
Help us to believe the fact of your love, forgiveness
and grace.
Help us to find the freedom to live the Jesus way.
Amen.

A personal prayer

Compassionate God,
always loving to those who seek you,
mend us where we hurt,
then send us where you will:
that we might speak, live and act as people who know
the love that makes all things whole,
and offer your hand of peace to a world that needs to
know your word of life and hope.
Amen.

A prayer of intercession

Lord, you demand of us hard answers to the
demands of your call. We are ready to respond and
we bring to you the concerns of our world…
Lord of the helpless and lost, the homeless and
rootless people, the warring and desperate people:
help us to help them, so that a future is not only
possible, but assured.

We bring the concerns of our national life…
Lord of mercy, we bring before you the people
struggling to make ends meet, families torn apart,
victims of violence and abuse, communities
where gangs rule and the effects of drug abuse
are witnessed on every street corner, farming
communities struggling with climate and economy:
help us to help them, so that hope is real.
We bring the concerns of this church community and
our local neighbourhood…
Lord of the suffering ones, of those who feel loss and
are bereft, of those yearning for release from pain,
those dreading each new day:
help us to help them, to care without reserve, to love
without thinking twice.
In word and action,
may we humbly follow both the call and the path of
discipleship in Jesus' name.
Amen.

A prayer for all ages

Loving God, make us welcomers
and proclaimers for you.
When people need a welcome
help us to be those who offer one.
When there is an opportunity to share the good news,
give us the confidence to do so.
When we meet people who don't understand us,
who call us names and make trouble for us,
make us strong in the knowledge of your love.
Loving God, make us welcomers
and proclaimers for you.
Amen.

A prayer activity

*Cut pieces of paper into stone shapes and write on
them the following words: Prayer, Bible reading, The
Holy Spirit, Going to church, Learning from others.
Leave some stones blank. Set the stones out as a
path. Ask the group to divide into pairs and look at the
stepping stones together. Invite them to walk along
the stepping-stone path. When they come to a stone
with words on, ask them to consider how God helps
them to share the good news. When they get to a
blank stone they write on it something that might help
them with their mission.*

A sending out prayer

Send us out, Lord, into the places that we know,
bearing the good news of your risen life.
Send us out, Lord, into the less familiar places:
the unknown and less trodden paths.
Give us strength there to speak your word,
to live your truth and to make known the story
of a people and a world made new.
Amen.

Year B   PROPER 10

Sunday between July 10 and July 16 inclusive

Amos 7.7–15; Psalm 85.8–13; Ephesians 1.3–14;
Mark 6.14–29 *Herod knew John to be a good and holy man.*

Call to worship

God calls us together to worship.
God calls us to hear God's word.
God calls us to journey with Jesus.
God calls us to work together to bring
about the purposes of God in the world.

A prayer of approach

Great God of time and eternity,
who inspired the prophets with your word
and gave them the will to speak to your people,
we gather in your name and seek your blessing on
the mission of this community.
May we listen and resolve, celebrate and sing,
in the knowledge of your love and of your gracious
calling.
Make us prophets to discern your will,
disciples to understand it and apostles to share it,
inspired by your Spirit.
Amen.

A prayer of confession

We ask your forgiveness, Lord,
for the times we forget to acknowledge you,
when the actions of our lives fail to reflect your
justice, your mercy and your love.
Forgive us, too, for those times when we diminish
others and fail to acknowledge the gifts they bring.
Forgive us for the times we demand certainty and
direction and are too afraid to step out in faith.
Change our hearts, God, strengthen our will,
that everything we are, and will be, is yours.
This we pray in Jesus' name.
Amen.

A prayer of intercession

The Lord calls us to follow.
We walk in your strength, O Lord.
We pray for situations where we struggle to follow
Christ, offering them to God in the silence…
The Lord calls us to follow.
We walk in your strength, O Lord.

We pray for our country and the places where God
seems absent…
The Lord calls us to follow.
We walk in your strength, O Lord.

We pray for our church, our home, our
neighbourhood, and the struggles we have in centring
our lives on God's love. We offer into God's care the
situations and people with whom we struggle.
The Lord calls us to follow.
We walk in your strength, O Lord.

We pray for areas of the world where Christians face
persecution; and we pray for ourselves when we face
situations where standing up for right is hard and
painful…
The Lord calls us to follow.
We walk in your strength, O Lord.

We pray for people who find themselves alone, and
for all who suffer, naming them before God and
trusting in God's faithful love…
The Lord calls us to follow.
We walk in your strength, O Lord.
Amen.

A prayer for all ages

Help us to be brave like John the Baptist
and to speak out when we see people doing wrong
things.
Help us to encourage people to come and say sorry
to you and to help others to live good lives.
Help us to be brave like John the Baptist,
when people don't like what we say.
Amen.

A prayer activity

*Give the children pieces of string with a lolly stick
tied to one end to represent plumb lines. Ask them
hold their plumb lines up while you pray this prayer
together:*
Let's ask God to help us stay close to what is right…
When we don't know what is right,
help us stay straight and true,
help us stay close to you.
When we want to stand up for what's right,
help us stay straight and true,
help us stay close to you.
When the truth is hard to take,
help us stay straight and true,
help us stay close to you.
As we try to live like disciples,
help us stay straight and true,
help us stay close to you.
Amen.

A sending out prayer

Loving God, you have come close to us and called us
as your own.
Help us to remember in the days ahead
that your love stays with us always and never ends.
Inspire our hearts and minds
to share your gifts with others
as we go out into the world every day.
In Jesus' name we pray.
Amen.

Year B   PROPER 11

Sunday between July 17 and July 23 inclusive

Jeremiah 23.1–6; Psalm 23; Ephesians 2.11–22;
Mark 6.30–34, 53–56 *Jesus said, 'Come with me …
and rest a while.'*

Call to worship

God calls us to worship.
Those from north, south, east and west are invited.
Children, young people, women and men, are invited.
Poor or rich, struggling or prosperous are invited.
Those from each and every kind of family are invited.
All of us, with our strengths and our weaknesses,
are invited.
God calls us to worship.

A prayer of approach

Lord Jesus, even when you're tired
and you might have had enough,
you never send people away.
You always give people time,
to listen to them, to help them,
to meet their needs.
Compassionate Lord, may we come to you
and share all that we are.
Amen.

A prayer of confession

Loving God,
gather us in from the busyness of our lives,
from the pressures of everyday living
and the anticipation of holidays and outings,
so that we still ourselves in your presence and
recover our balance, knowing that in you, we find
peace and fulfilment.
In this deep stillness,
we acknowledge our distorted priorities and ask you
to forgive our blustering and hurried habits.
Remind us always of our need to regain the peace
of treasured moments with friends and family, which,
in turn, allow our closeness to you, our creator, to
Jesus, our shepherd, and to your renewing Spirit.
Amen.

A prayer of intercession

We pray for those who have laid down responsibility
during the holiday season.
Lord, give them rest.

We pray for all exploring new ideas and options
for their life, because of changes in personal and
financial circumstances. For all who struggle in
adverse circumstances.
Lord, give them rest.

We pray for all who are sick or distressed.
Lord, give them rest.

We pray for leaders: on the world stage, in our local
authorities, in our churches.
Lord, give them rest.

We pray for those who care for the sick and needy in
their homes, often struggling to manage.
Lord, give them rest.

We pray for all who come to you.
Lord, give them rest.
Amen.

A prayer for all ages

You say, 'Come away to a deserted place all by
yourselves and rest a while.'
In the business of life,
its many words and deeds,
its arguments and temptations,
hopes and frustrations, be our still place.
Our place of recreation, healing and forgiveness,
our centre and our safe place.
Help us find in you the stillness that we need,
to regain our perspective
and our sense of you.
Amen.

A prayer activity

*Invite the group to kneel or sit on the floor around
a throw or tablecloth (preferably one with a fringed
edge) which has been spread out. Ask everyone to
hold onto the material with both hands. Gently waft
it up and down, everyone working in unison without
talking. Read the following prayer:*
Lord, who healed the sick and cured the blind,
help us to feel your healing presence.
Jesus, who always made time to care for others,
help us to feel your healing presence.
Whenever we feel crushed and overwhelmed
with life,
help us to feel your healing presence.
When we need a breathing space to rest and
recuperate,
help us to feel your healing presence.
Amen.

A sending out prayer

At work, at rest, at leisure,
the peace of God the Creator to you.
God the Father,
God the Son,
God the Holy Spirit,
go with you on every side and at every turn,
each day and each night,
for all eternity.
Amen.

Year B   PROPER 12

2 Kings 4.42–44; Psalm 145.10–18; Ephesians
3.14–21; **John 6.1–21** *Jesus said to Philip, 'Where
are we to buy bread to feed these people?'*

Call to worship

Loving God, you fed your people in the past: feed us
now. We come to hear your living word. Loving God,
you fed your people in the desert: feed us now. We
come searching for truth. Loving God, you fed your
people on the hillside: feed us now. We come for
sustenance for life. Loving God, you fed your people
in the past: feed us now.

A prayer of confession

Forgive us, when we follow the crowd
because we are afraid to stand out
and follow our conscience…

Forgive us, when we hide behind the crowd
because we are afraid to show our face
and speak up for what is right…

Forgive us, when we avoid the crowd
because we are afraid to join in their protest
and the cost that might involve…

Forgive us, when we swim in the crowd
because we are afraid to show our hand
and share what we have with those in need…

Be no more afraid; and rest assured of the
forgiveness of the one who gave of himself
and taught us how to share our bread.
Amen.

A prayer of intercession

Lord Jesus Christ, who fed a waiting multitude,
feed us this day.
Feed us the bread of life, so that we no longer hunger
for the things that harm our lives.
Feed us the bread of life, so that we no longer crave
for that which leads us astray.
Feed us the bread of life, so that we no longer yearn
for easy options.
Feed us the bread of life, so that we no longer need
to rely on our own strength.
We pray for those in our world who do hunger,
not only for food, but also for freedom and justice.
We pray for those in our world whose cravings are
out of control, for addicts and their families who go
through so much pain.
We pray for those in our world who succumb to the
easy option of stealing and cheating others rather
than working for what they want.
Lord Jesus, who fed a waiting multitude, feed all your
children this day and every day.
Amen.

An offertory prayer

Receive from our hands, God,
our small gifts, just as you received the bread and
fishes from the child on the hillside.
Take, too, what little we have of faith and love and
hope.
Bless them, break them and distribute them
so that people may take until they are satisfied
by the abundance of your love, and worship you,
source of all life and prosperity and peace.
Amen.

A prayer for all ages

Two fish and five loaves of bread
was all it took for thousands of people
to see you, God, who loves us.
Two fish and five loaves of bread
allowed people to see you, God, who works with us.
Two fish and five loaves of bread
meant people were fed by you, God, who provides.
Two fish and five loaves of bread
reminds us that you, God, will provide.
Amen.

A prayer activity

*Draw a large smiling face on a piece of card. Cut the
face into jigsaw pieces and give one to each child
present. Ask them to record on the back of their
jigsaw piece (either in words or pictures) one good
thing they think they could do in the week ahead,
then to sit quietly, with eyes closed, and picture
themselves doing the thing they've put on their
jigsaw piece. Then slowly, to some gentle music, the
children put down their jigsaw pieces in turn, to make
the smiling face. They gather around the face while
the following prayer is read:*
Dear God, in the story of the feeding of the five
thousand one boy was generous with his food and
that led to the whole crowd having enough to eat.
Help us to remember that every little good thing we
do makes the world a happier place; and help us to
do our bit in the week ahead.
Amen.

A sending out prayer

As the multitude came seeking Jesus,
we, too, have gathered here today.
As the people were fed,
we, too, have received nourishment.
As Jesus calmed the fears of his disciples,
we, too, can face this day with confidence that God is
with us.
Fed by Christ, empowered by the Spirit, loved by
God, go in assurance. Go in peace.
Amen.

Year B   PROPER 13

Exodus 16.2–4, 9–15; Psalm 78.23–29; Ephesians 4.1–16; **John 6.24–35** *Jesus said, 'It is not because you saw signs that you came looking for me, but because you ate the bread and your hunger was satisfied.'*

Call to worship

What must we do to perform the works of God?
We will believe in him who God has sent.
Give us the bread which comes down from heaven:
Lord Jesus, feed us.

A prayer of approach

Mysterious God,
We come looking for a sign of your power and greatness
and find you come among us as one of us.
We come looking for proof that you are the God of our salvation
and find you crucified upon a cross.
We come wanting a miracle to make you known to us
and find you present with us as we share our bread.
Amen.

A prayer of confession

Giver of life,
when we have seen your greatness
and sought to tame you to our cause,
forgive our unworthiness.
When we have seen your goodness
and claimed it as our right,
forgive our ingratitude.
When we have seen your mercy
and continued to harbour grudges,
forgive our lack of compassion.
When we have seen your love
and complained about our lot,
forgive our lack of generosity.
Amen.

A prayer of intercession

Lord Jesus, the crowd came to hear good news.
They came expecting to be fed.
We pray for those in our world who wait expectantly to be fed.
We pray for those who hunger for words that will feed their spirits, words that will change the situations that they live in.
We pray for politicians and administrators,
for those in power, that all might be able to share the bread of your creation.
The crowd came as many still come.
Lord, we pray for those agencies whose work supports the needy, the homeless, those devastated by life.
We pray for all who work to bring food to a world where many are still waiting to be fed.

We pray especially for the work of...
The crowd sat and were fed.
Lord, we pray that we may use all the resources we have to feed the world, to share and support one another; we are all part of your family.
We pray for your family here in this place.
May all be fed with your living bread.
Amen.

A prayer for all ages *based on Ephesians 4*

You have called some to be apostles,
starting up new congregations and leading them forward in your name.
Bless them and make them strong.
You have called some to be prophets,
challenging us to see your word in the Bible and in daily life.
Bless them and make them strong.
You have called some to be evangelists,
taking the good news of Jesus wherever they go.
Bless them and make them strong.
You have called some to be pastors,
caring for those in need with compassion and commitment.
Bless them and make them strong.
You have called some to be teachers,
explaining your word to people of all ages.
Bless them and make them strong.
You have called us, too, to discover our gifts,
so that we can use them in your service.
Bless us and make us strong.
For we ask it in Jesus' name.
Amen.

A prayer activity

Make a prayer poster. Across the top of a large piece of paper write, 'Do not work for the food that perishes'. In the middle, draw a loaf of bread and write, 'I am the bread of life'. Round the edge write brand slogans and logos. Then be silent together. Share some bread together as a reminder of Jesus as the bread of life. Take advertising slogans that you can think of and use them for prayer. For example:
Just do it – every day, let me remember your goodness to me, Jesus.
Work, rest and play – are all gifts from you:
thank you, God.
Don't live a little, live a lot – as Jesus showed us.

A sending out prayer

Jesus' hands reach out and he says,
'I am the Bread of Life. I am the living bread of God.'
Lord Jesus, give us this day that living bread.
May our lives enrich those about us with the love which is everlasting and will never perish.
Amen.

Year B PROPER 14

Sunday between August 7 and August 13 inclusive

1 Kings 19.4–8; Psalm 34.1–8; Ephesians 4.25–5.2;
John 6.35, 41–51 *Jesus said, 'I am the bread of life.
Whoever comes to me will never be hungry.'*

Call to worship

Come to me and find a welcome.
Come to me and find the peace you crave.
Come to me and find the assurance you long for.
Come to me to find food from heaven.
Come to me to find the cup of salvation.
Come to me to find the challenge of eternal living.
Come, Lord Jesus. Come.

A prayer of confession

God of life, of heaven and of earth, give us this day
our daily bread.
Forgive us the times when we forget those who are
living in lands where food is scarce and difficult to
obtain.
Forgive us, Lord.

Forgive us the times when we see and read about
those who are malnourished and yet do nothing.
Forgive us, Lord.

Forgive us the times when we ignore those who do
not know how they will feed their families.
Forgive us, Lord.

Yet still we ask – give us today the bread of life,
that we might share it with our needy world.
Amen.

A prayer of praise

Gracious God of every day,
not a Sunday treat, or kept for holy days
and high feasts and holidays,
but our bread and our necessity.
You are the substance of life,
the ground on which we tread,
the staple of our diet, the air we breathe,
the place we rest, and the breeze that makes us
restless.
The hope we have to come,
and the treasure of our past.
The source of life, and destiny, beginning and ending,
our history and our future.
Everyday God, broken as bread, that we may be
made whole, given as bread that we may eat and be
strong. Bread for the journey, that we may find you
and know you for ever.
Amen.

A prayer of intercession

Lord, we pray for all who hunger:
those who hunger for food in countries where there
is famine; those who hunger for peace where there is
political unrest or warfare.
We pray for those who hunger for a new beginning.

Lord, we pray for those who thirst:
for countries where there are droughts and water
shortages; for those whose water supplies are
contaminated.
We pray for a thirst for justice where wrong has been
done, and we pray for those who thirst for
righteousness.

Lord Jesus, the crowd came to you and you fed them.
Help us to feed our neighbours. We pray especially
for ....

Lord Jesus, you gave the crowd hope.
We pray for those who are going through difficult
times. We pray for ....

Lord Jesus, you had gone away to be alone and
find rest. We pray for those who need to find time to
recover and rebuild. We pray for ....

Lord Jesus, you listened to the crowd and gave them
answers. Listen to our prayers for ....
Lord, in your mercy,
hear our prayer.
Amen.

A prayer for all ages

Help us, Lord, to work for what lasts:
love, kindness, generosity and thankfulness.
Help us, Lord, to be real:
**to love as we are loved, to do what is right, rather
than what is popular.**
Jesus said, 'I am the bread of life.'
Give us this bread always.
Amen.

A prayer activity

*Invite everyone to sit in a circle. Hold some bread in
your hands. Explain that Jesus said when we break
bread together we should remember him. Invite the
children to pass the bread around the circle, breaking
a piece off as they go. As they do this, ask them to
name, aloud or in their heads, someone who they
would like to pray for. Once everyone has some
bread, say a simple prayer, asking Jesus to receive
you and your prayers as you remember him. Invite
everyone to eat together.*

A sending out prayer

Lord Jesus, let us not settle for things that perish
but let us yearn for the day when all will know you.
Let us desire the peace which passes all
understanding.
Let us be eager to follow you.
Let us long to share your love with all whom we meet
as we travel on.
Amen.

Year B   PROPER 15

Sunday between August 14 and August 20 inclusive

Proverbs 9.1–6; Psalm 34.9–14; Ephesians 5.15–20;
John 6.51–58 *Jesus said, 'Whoever eats this bread will live for ever.'*

Call to worship *based on Psalm 34*

Come with me, and listen to God:
teach us respect, O Lord.
Come, all you who long for life:
fill our days with meaning and purpose.
Come, all you who seek for truth:
help us find good, find peace and find life.
O taste and see how gracious the Lord is:
blessed are those who take refuge in him.

A prayer of confession

For expectations of appreciation
and reluctance to show gratitude:
forgive us and help us.

For greed and waste
and unwillingness to share:
forgive us and help us.

For unkind thoughts and lack of charity:
forgive us and help us.

For all we have failed to do
and all we would like to undo:
Lord, forgive us and help us.
Amen.

A prayer of thanks *based on Ephesians 5.20*

Let us give thanks to God in all things, for in
thanksgiving lies hope:
for a better future for everyone…
for a chance to make a real difference…
for a way of coping through good times and bad…
Let us give thanks to God in all things.

Let us give thanks to God in all things,
for in thanksgiving lies gratitude:
for the good things we have and enjoy…
for the opportunities and chances we get…
for the friendships and relationships that shape us…
Let us give thanks to God in all things.

Let us give thanks to God in all things,
for in thanksgiving lies praise:
for creation and its creator…
for salvation and our saviour…
for spirit and spirituality…
Let us give thanks to God in all things.
Amen.

A prayer of intercession

Loving God, you are the living bread that recreates
and sustains us, the bread that brings life to the
world, the crucified and living Christ whose Spirit
teaches us to dance to the rhythm of your heartbeat.

As you have called us to be wise, we pray for those
who seem to rely on their own strength and wisdom,
those who turn away from faith, those who believe
they are never wrong…
Living bread: **bring life to your world.**

As you have filled us with your Spirit, we pray for a
world so often filled with its own importance, those
who will not look for the kingdom of God…
Living bread: **bring life to your world.**

As you teach us to sing, we pray for a world crying in
pain, victims of injustice, those on the margins…
Living bread: **bring life to your world.**

As you ask us to give thanks,
we pray for those whose pain is too much,
the friend and stranger asking to be healed…
Living bread: **bring life to your world.**

As you accept our offering,
we pray for those who feel they have nothing to offer,
the bullied, the different, and the poor…
Living bread: **bring life to your world.**

You are the living bread. You call us to feed your
world. Bless us, challenge us, feed us and nurture us,
as you hear our prayers.
Amen.

A prayer for all ages

Jesus is the living bread that came down from heaven:
Dear God, we pray that we may make Jesus a part
of our lives as the food we eat becomes part of our
bodies.
As our food strengthens our bones, so may Jesus
make us strong to stand up for what's right.
As our food builds our muscles, so may Jesus
empower us to carry each other's burdens.
As our food gives us energy, so may Jesus make us
eager to do his work in the world.
Amen.

A prayer activity

*Write short prayers on squares of card. Place them in
an empty bread wrapper, as though they were slices
of bread. Pass the 'loaf' around the group so that
anyone who wants to can pull out a 'slice' and read a
prayer or part of a prayer.*

A sending out prayer *based on Ephesians 5*

Go out into the world as those who are wise,
making the most of the time, and giving thanks to
God the Father at all times, and for everything.
In the name of our Lord Jesus Christ.
Amen.

Year B PROPER 16

Sunday between August 21 and August 27 inclusive

Joshua 24.1–2a, 14–18; Psalm 34.15–22; Ephesians 6.10–20; **John 6.56–69** *Peter said, 'Lord, to whom shall we go? You have the words of eternal life.'*

Call to worship

Welcome to you:
those who come filled with joy and thankful hearts,
those who come filled with doubt and sorrow,
those who hunger for more than food:
you are welcome in this place.
A welcome to one and all:
those without and those within,
those who conform and those who confront,
those whose difference enriches our lives,
those who guide us into the very presence of God:
you are all welcome in this place.

A prayer of approach

Jesus is the bread of life,
and whoever eats of him will live for ever.
Heavenly Father, in our worship,
help us to unravel the puzzles of Jesus' words,
to accept the challenge of discipleship,
and to discover the fulfilment of following your Son,
the Holy One of God.
Amen.

A prayer of confession

Forgive us, gentle God,
For we like to be in control of our lives,
to make our decisions, based on what we know.
Burdening ourselves with luggage for every eventuality.
We want to be one of the crowd,
not out of step with others.
But sometimes that is what you ask of us –
to tread a different route, to test uncharted ways,
to make new discoveries of when and where you are to be found.
God of travelling mercies,
give us the courage to walk in faith,
strength to negotiate the rough places,
energy for the mountain peaks,
comfort for the lonely places,
and yourself as bread for the journey.
Amen.

A prayer of intercession

Pray for those who long to lay down their burdens:
for those overtaken by things they cannot control…
for those overburdened by worry…
for those overwhelmed by grief…

Pray for those who long to lay down their burdens:
for those embroiled in conflict…
for those embittered by memories…
for those embarrassed by shame…

Pray for those who long to lay down their burdens:
for those concerned by ethical dilemmas…
for those considering life-changing decisions…
for those condemned by others…
We pray for those who long to lay down their burdens.
Amen.

A prayer for all ages

Give each person a small chunk of bread, to hold in their palm:
We thank you, God, for choosing to create such a wonderful world.
We choose to follow you.
We thank you, God, for creating us and giving us a new day today.
We choose to follow you.
We are sorry that some of our choices hurt you.
We choose to follow you.
We thank you, Jesus, for being the bread of life.
We choose to follow you.
We thank you for the choices you give us every day.
We choose to follow you.
Thank you for trusting us with your world.
We choose to follow you.
Amen.

A prayer activity *based on Ephesians 6.10–20*

Prepare a large shield made of paper or card, or draw the outline of a shield on a whiteboard or in chalk on the floor. Then ask the group to think of all the occasions when they might need God's help and protection. Give everyone a small square of paper and ask them to write or draw one or more of those times. When they have finished, invite them to stick what they have written onto the shield. Then pray:
Loving, powerful, protecting God,
please keep us safe.
Amen.

A sending out prayer

Send us out,
equipped with your gifts,
to be bearers of your saving word:
in prayer, draw us deeper and deeper to your heart;
in service, help us to make your love real;
in stillness and silence, may we know our need of you;
and in action may we serve others
as you have here served us.
We ask this through Jesus the Lord,
for your words are spirit and they are life.
Amen.

Year B   PROPER 17

Sunday between August 28 and September 3 inclusive

Deuteronomy 4.1–2, 6–9; Psalm 15; James
1.17–27; **Mark 7.1–8, 14–15, 21–23** *Jesus said to the
Pharisees, 'You neglect the commandments of God
to maintain the tradition of men.'*

Call to worship

Purify our hearts, O God,
and fit us for your company.
Call us to worship you,
that we may be cleansed by your light,
healed by your love,
and filled by your spirit.

A prayer of confession

Lord God, we acknowledge before you that
sometimes religion can be soul-destroying rather than
life-enhancing: an end in itself, rather than a growing
in your grace.
It can spawn divisions, rather than the search for
justice, truth and freedom.
We confess the brokenness of the Church which
denies your one-ness.
We beg forgiveness where our disputes mar the
proclamation of your love for all people.
So we pray for our churches, that we might show your
unity to a broken world, and pray the prayers of the
world, not of our own self-interest.
May we have courage to obey,
courage to live the gospel in a world that rejects you,
courage to accept your healing for our own wounds.
Amen.

A prayer for purity

Lord, may I not be like the Pharisees,
eager to condemn others and more keen on tradition
than on knowing you.
Instead, may I hear your voice and feel your inward
call, that my soul may be cleansed by the renewing
power of your Holy Spirit,
and my life given the new direction and purpose of
Jesus Christ our Lord.
Amen.

A prayer of intercession

Lord, we pray for the Church, especially for those
who order and lead our worship, and those who help
us to understand it.
We pray for the world that you created. May we see
things always through the eyes of faith and delight.
We pray for those who lead us, that they may always
be open to new solutions, that the world may be a
better place for all its children.
We pray for our own community, that it may be a
place of adventure where all are included and
new solutions for a just society are constantly
welcomed.

We pray for the sick and those who care for them,
and those who pursue research to find new ways to
alleviate suffering. Lord, help us never to overlook our
response to the vulnerable.
We pray for those who find change difficult
and those trapped in unhelpful routines.
We give thanks for those who have gone before us:
those who have developed supportive and creative
traditions and those who have been responsible for
radical and life-giving change.
Amen.

A prayer for all ages

Lord God, may we see our hearts the way you see
them.
Help us to read your word so we can hear you
speaking.
Help us to think about your word so we can see why
you think what you think.
Help us to remember your word so we don't forget
what we're like.
Help us to see the things that are wrong with us, so
we can start changing.
Help us to see the things you like about us, so we
can grow in goodness.
Help us to remember that you love us very much – so
much that Jesus came especially to die for us, so that
we could share eternal life with you,
even though we don't deserve it.
Amen.

A prayer activity

*Invite everyone to think of one thing about
themselves they would like to change. Tell them that
it's not about having blue eyes rather than brown,
etc., it's about things inside – what we're like as
people. Give each child a slip of paper and a pencil,
and time to think. No one is going to know what they
write other than themselves. Lay a mirror flat and
invite them to crumple up the paper into a ball once
they've written something, and to look into the mirror.
Say the following prayer or something similar:*
We offer you, Lord, our imperfections.
Help us instead to be reflections of your
goodness and glory.
Amen.

A sending out prayer

Surround one another
in the warmth of love.
Enfold one another
in the strength of prayer.
Encourage one another
in the journey of faith.
Surprise one another
in the wonder of life,
and so bless one another
as God blesses you.
Amen.

Year B   PROPER 18

Isaiah 35.4–7a; Psalm 146; James 2.1–10 (11–13), 14–17; **Mark 7.24–37** *The crowd were astonished beyond measure, saying, 'He does all things well.'*

Call to worship

Come, strangers and friends, to worship the Lord.
We come in joy!
Come to sit at the feet of your teacher and master.
We come to sing his praises!
Come and bear witness to God's goodness and love.
We come to be filled, inspired and challenged!
Know how close God is, now and always.
Closer than our closest friend.
Hallelujah!

A prayer of confession

Wise and loving God, source of our being, answer to all our neediness: we come before you as people who do not live as we might, people who fall short of your glory. May we know and experience our forgiveness through your love, and live our lives in the light of your knowledge and truth.
Lord, in your mercy: **hear our prayer.**
Amen.

A prayer of intercession

Let us pray for those on the edge of the church, those who would like to be more involved but feel excluded, and those who find the church a painful place but cannot leave.
God, let us into your love so that we may
with one voice and one heart
love our neighbour.

Let us pray for those whom society considers beyond the pale, those whose crimes are so horrific that forgiveness is foreign, and those who are so desperate that they come anyway.
God, let us into your love so that we may
with one voice and one heart
love our neighbour.

Let us pray for those separated from us by boundaries of belief, those who cannot accept that there is a God, and those whose faith we find untenable.
God, let us into your love so that we may
with one voice and one heart
love our neighbour.

Let us pray for those who belong to a different class of people, those who are of a different gender, age, race, education, and for ourselves who are less 'normal' than we think we are.
God, let us into your love so that we may
with one voice and one heart
love our neighbour.
Amen.

A prayer of adoration

Wonderful God,
above and beyond us
and yet right beside us,
we thank you for your unlimited patience with us,
for your endless concern for our well-being,
for your amazing depth of commitment to us
and to all your people everywhere.
Teach us to respond to you with the whole of our being,
holding back nothing,
offering ourselves in your service and in your name,
in the service of others.
For you are God who deserves our all
and who asks only that we love one another
as you love us.
Amen.

A prayer for all ages

Lord Jesus, you made a deaf man hear.
When we refuse to hear your voice,
open our ears to your words of love.
Living Lord Jesus, hear us.

Lord Jesus, you made a dumb man speak.
When we do not know what to say,
open our mouths to praise you and speak your words of love.
Living Lord Jesus, hear us.

Lord Jesus, you made a blind man see.
When we cannot see the signs of your presence in the world around us,
open our eyes and show us your works of love.
Living Lord Jesus, help us.
Amen.

A prayer activity

Give each person a picture from newspaper reports from around the world. Pass around a plate with crumbs on it. Take turns to press a finger onto a few crumbs and sprinkle them onto the picture, silently praying for people in that country. When everyone has finished, each person quietly folds their picture, trapping the crumbs inside, and drops it into a bin, to symbolize committing the prayer to God.

A sending out prayer

Go now in the love of God,
to love God and one another.
Go with open hearts and hands and minds,
in his name and for his sake.
And may the blessing of God almighty
be with you and all his people everywhere,
now and always.
Amen.

Year B PROPER 19

Sunday between September 11 and September 17 inclusive

Isaiah 50.4–9a; Psalm 116.1–9; James 3.1–12;
Mark 8.27–38 *Jesus asked them, 'Who do you say that I am?'*

Call to worship

May the words of our mouth
and the meditation of all our hearts
be acceptable in your sight,
O God, our creator, Saviour and redeemer.

A prayer of praise *based on Psalm 19*
(in the semi-continuous readings)

Heavenly God, we praise and adore you.
We lift our hearts to you, for you are our all.
We see you in the landscape, in the sky, in the hills
and trees, the mountains and streams.
We see you on the face of the child looking up in
love. We see you on the face of elderly people
sleeping in peace. We look for you now, Lord: we
listen for your voice. We seek your wisdom: may she
come and be with us as we worship together today.
Amen.

A prayer of confession for all ages

Who do you say that I am?
Christ, forgive us,
if we see you like Madonna
and make you into a star,
when you see yourself as a suffering servant.
Christ, forgive us,
if we see you like Churchill
and make you into a monument,
when you see yourself as a mocked messiah.
Christ, forgive us,
if we see you like Superman,
and make you into a fantasy figure,
when you see yourself as a true friend.
Christ, forgive us,
if we see you like the 'Nice Guy' next door
and make you a mirror of ourselves,
when you see yourself as a rejected radical.
Christ, you are hard to understand,
and hard to follow.
But give us wisdom to see,
faith to follow
and courage to carry
the cross with you.
Amen.

A prayer of intercession

Father, your son Jesus Christ asks his friends to
follow him in carrying the cross.
In your Church, we pray for those who try to follow
Jesus in places where Christians are oppressed,
abused or killed for their beliefs.
Give them strength to carry their cross
and follow in his way.

In your world, we pray for those who struggle to live
without proper food or clean water,
and for those who have lost homes and family in war.
Give them strength to carry their cross
and follow in his way.

In our community, we pray for those who are uncared
for and unwanted,
for those who have been hurt and cannot forget,
for those who are depressed and see no purpose in
living, and for those who are ill.
Give them strength to carry their cross
and follow in his way.

In our own lives, we pray for courage to choose the
way of Christ, whatever it may cost,
and to see him in the faces of all who suffer in your
world.
Give us strength to carry our cross
and follow in his way.
Amen.

A prayer for all ages *based on Proverbs 1.20–23*
(in the semi-continuous readings)

Lord, you have given us lots of wise sayings
in the Bible.
Give me the courage to stand up for the things I know
to be right, and for those who cannot stand up for
themselves.
Give me the wise words I need when others laugh
at me, or try to make me do things that I know to be
wrong.
Help me to remember that you are always with me.
Amen.

A prayer activity

*Place a cross centrally and invite everyone to make
a cross from two pieces of wood tied together with
wool. Ask them to sit quietly and hold the cross in
their hand. The group could say together:*
Lord Jesus, help me to follow you.
Amen.

A sending out prayer

Loving God, as we leave this time of worship,
we remember you are with us in our pain.
We remember you are with us in our
struggle to bring goodness.
We remember you are with us in the fun we have.
We remember that nothing in all of creation
can separate us from your love.
Amen.

Year B   PROPER 20

Sunday between September 18 and September 24 inclusive

Wisdom of Solomon 1.16–2.1, 12–22, or Jeremiah
11.18–20; Psalm 54; James 3.13–4.3, 7–8a;
Mark 9.30–37 *Jesus said, 'Whoever receives a child
in my name, receives me.'*

Call to worship

Let us worship God.
We come as we are to meet God here.
God's arms are open wide in welcome.
Our hearts are open wide to receive him.
God's Spirit draws us closer now to him
and to one another.
**May we, together, worship in Spirit
and in truth.**

A prayer of welcome

Holy Spirit, source of heavenly wisdom,
pure, peaceful, gentle and compassionate:
we welcome you.
Loving Lord Jesus, who came as a servant,
humble and obedient to your Father's will:
we welcome you.
Gracious heavenly Father,
drawing near to all who draw near to you:
we welcome you.
All who come here in sincere humility,
little children in the eyes of God:
**we welcome you in the name of Christ.
Amen.**

A prayer of confession

Forgive us, God, it's just the way we are.
We are fooled by fancy appearance and miss you,
the simple soul by our side. We are dazzled by the
dramatic entrance and ignore you, the constant
child by our side. We are bewitched by the powerful
presentation and abandon you, the faithful friend by
our side. Open our eyes; clear our thinking; help us to
learn wisdom and in humble honesty to be glad you
are by our side.
Amen.

A prayer of intercession

*Use the Taizé chant 'O Lord, hear my prayer' as a
sung response:*
We pray for peace, Lord God. For peace in homes, in
communities, in the world. Ease tensions and lessen
violence, and teach us to live in respect and unity.
(Sung response)
We pray for peace in your Church, Lord God. Unite
us by your Spirit, that your people may live by your
word, expressing your gracious love to the glory of
your name. *(Sung response)*
We pray for peace of mind for the searching, the
unhappy, the guilty. Make this community of yours a
harbour of tranquillity for all who need to know peace.
(Sung response)
Amen.

A prayer of adoration

Lord Jesus, you come among us to show us your
father's love. You speak of light and water, salt and
dough, wind and fire. You ask us to look at a bird, a
flower, a seed, a grain of wheat.
You touch a leper and take a little child in your arms.
Help us to see as you see. Open our eyes to your
father's love.
Amen.

A prayer for all ages

Lord, we look for you in the helpless baby who trusts
us to meet all her needs.
Show us your face, **and we shall be satisfied.**

Lord, we look for you in the child who challenges us
with his questions and tires us with his boundless
energy.
Show us your face, **and we shall be satisfied.**

Lord, we look for you in the teenager who rejects our
values and disturbs our peace.
Show us your face, **and we shall be satisfied.**

Lord, we look for you in the old man who slows our
path as we hurry on the street.
Show us your face, **and we shall be satisfied.**

Lord, we look for you in the beggar who bothers us at
the corner.
Show us your face, **and we shall be satisfied.**

Lord, we look for you in our classmates, our
colleagues at work and in the people next door.
Show us your face, **and we shall be satisfied.**

Lord, we look for you here in the person beside us, in
your gospel of love, in bread and in wine.
Show us your face, **and we shall be satisfied.
Amen.**

A prayer activity

*Make name cards. Each child writes, or is helped
to write, their name on a card. They decorate it and
make it look special, using patterns, sequins, ribbons,
etc. Then each child sticks their name to a central
cross using sticky tac. When all the names have been
added, the leader says (for the children to repeat):*
**We are the body of Christ.
Amen.**

A sending out prayer

Go now, knowing you are one.
We are one in the Spirit.
Go now as Christ's body in this community and world.
**We go in his peace and strength.
Amen.**

Year B PROPER 21

Sunday between September 25 and October 1 inclusive

Numbers 11.4–6, 10–16, 24–29; Psalm 19.7–14;
James 5.13–20; **Mark 9.38–50** *Jesus said, 'He who is
not against us, is on our side.'*

Call to worship

The touch of God **caresses our brokenness.**
The suffering of God **meets us in this world.**
The power of God **supports us on our journey.**
The justice of God **calls us into right living.**
The voice of God **whispers each of our names.**
The grace of God **shapes us a new community.**
The love of God **holds each of us together.**
The peace of God **makes this a safe place.**
The presence of God **welcomes us, upholds us and
loves us through everything.**

A prayer of confession *based on
Esther 7.1–6, 9–10, 9.20–22*
(in the semi-continuous readings)

For covenants abandoned – **pardon us.**
For promises broken – **forgive us.**
For friendships betrayed – **renew us.**
For faith denied – **re-equip us.**
In the name of the one who created us, died for us
and sent us out to serve: the God of all creation.
Amen.

A personal prayer

If we took your words literally, God's kingdom would
contain only handless, footless and eyeless people!
But do I take my sin seriously enough?
I'm quick to see and judge the sins of others but find
it easy to explain away my own faults and failings.
Loving God, help me to respond to this teaching
in love, not fear. Help me to see my sin from your
perspective, to deal with it lovingly and effectively,
so that I may become more fully human
and more like Jesus.
Keep me from setting a bad example
or being a stumbling block,
so that others may also find fulfilment
in the company of Jesus.
Amen.

A prayer of intercession

Let us pray for all people, of whatever faith, politics,
or race, who care for the poor, sick and needy.
They are working for you.
Bless their love.

Let us pray for all people, of whatever church,
community or tradition, who welcome and include
outsiders.
They are working for you.
Bless their hospitality.

Let us pray for all people, of whatever age, gender or
class, who work for reconciliation despite opposition.
They are working for you.
Bless their commitment.

Let us pray for all people, of whatever education, skill
or experience, who help those who suffer loss.
They are working for you.
Bless their compassion.

Bless and enable us all
as we partner you in service,
in the name and spirit of Jesus Christ.
Amen.

A prayer for all ages

Where there is hurt in our neighbourhood,
we pray… *(Pause)*
With love we surround you. *(Cross arms over heart)*
With grace we enfold you. *(Stretch arms out to sides)*
With peace we pray for you. *(Bring hands together
into praying hands)*
Where there is division in our community…
Where there is loneliness in our parish…
Where there are too many memories in our district…
Where there is illness in our homes…
Amen.

A prayer activity

*Give each child two pieces of paper. On one piece
they write something that stops them doing what God
wants. On the other piece they write a problem that
someone else has. The problems may be things that
stop them coming to church, e.g. family problems
or problems with teasing. When they've all written
something, fold the pieces of paper and put them into
a box, then pray:*
Dear God, may we clear away the obstacles in our
lives that stop us from getting to know you better,
with your help.
May we avoid the things that we shouldn't be doing,
with your help.
May we see how we can help those around us,
with your help.
Amen.
*You could then stamp on the box to symbolize the
transfer of our stumbling blocks to God's care.*

A sending out prayer

Come, Lord, to hold us and meet us in all our
mistakes. Come, guide us through our faults and
soothe us in all our complaints. Come to us, and
make us complete, standing with us as we pray.
Smile at us through the people we meet, and wave
as we go on our way. Help us to rest in the warmth of
your love, in the grace that we give and receive. And
after we sing of your glory above, take us by the hand
as we leave.
Amen.

Year B   PROPER 22

Sunday between October 2 and October 8 inclusive

Genesis 2.18–24; Psalm 8; Hebrews 1.1–4, 2.5–12;
Mark 10.2–16 *Jesus said, 'Let the children come to me.'*

Call to worship *based on Psalm 8*

O Lord, how majestic is your name in all the earth!
When I look at the heavens, the work of your fingers,
what are human beings that you are mindful of them?
Yet you have made them a little lower than God,
and crowned them with glory and honour.
O Lord, how majestic is your name in all the earth.

A prayer of confession

I confess to God, to my loved one,
to my family, and to my sisters and brothers:
I let you down when I forget you to enjoy myself.
I let you down when I use you to satisfy myself.
I let you down when I hurt you to defend myself.
I ask you to forgive me, and help me to be one with
you again, like children playing together and giving as
well as receiving.
I ask you in the name and spirit of Jesus
our mutual friend and saviour.
Amen.

A prayer of intercession

God of rainbows and wellingtons,
we pray for anyone who finds life grey and dull.
Help us to find ways of sharing with them
the joys of play and the delights of puddles.

God of roses and whispers,
we pray for anyone who finds life cold and lonely.
Help us to find ways of sharing with them
the warmth of laughter and the intimacy of love.

God of rest and wonder,
we pray for anyone who finds life hard and painful.
Help us to find ways of sharing with them
the release of healing and the promise of hope.

We pray, knowing that we ourselves are in need,
and trusting that you are faithful, in the name and
Spirit of Jesus Christ.
Amen.

A prayer of petition

Make our church a playground, O God,
where hearts are joyful,
minds are full of play and incredible dreams,
love and laughter rule OK.
Turn our ritual into creativity,
colleagues into playmates,
old ways into daring adventures,
and tradition into the grass beneath our feet.
Then, between the slides and see-saws
of all we experience,
may we learn to trust those we dance with,
and renew our strength in the comfort
of your care for us all.
Amen.

An offertory prayer *based on Job 1.1, 2.1–10*
(in the semi-continuous readings)

All our possessions are worthless unless dedicated to
you. All our belongings are of no value, if owned with
thankless hearts. So we offer back to you what was
always yours, asking for your blessing.
The Lord gives and the Lord takes away.
Blessed be the name of the Lord for ever.
Amen.

A prayer for all ages

Loving God, we pray for people around the world
who experience loss; those who have faith in you and
those who have no faith; those who have friends and
family to support them and those who have none.
We pray for ourselves, that we may be people of
faith who trust in you and seek to help those in need
wherever we can.
We ask this in Jesus' name.
Amen.

A prayer activity

*The children sit in a circle with pictures or
photographs of family members in front of them. Pray
that God will protect and watch over every member
of every family. At this point the children could put
their pictures into a bowl as a symbol of placing their
relatives into God's care.*

A sending out prayer

Lord Jesus, help us to become like children again.
Take us in your arms, place your hands on us
and bless us.
And may Christ the supreme one reign over us.
May Christ the suffering one sustain us.
May Christ our brother be close to us,
today and every day.
Amen.

Year B   PROPER 23

Sunday between October 9 and October 15 inclusive

Amos 5.6–7, 10–15; Psalm 90.12–17; Hebrews 4.12–16; **Mark 10.17–31** *Jesus replied, 'Sell everything you have and give to the poor, and you will have treasure in heaven.'*

Call to worship

We come from all walks of life.
We bring all that we are,
our burdens of joys and woes,
and Jesus knows.
We are a tangle of worry and wonder.
We live in both darkness and light,
and Jesus knows.
We meet here with all kinds of experiences.
We come with questions and anxieties,
and Jesus knows.
We come fully as ourselves,
and Jesus knows.

A prayer of approach

Your love is difficult, O God,
for you speak words that delve deep,
uncovering those things we would hide.
Then you open the doors wide, calling us out into you. You hold out open arms, and, as we respond, uncomfortable in our nakedness, so you wrap your care around us and speak words of peace.
Call us, O God, and help us to hear.
Amen.

A prayer of confession

To you who have had to give up your home
and flee your country, God says: 'You will be one of the family in the promised land.'
To you who use your wealth to buy possessions and protection, God says: 'Justice threatens your comfort and your conscience.'
To you who have had to lose your security
and know real poverty, God says: 'You will be granted a place full of peace.'
To you who save your surpluses and benefit from stocks and shares, God says: 'The poor disturb your serenity and security.'
Help us, Word of Truth, to hear the comfort and the challenge in the teaching of Christ.
Help us, Word of Life, to repent and respond
to the Gospel of Christ.
Amen.

A prayer of intercession

We pray that those who need shelter, safe homes and protection,
may find a place to be in God's promised paradise.
God, may we share what we have to answer these prayers.

We pray that those who need love and affirmation, may find the welcome they need among God's pilgrim people.
God, may we share what we have to answer these prayers.

We pray that those who need truth and reality checks, may find the courage to change in God's powerful presence.
God, may we share what we have to answer these prayers.

We pray that we who need you, soul searcher and gracious God, may find a message of mercy in your prophetic preaching.
Help us when you ask us for something to give it with all our heart.
Amen.

A prayer for all ages

Loving God, you have given us more good things than we need.
Help us to share them with those who have less.
Loving God, **help us to be generous in giving.**

Loving God, you have given us families and friends and neighbours to care for us.
Help us to show love for those who are unhappy or alone.
Loving God, **help us to be generous in giving.**

Loving God, you have given us different gifts and talents and many opportunities to learn.
Help us to use them creatively to make your world a richer and a lovelier place.
Loving God, **help us to be generous in giving.**

Loving God, you have given us freedom to live how we choose.
Help us to use it wisely for those deprived of basic human needs and rights.
Loving God, **help us to be generous in giving.**
Amen.

A prayer activity

Ask the children to think of their favourite thing. Then pray:
Dear God, these are our favourite things.
The children shout them out
Help us to share them with you.
Help us to share them with others,
as you share so many good things with us.
Amen.

A sending out prayer

Send us out as hearers of your voice, to listen to troubled hearts, to speak words of love and to act with compassion.
Amen.

Year B   PROPER 24

Isaiah 53.4–12; Psalm 91.9–16; Hebrews 5.1–10;
Mark 10.35–45 *Jesus said, 'Whoever wants to be
great among you must be your servant.'*

Call to worship

God calls the weak and the poor.
God calls the suffering and the gentle.
God calls the needy and the sick.
For these are kingdom people,
who hear the voice of God.

A prayer of confession

O God, so often we understand greatness
in outward signs of status and position,
of power and rank. We push ourselves forward.
We want to have the last word. We strive to be
noticed and care about how others see us.
We are proud on the outside and fearful within.
We are truly sorry, and ask to be forgiven.
Jesus, we hear your words of acceptance
and life, 'but it is not so among you'.
Transform us. Make us want to change.
Help us understand your way of greatness
that comes in serving one another in love.
Help us find our true selves in the giving
of ourselves.
Holy Spirit, enable us to cherish others
with your love.
Give us joy in simple acts of caring,
loving others as much as we love ourselves.
May we impress others only in our
commitment to them,
offering all we are able in the name and
strength of Jesus.
Amen.

A prayer for all ages

God, thank you for all the ways we can serve
one another in your name.
Thank you for those who have served
and cared for us throughout our lives.
Thank you for giving us hearts that find joy
in serving for your love's sake.
As we listen to your word to us this day,
come to us afresh through your Spirit.
Help us know that we are great in your eyes
when we serve one another,
when we prize others as highly
as we prize ourselves.
O Jesus, you kneel at the feet of your friends
and wash each one of us clean.
Help us to look for ways to kneel at the feet of friend
and stranger,
and receive from them whatever they need to give us.
All this we can only do in the name and the Spirit of
Jesus, who serves us unto death
and brings us into life.
Amen.

A prayer of intercession

We pray for those who wrestle with media attention
when they only want to serve; and for those whose
reputations are ruined by rumour.
We pray for those who work in the spotlight
but sacrifice their comfort for others.
For those who are casualties of celebrity.
For those who weather the storms of success in
selfless commitment to justice; and for those who find
fame too fearful.
We pray for those who win respect from their critics
because of their integrity and humility;
and for those who are shown to be self-seeking.
For those who watch others claim fame, content to
have contributed to change; and for those whose
credibility is cheapened by corruption.
We pray for all who serve, sacrifice and slave willingly
for the sake of others. And we pray that all who are
exploited, oppressed and abused may be set free to
find fulfilment.
God, help us to think more of what needs to be done
than what we might get out of doing it.
Amen.

A prayer with children

You call me friend and so I am,
for I know you by your name.
You call me servant and that may be,
as I like to be of help to you.
You call me disciple and that seems so,
for I follow the words passed on to me.
You call me loved and so I'm glad,
for that changes the world around me.
Amen.

A prayer activity

*Lay a tray of little twigs in front of the group. Ask
everyone to take one. Explain that the twig represents
the staff that a servant carries, and ask them to carry
that twig in their pocket to remember what it means to
serve other people for Jesus. Then pray:*
Lord Jesus Christ, help us to serve you each day.
Make us your servants, this we would pray.
Help us to see all the people who need you,
to be caring and kind, to make the world new!
Amen.

A sending out prayer

Go from this place, not to be served but to serve:
in the name of Christ, who has gone before us;
in the love of God, our heavenly Father;
in the power of the Spirit, source of humility.
Go with assurance.
Go with God's blessing.
Go in peace.
Amen.

Year B   PROPER 25

Jeremiah 31.7–9; Psalm 126; Hebrews 7.23–28;
Mark 10.46–52 *Take heart, get up, Jesus is calling you.*

Call to worship

Open our eyes to see Christ among us.
Open our ears to hear the living word.
Open our mouths to speak and sing praises.
Open our hearts to receive you now.
Amen.

A prayer of approach

Gathering God,
your love attracts everyone who looks for help
and gives hope, healing and wholeness.
Welcoming God,
your love accepts everyone who comes for help
and gives peace, pleasure and purpose.
Gracious God,
help us to see when we are indifferent, insensitive
and unjust.
Generous God,
give us grace to heal, welcome and transform
so that we might also follow Christ.
Amen.

A personal prayer

God, help us to be like Bartimaeus,
someone who asks, receives and follows.
Amen.

A prayer of confession

When we have not best cared for those nearest to us,
our families, our friends,
good Lord, forgive us.
When we have not best cared for those close to us, in
our church, our street, our community,
good Lord, forgive us.
When we have not best cared for those far from us, in
our country, in our world,
good Lord, forgive us.
When we have not best cared for you, in worship, in
word, in prayer,
good Lord, forgive us.
Amen.

A prayer of intercession

Softly, quietly, children die and mothers weep.
Softly, quietly, crops fail and wither in the land.
Softly, quietly, arms are sold and taken up.
Softly, quietly, the poor get poorer, the rich richer.
Softly, quietly, lives are sold and passed along.
Softly, quietly, death creeps in, decay takes over.
For we do not hear or see, so we do not shout.
God, open our eyes and ears to see the trouble you
see, to hear the torment you hear, and to cry out loud
for justice in the land.

Let us hold the grieving mothers in our arms, send
the good seed to grow, fight the trade in weapons,
speak up for the rights of the poor, demand justice
among the nations, value each human life, end our
dealing in death.
In all this, let us not be blind to what the world does,
nor to what we can do. Let us not be deaf to the cries
of those who need mercy, nor turn away from all who
need our help. Let us not be silent as long as others
suffer mutely, but shout out our solidarity with them.
Softly, quietly, the Holy Spirit comes among us,
then with flames and like the wind stirs and moves
us, opens our ears and eyes and gives us a voice to
shout out for justice, goodness and peace
throughout the earth.
Come, Holy Spirit, come.
Amen.

A prayer for all ages

When darkness descends and courage fails,
when even the sun has lost its warmth,
take heart, Jesus is calling you.

When the words you speak seem feeble and tired,
when the news you hear is full of gloom,
take heart, Jesus is calling you.

When other people have let you down,
when the trust you shared has been destroyed,
take heart, Jesus is calling you.

When precious hopes have come to grief,
when time is filled with emptiness,
take heart, Jesus is calling you.

When those you love have left you behind,
when you feel so very alone,
take heart, Jesus is calling you.
Amen.

A prayer activity

*Put some spectacles, magnifying glasses and
binoculars on a tray. Ask each child to choose
something from the tray and try using it, and then
afterwards all say:*
**Lord God, we thank you that you have given us
eyes to see. Help us to use our eyes always to
see those people who are sad or lonely or afraid.
Help us to remember that you have made all of us
and that you love us as your children.**
Amen.

A sending out prayer

God of beauty in our broken world, help us to be
transformers, mending shattered lives.
Help us to be restorers, bringing comfort and hope.
Help us to be accepters, finding peace in your love.
Amen.

Year B   PROPER 26

Sunday between October 30 and November 5 inclusive

Deuteronomy 6.1–9; Psalm 119.1–8; Hebrews 9.11–14; **Mark 12.28–34** *Jesus said to the Scribe, 'You are not far from the kingdom of God.'*

Call to worship

Come to worship,
not out of habit,
not out of duty,
not because your name is on a rota,
not because you will earn points in heaven.
Come to worship
because you love God,
because you love yourself,
because you love God's world,
because you love God's people.
We come to celebrate the living God.

A prayer of confession

Forgive us in our busyness and compulsion
to get through the chores or business of the day,
when we rush past or forget about those we take
for granted,
when we fail to stop and truly listen,
or get angry far too quickly,
or once again put off making that call
that would mean so much to the person at the
other end.
**Forgive us and love us, so that we may reach
out in love to others.
Amen.**

A prayer of intercession

Living God, if your kingdom is to come you need
workers for the kingdom.
We pray for those who try to love you and other
people.
We pray for those who use their hearts:
artists, musicians, carers…
We pray for those who use their souls:
preachers, church workers, aid workers…
We pray for those who use their minds:
scientists, lawyers, teachers…
We pray for those who use their strength:
builders, workers, soldiers…
Touch us all with your love.
Strengthen each one to know and love you more
and help us learn to love others.
So may we make this world more like your kingdom,
a place of love, hope, joy and healing,
and make us more like Jesus Christ,
our love and Saviour, strength and song.
Amen.

A prayer of supplication

When you called your people to hear you, loving God,
you told them that you are one.
May we be one in our love for you,
in all that we are together.
Teach us, great God, to love
with our heart and soul, our mind and strength.

Patient Saviour, the temptations are many,
and the pathways of love are hard going.
May we love you with determination;
let us not turn aside or grow weary.
Teach us, great God, to love
with our heart and soul, our mind and strength.

Our neighbours are many, their lives are diverse;
help us to hear them and learn from them,
to love them as you love us.
Teach us, great God, to love
with our heart and soul, our mind and strength.

May love be our journey, our goal and our lifestyle.
May love be our hope and our deepest desire, that
we may grow closer and give you the glory.
Teach us, great God, to love
**with our heart and soul, our mind and strength.
Amen.**

A prayer for all ages

God, we want to love you with
all of our hearts, *(Hold hands over heart)*
all of our souls, *(Hold hands out)*
all of our minds, *(Point to head)*
and all of our strength. *(Flex arm muscles)*
Help us to love you more every day.
God, we want to love other people *(Point to each other)*
just as we love ourselves. *(Point to yourself)*
Help us to show other people we love them.
Amen.

A prayer activity

*Light three tealights in turn as you invite the children
to think about loving God, loving our neighbours and
loving ourselves and pray:*
We light this light to show our love of God.
We light this light to show our love for our neighbours.
We light this light to show that God loves us.
Amen.

A sending out prayer

Living God, you love each one of us; everywhere,
always, with all the love you have.
Help us to love you and to love other people with all
the love we have, as Jesus did.
Amen.

Year B   PROPER 27

1 Kings 17.8–16; Psalm 146; Hebrews 9.24–28;
Mark 12.38–44 *Jesus said, 'Truly I tell you, this poor widow has given more than all the others, for she has given all she had to live on.'*

Call to worship

Come not to create power and wealth,
but to become a community of peace.
Come not to climb lofty branches,
but to plant a small seed in the ground.
Come not to savour the feast of kings,
but to ferment yeast into bread.
Come not to flaunt precious jewels,
but to find the hidden treasure within you.
Come not to trade in the things of this world,
but to find what is precious.
**Come, for it is Christ the valuer of the small things, who meets us here.
Amen.**

A prayer of confession

We cannot pray for the poor if we walk by on the other side.
We cannot pray for the sick if we remain unmoved.
We cannot pray for the hungry, and continue to waste our food.
We cannot pray for the exploited,
and continue to buy products that enslave them.
We cannot pray for the victims of war,
and continue to wage war.
We cannot pray for the persecuted
if we support the bully.
We cannot pray for the unemployed,
and continue to value only the lowest price.

God of forgiveness,
in this world of sin, we dare not pray,
for we, ourselves, are ensnared in sin.
Forgive us, that we cannot live lives without sin,
that we cannot escape the systems of death,
that we cannot change the world.
**Forgive us. Hear our prayers,
and change us to become part of the solution,
not the problem. In the name of the one who shows us the way,
Amen.**

A prayer of intercession

The world dictates that everything must be bigger, better, faster, yet walking and cycling are healthier for us and for the environment, consuming less means there is more to share with others, and shopping locally helps strengthen our community.
Teach us to see the greatness of the small.

The world says that power belongs to the young, the ambitious, the wealthy, yet…
Teach us to see the greatness of the small.
The world listens to those with influence, media access and technology, yet…
**Teach us to see the greatness of the small.
Amen.**

A prayer of offering *based on 1 Kings 17.8–16*

An offering of love for others is like the widow's jar of meal. It can never be exhausted.

An offering of hope for others is like the jug of oil. It can never run dry.

An offering of life for others is like the bread and wine. Its remembrance stirs up life in its fullness.

Loving God, help us to give of ourselves,
as we celebrate what others have given.
May we bring love and hope and life into a needy world, and so glorify your name.
Amen.

A prayer for all ages

Jesus, the scribes said,
'Look at me, me, me! *(Point to yourself)*
I am great, great, great!' *(Thumbs up)*
The widow said,
'Don't look at me, me, me! *(Shake head)*
Look at God, God, God! *(Point up)*
God is great, great, great!' *(Thumbs up)*
Help us say,
'Don't look at me, me, me! *(Shake head)*
Look at God, God, God! *(Point up)*
God is great, great, great!' *(Thumbs up)*
Amen.

A prayer activity

On pieces of card cut to the shape of a money bag write or draw something you could give to God by giving to other people. What you give may not necessarily be money, but it should be something that will cost you time or effort. Pass a basket around for the children to put their cards in. When everyone has done this, one person should pray that all present will be generous in what they give, and ask for God's help to actually do these things.

A sending out prayer

Go into a needy world filled with the knowledge of all the good things God gives you. And may God grant you joyful lives to spend in the service of others.
Amen.

Year B   PROPER 28

Daniel 12.1–3; Psalm 16; Hebrews 10.11–14 (15–18), 19–25; **Mark 13.1–8** *Jesus said, 'Do not be alarmed.'*

Call to worship

Come to him, a living stone, though rejected by mortals yet chosen and precious in God's sight.

A prayer of approach

When we stand in awe of the magnificence of the Temple,
Jesus calls us to look for the kingdom hidden among us.
When we value the security of wealth and insurance premiums,
Jesus reminds us that we cannot predict the future.
When we allow corruption and injustice to go unchallenged,
Jesus prompts us to ask the difficult questions.
When we are overwhelmed by the pain and struggles of living,
Jesus teaches us to hope and dream of a new birth.
We draw near – hesitant, afraid, searching, hoping – to worship the one who calls us to one another, who calls us to a new way of living for ourselves and the world.
Amen.

A prayer of confession

God of the generations who have gone before us,
we give you thanks for our sense of identity, forged
from the mix of family and culture,
from nationality and religion.
We confess that we have sometimes denied the identity of others and have sought to make others in our own image.
God of our turbulent, insecure world, we give you
thanks when life feels safe and secure, for the ways
we can plan for difficult times and plan for our future.
We confess that we have sometimes hidden behind our policies and pensions,
and buffered ourselves from the pain of the world.
God who is birthing new life, we give you thanks
for the differences and dissonance that give life its
vibrancy and colour, its energy and excitement.
We confess that we have sometimes preferred the drabness of the familiar, and denied others their dreams and aspirations.
Amen.

A prayer of intercession *based on Psalm 16*

The Lord our God is our refuge; our protector; our
rescuer; and our joy.
Let us come to the Lord our God in prayer.

Ever-living God, God our refuge,
we pray for all who need your safety this day.
Those who fear violence, who have no stability, who
have no home (especially in…)
God our refuge, in your mercy,
hear our prayer.
God our protector,
we pray for all whose future is uncertain.
Those without work, awaiting news, ending a chapter
of life (especially…)
God our protector, in your mercy,
hear our prayer.
God our rescuer,
we pray for all who are in deep trouble.
Those addicted to drink or drugs, those without hope,
those in debt (especially…)
God our rescuer, in your mercy,
hear our prayer.
God our joy,
we give thanks for all who have passed through death
and are now safe with you (especially…)
Bring us, with them, to your kingdom of everlasting
life and peace.
God our joy, in your mercy,
hear our prayer.
God who hears all our prayers,
grant the peace and power of your presence,
for each one of us and all those for whom we have
prayed, today and always.
Amen.

A prayer for all ages

God of strength, there are things in our world that
frighten us. **Jesus said, 'Do not be alarmed.'**
There are wars and fighting and people are hurt.
Jesus said, 'Do not be alarmed.'
There are arguments and fear in some people's
homes. **Jesus said, 'Do not be alarmed.'**
We see bad things happening on television.
Jesus said, 'Do not be alarmed.'
But we know you are with us, and will help us to get
through things that frighten us.
Help us to learn to trust you.
Amen.

A prayer activity

With building bricks, make something together. Have fun knocking it down! Then pray:
Dear Jesus, sometimes things are built up.
Sometimes they fall down.
Thank you that you are with us always,
in the good times and the bad.
Amen.

A sending out prayer

Awesome God, you call us to come and follow you.
Help us to hear your voice speaking into our hearts
and minds. Give us the courage to live for you.
Amen.

Year B   PROPER 29/CHRIST THE KING

Sunday between November 20 and November 26 inclusive

Daniel 7.9–10, 13–14; Psalm 93; Revelation 1.4b–8;
John 18.33–37 *Pilate said to Jesus, 'You are a king then?'*

Call to worship

Within God and before God, we offer our hearts and minds in worship.
In the air we breathe, in the world we walk.
In the people we meet, in the life we share, **God is.**
In our words, in our actions, in all we do in love for each other, **God is.**
Through the goodness of the world, **God speaks.**
Through justice, **God speaks.**
Through mercy, **God speaks.**
God calls us now to walk a right path,
to live in love, to know that God is one.

A prayer of confession

Loving God, maker of all that is,
we come before you now in all our weakness.
We have turned away from your goodness
and forgotten your love for us.
We have not kept your command to love you with our whole selves.
We have not loved others as we love ourselves.
Forgive us when we forget you.
Forgive us when we fail you.
Give us grace to face our mistakes and to try again.
We ask this in the name of Jesus Christ.
Amen.

A prayer of intercession for all ages

Jesus, where people hate each other:
may your kingdom come.
Where people are greedy:
may your kingdom come.
Where people don't have the things they need:
may your kingdom come.
Where people are scared or lonely:
may your kingdom come.
Where people are hurting or ill:
may your kingdom come.
Where people are sad:
may your kingdom come.
Your kingdom will last for ever and ever.
Amen.

A prayer of adoration

Lord Jesus Christ, king of all creation,
alpha and omega, the beginning and end of all things,
we worship you.
When the universe began, spiralling outward, the newborn stars reflected your glory, for you are the beginning of all things.
When you walked along the shores of Lake Galilee and healed broken hearts, touched lepers and gave tax collectors and prostitutes self-respect, your kingdom came near.

When you were betrayed, mocked, beaten, crucified, you revealed the kingdom of the servant king – a kingdom not of this world.
And when, beyond all our imagining, there shall be a new heaven, and a new earth, and tears and death shall be no more, all people will see, all people will know that you are the Everlasting King. Lord Jesus Christ, king of all creation, alpha and omega, the beginning and end of all things, we worship you.
Amen.

A prayer for all ages

Jesus, you were born in a stable; that's not the way kings are born, yet shepherds and kings came to worship you.
You are not like a king of this world,
but you are King of our lives.
You worked as a carpenter, your friends were ordinary folk, yet they followed you as their leader and king.
You are not like a king of this world,
but you are King of our lives.
You rode on a humble donkey, not on a camel with a train, yet people waved palms and hailed you as king.
You are not like a king of this world,
but you are King of our lives.
You died as 'King of the Jews', wearing a crown of thorns, yet Pilate failed to recognize that you were the king of all.
You are not like a king of this world,
but you are King of our lives.
You appeared quietly to your friends, to show that you had defeated death. Today you are still alive as our friend and king.
You are not like a king of this world,
but you are King of our lives.
Amen.

A prayer activity

In silence, or with soft music playing, pass around a model of a crown of thorns. Each child weaves into it a small piece of red ribbon or wool. Ask them to think about the sort of king who would choose to wear this crown rather than a golden, jewelled one. They could pray aloud or silently for everyone who has power over other people. Pray:
Jesus, you wore a crown of thorns instead of a crown of gold. You are a new kind of king. You suffered and died because you loved your people. Thank you. Help us to know what you want us to do. Give us strength to serve you.
Amen.

A sending out prayer

Lord God, you are the Almighty God, and ruler of the kings of the earth. You invite us into relationship with you as our King, our Lord, our Saviour and our friend. Help us to draw close to you this week.
Amen.

Year C

Year C   ADVENT 1

Jeremiah 33.14–16; Psalm 25.1–10; 1 Thessalonians 3.9–13; **Luke 21.25–36** *There will be signs in the sun, the moon and the stars.*

Call to worship

God, who made earth and heaven
and fills creation with the Spirit,
calls us into friendship.
God, who loves creation as a mother and a father,
values us.
God speaks through wind and rain,
through heat and ice.
We will find God in the hearts of those who love us.
We will find God in the outstretched hands of those
who seek our help.
We will find God in the energy of the universe.
We will find God because God looks for us.
Here, now, in this place, with these people, we come
before God and lift up our heads because the God of
glory loves us.

A prayer of confession

Loving God, the world is yours,
but we behave as if it were ours.
Just God, merciful God,
we will put our trust in you.
Loving God, we belong to each other,
but we behave as if we stand alone.
Just God, merciful God,
we will put our trust in you.
Loving God, we are your family,
but we behave as if we were our own creation.
Just God, merciful God,
we will put our trust in you.
We forget you. We act against you.
We break what we should cherish.
Do not give us what we deserve, O Lord.
Fill us with your Spirit.
Change us. Help us to start again.
Just God, merciful God,
we will put our trust in you.
Amen.

A prayer activity

*Write a prayer together as a group that
identifies and thanks God for the different
priorities of those who follow Christ.*

A responsorial prayer for children

Jesus, when bad things happen,
help us to remember:
Your words will last for ever.
When we are worried or scared,
help us to remember:
Your words will last for ever.
When everything seems to keep changing,
help us to remember:
Your words will last for ever.
Keep us safe in your love for ever and ever.
Amen.

A prayer for all ages

Gentle God, when there is trouble, when people fight,
give us the courage to be your peacemaker.
Powerful God, **make us strong in you.**
Tender God, when there is sadness, when people cry,
give us kind hearts to be your comforters.
Powerful God, **make us strong in you.**
Glorious God, when there is fear, when people
tremble, give us the confidence to be your
encouragers.
Powerful God, **make us strong in you.**
Loving God, when there is hopelessness, when
people give up, give us the fire of your Spirit so that
we may share your light.
Powerful God, **make us strong in you.**
Gentle, glorious, loving God, help us to be your
messengers.
Let us live in the faith of Jesus Christ so that all the
world will see your love working in us.
Powerful God, **make us strong in you.**
Amen.

Prayer for young people, that God would help us to hear and obey his call

Dear God,
Your call can be hard to hear,
or hard to accept.
It can sound silly,
or scary.
Mary's call was terrifying.
Help us to accept your call as she did.
Through an experience with the supernatural,
through a difficult time with Joseph,
through pregnancy and laborious travelling,
Mary kept her faith in you.
Help us to trust you as we do your will.
So many things can look impossible:
too big, too important.
Help us to trust in you,
to trust in your impossibilities.
All over the world,
people have heard your call.
We pray for those in difficult situations,
for those living your word through tough times.
Lord, help us, like Mary,
to do your will,
however hard it is.
Amen.

A sending out prayer

God of peace,
We pray for peace throughout the world.
Help us to be peacemakers and to set things right
where there is disagreement and violence.
Show us the way of peace in our own lives and in our
homes, schools and streets.
Amen.

Year C ADVENT 2

Baruch 5.1–9, or Malachi 3.1–4; Luke 1.68–79,
Philippians 1.3–11; **Luke 3.1–6** *He went into all the region around the Jordan, proclaiming a baptism of repentance for the forgiveness of sins.*

Call to worship

Let the heavens rejoice and let the earth be glad, for God comes.
God comes to judge the world with righteousness and people with truth.
Sing and rejoice, people of God, for God comes to dwell in your midst.
Happy are those who are watching when God comes.
Look, God sends a messenger to prepare the way of the Lord.
Listen and pay attention to him.
Turn around, mend your ways,
and be ready when God comes.
For God is coming soon.

A prayer of confession

God of all the world, our world is lost without you.
We make war with each other.
Some have too much while others have little.
Our differences confuse us, and we lack understanding.
Come amongst us, God, and help us.
God of the Church, we have lost the excitement of pilgrimage.
We avoid adventure and sharing in challenging service.
We shrink from mission and evangelism.
Come amongst us, God, and help us.
God of our life, you have called us and we have not heard well.
You have real things for us to do, and we have not always done them.
You call us to a life of Christian love and discipleship and we have fallen from your ways.
Come amongst us, God, and help us.
For the sake of Jesus Christ.
Amen.

A prayer of petition for children

Lord Jesus,
Show us now and every day,
How to live and how to pray,
How to listen when you say,
'It's time for you to prepare my way.'
Amen.

A prayer activity

Cut a photocopied map of your area into large pieces. Ask each person to write a prayer for your local community on one of the pieces of the map and then assemble it together.

A prayer of intercession

In the desert John spoke his words of judgement, challenging people to change, to repent, to be baptized with water.

We remember today:
those who hear only words of judgement;
those struggling in a desert of despair;
those who are afraid for their future;
those who feel worthless and unloved.
By the lake and in the marketplace Jesus spoke his words of invitation,
challenging people to follow him,
transforming them with his spirit of love.
We remember today:
those who speak words of encouragement;
those who walk with the despairing;
those who give hope to the fearful;
those who offer friendship to the unloved.
We pray for those who find it difficult to say sorry,
and those who find forgiveness too difficult.
We give thanks for John the Baptist
who prepared the way for something new to happen,
bridging the gap between old and new,
judgement and forgiveness.
Amen.

A prayer for all ages together

Invite people to shout out the response as if they were at a pantomime
Can a leopard change its spots
or an oak tree turn into a pine;
a trout into a whale, a tortoise into a hare;
a frog into a prince?
Well, what do you think? – Yes?
Oh no they can't.
Can water freeze into ice?
Can snow turn into water?
Can an acorn grow into an oak,
a bud into a flower, a caterpillar into a butterfly?
Well, what do you think? – No?
Oh yes they can.
It's more than the eye can see
but we know it happens.
Now can we change?
Oh yes we can.
For God's love changes everything.
Amen.

A prayer of dedication

Journeying God,
You have a great journey mapped out for us.
We want to travel with you.
Help us to prepare well, to shake off the past,
to take on the future and go forward with you.
We will not fear the heights,
for you will steady us.
We will not fear the rough places,
for you will equip us.
We will not fear the valleys,
for you will sustain us.
With you we go forward,
and we trust you to bring us home.
Amen.

Year C   ADVENT 3

Zephaniah 3.14–20; Isaiah 12.2–6; Philippians 4.4–7;
Luke 3.7–18 *Whoever has two coats must share with anyone who has none; and whoever has food must do likewise.*

Call to worship

Sing to God a new song:
Give thanks and shout in triumph!
God loves righteousness and justice:
God's love unfailing fills the earth.
Let the whole world fear God:
Let all on earth stand in awe!

A prayer of confession

We are afraid:
disaster stalks the planet
and can seem quite close.
We are afraid:
as age changes us,
weakness and loss are real possibilities.
We are afraid:
of those different from us in lifestyle, ability, culture
and beliefs.
We turn to you again.
We want you to make us new.
We are ready to embrace your promise to save us.
Please deal with our fears.
Please release us.
Amen.

A prayer of petition

Lord Jesus,
When our lives have gone wrong
and we don't know how to put them right,
show us your love.
Teach us what we should do.
When our thinking is confused
and we don't know how to sort it out,
show us your love.
Teach us what we should do.
When our intentions are good
but we don't know how to put them into practice,
show us your love.
Teach us what we should do.
Lord Jesus,
You separate the wheat from the chaff,
the sheep from the goats;
help us to prepare for your coming.
Show us your love.
Teach us what we should do,
that we may be baptized with the Holy
Spirit and with fire.
Amen.

A prayer activity

Give each of your group some Fairtrade chocolate or other product. Talk about the similarities to and differences from the non-fair trade version. Pray together for the producers.

A prayer of intercession

God of truth, we pray for all whom you call to the task of being prophets.
To those crying for justice in a world controlled by material profit,
Holy God, bring strength and perseverance.
To those imprisoned for having dared to challenge the powers,
Holy God, bring courage and hope.
To those vilified or misunderstood for threatening closely held assumptions,
Holy God, bring wisdom and determination.
To those ridiculed or ignored for speaking peace in the midst of violence,
Holy God, bring a sense of your kingdom.
And to your Church, unsure how to speak and be heard, but struggling to find a prophetic voice,
Holy God, bring faith
and the confidence that comes from
confessing Christ as Lord.
Amen.

A prayer for all ages together

Invite people to get into twos facing each other. As the prayer below is said, one person makes the facial expressions and the other winks (or blinks):
God loves a happy face
but in the twinkling of an eye things can change –
to a sad face.
In the twinkling of an eye things can change –
to an angry face.
In the twinkling of an eye things can change –
to a worried face.
In the twinkling of an eye things can change –
to a puzzled face.
Lord Jesus,
help us to be people who change things for the better.
Amen.

A sending out prayer

God of welcome,
may we have welcoming hearts full of your love;
may we have welcoming words sharing your love;
may we have welcoming hands showing your love.
Amen.

Year C ADVENT 4

Micah 5.2–5a; Luke 1.46b–55, or Psalm 80.1–7; Hebrews 10.5–10; **Luke 1.39–45 (46–55)** *My soul magnifies the Lord, and my spirit rejoices in God my Saviour.*

Call to worship

The Holy One is merciful and strong.
Magnify the Lord with us.
The Holy One is unimpressed by power.
Magnify the Lord with us.
The Holy One feeds the hungry.
Magnify the Lord with us.
The Holy One keeps ageless promises.
Magnify the Lord with us.

A prayer of confession

Lord God, there are times in our lives when we fail to understand.
In reliving the past, we do not live in love.
In fearing the future, we do not offer hope.
In depending on ourselves, we do not trust.
We avoid the risks of discipleship and turn away from the challenges of transformation and change.
Renew our sense of vision.
Plant the seed of expectation in us and help us to live as a people in mission.
Bring your kingdom to birth through us.
For Jesus' sake.
Amen.

A prayer of praise

Holy God,
Before we ever had faith in you,
you already had faith in us.
You sought us out from afar,
longing to include us in your purposes.
**Holy is your name,
your mercy everlasting.**

Before we ever hoped in you,
you already hoped in us.
You entrusted us with a vision of the world transformed,
knowing what our humanity could be.
**Holy is your name,
your mercy everlasting.**

Before we ever came to love you,
you already loved us.
You wooed and welcomed us,
inviting us to be your partners.
**Holy is your name,
your mercy everlasting.**

Kind and trusting God,
you have said 'yes' to us.
Give us strength to say 'yes' to you.
Amen.

A prayer for children

Ask the children to repeat the refrain
When you ask us to listen to you…
Yes, God, we say yes.
When you whisper that someone needs a hug…
Yes, God, we say yes.
When you show us that it's time to share…
Yes, God, we say yes.
When you tell us to shout that Jesus has come…
Yes, God, we say yes.
When you ask for our love…
Yes, God, we say yes.
Amen.

A prayer for all ages

There are just a few more days to go.
Soon the waiting will be over.
It will be time to unwrap presents.
It will be time for turkey and tinsel, crackers and chocolate.
It will be time for surprises.
It has been a long time coming, but now it is almost here.
We have spent so long preparing. We are looking forward still, but now there is not long to wait.
Lord, your people looked forward for hundreds of years.
They waited for the Saviour you promised.
As we look forward to the celebration of his birth, be with us and bless us.
Be with us in our excitement and in all we share together, today, tomorrow and every day.
Amen.

A sending out prayer

Lord God, in worship you meet with us.
You are the God of celebration.
We celebrate your goodness and your faithfulness.
As we hear your call to us in the world, help us to respond.
Give us confidence and hope in your word.
Change us, so that we might change the world,
so that in us and in the world, we might see your kingdom come.
For Jesus' sake.
Amen.

Year C   CHRISTMAS 1

1 Samuel 2.18–20, 26; Psalm 148; Colossians 3.12–17; **Luke 2.41–52** *Did you not know that I must be in my Father's house?*

A gathering prayer for children

We gather now remembering that Jesus is with us.
Hip, hip, hooray!
We remember all we have been given.
Hip, hip, hooray!

A prayer of approach

Lord God,
In love you brought the universe into being.
In love you set your people on the path of pilgrimage and faith.
In love you bear witness in us.
In love you are with us now in our wandering and wondering.
In love you lead us onwards to maturity.
Deepen our faith and understanding.
Help us to see you more clearly.
Help us to know you more nearly.
Help us to love you more dearly.
Help us to follow you more nearly.
In the name of our Saviour Christ.
Amen.

A prayer of petition

When our lives are beset with hatred and hurt,
come, Lord,
teach us to forgive.
When our relationships are reduced by indifference or lack of care, come, Lord,
teach us to love.
When our learning is impaired by arrogance or closed mindedness, come, Lord,
teach us to ask questions.
When our world is harmed by injustice and apathy, come, Lord,
teach us to be angry.
When our trust is undermined by tragedy and trial, come, Lord,
teach us to hope.
Lord Jesus,
You come among us to show us what our humanity can be.
Give us hearts so open to your wisdom that we may grow more fully into your likeness.
Amen.

A prayer activity

Give each young person a piece of card to put their name on and decorate. Sitting in a circle prayerfully, invite them to pass around their cards and for each person to write a positive or affirming comment on them. When the cards have completed their journey, invite each person to read their card in silence, then conclude with a prayer of thanksgiving:

Creator God, thank you for all that I am. I am not the finished article yet, but with your help I can grow to be who you want me to be.
Amen.

A prayer of intercession

We pray for all those who are far away from home:
Lord, we pray,
hold them in your love.
That those sick in homes and hospitals
may know their value as whole people,
mind, body and spirit:
Lord, we pray,
hold them in your love.
That those in prisons and detention centres
may know that they are not written off
or forgotten by society:
Lord, we pray,
hold them in your love.
That those who flee violence, oppression and injustice
may know that hatred does not have to have the last word:
Lord, we pray,
hold them in your love.
That those who have no home or resting place may know that identity does not depend on having an address:
Lord, we pray,
hold them in your love.
That those who seek their home in your heart
may know that they are cherished and beloved:
Lord, we pray,
hold them in your love.
And for ourselves we pray.
Lord God, by the love we have seen in Jesus,
hold us, nurture us and sustain us,
that in your name,
we may draw others to you.
Amen.

A prayer for all ages

For the year that is passing,
we thank you.
For the friends we have made,
we thank you.
For the fun we have shared,
we thank you.
For the faith that has grown,
we thank you.
For the year that is dawning,
we thank you.
For all we shall learn,
we thank you.
For the love we will find,
we thank you.
For the lives we will live,
we thank you.
Amen.

Year C CHRISTMAS 2

Jeremiah 31.7–14, or Sirach 24.1–12; Psalm 147.12–20, or Wisdom of Solomon 10.15–21; Ephesians 1.3–14; **John 1.(1–9) 10–18** *In the beginning was the Word, and the Word was with God.*

Call to worship

In the beginning was the Word,
and the Word was with God and was God.
Begin in silence and as much darkness as possible. Then let a hidden drum beat a heartbeat rhythm into the silence:
The Word was life,
and that life was the light of all people.
Set a large candle in a prominent place in the worship space:
The Word became flesh and dwelt among us.
We saw his glory, full of grace and truth.
Place a cross beside the candle, or if there is a crib, light candles all round it. Then switch on all the lights and any Christmas lights.

A prayer of approach

Light of the world, shining in darkness:
Open our eyes to see your light.
Light of the world, dwelling among us:
Open our eyes to live in your light.
Light of the world, guiding your people:
Open our eyes to walk by your light.
Light of the world, freeing the captive:
Open our eyes to rejoice in your light.
Light of the world, offering blessing:
Open our eyes to receive your light.
Light of the world, reflecting God's glory:
Open our eyes to bathe in your light.
Amen.

Meditation: Christ-child come with us

Strip the tree,
revealing bare branches in naked green.
Pack away the doves and angels, along with Santa and his reindeer.
Seal into bags the pungent potpourri.
Close the advent doors.
Carefully wrap the carved figures.
But, leave out the Christ-child to live and grow
from innocent babe to fun-filled child,
rebellious adolescent to Easter man.

A prayer activity

Invite the children to remove the four outer candles and add fresh greenery to the Advent ring, then a leader lights the centre candle.
Each child in turn comes forward and a leader helps them to light their own tealight.
Each child then says:

Dear Jesus,
I am ………… *(own name)*
Here is my light.
It is burning for you.
They put their tealights around the centre candle. When the children have all had a turn, the leaders add their candles. Say:
Thank you, Jesus, for your light.
You make us feel alive and bright.
Amen.

A prayer for all ages

Lord Jesus, here we are at the end of another year's journey through life.
Thank you for all the good things we've enjoyed; and for the hard things that have helped us grow.
Lord Jesus, now we are starting on the next bit of the journey.
Help us to shine like polished gold for you wherever we go.
Help us to be the fragrance of the Spirit wherever we are, and make us unselfish with all that we meet.
We want the baby Jesus in us to grow and to mature, for your sake, for our sake, and for the sake of everyone we meet.
Amen.

A prayer of intercession

Let us remember that there is no place, no life, and no circumstance beyond God's presence.
Silence
Lord, we find it impossible to put into words what lies in the depth of our souls
when we remember people we love and those whose plight is known to us.
It can be tempting to ignore what robs others of a full life.
In the company of your people, we remember those for whom the light has gone out of their lives.
Silence
We remember those for whom the darkness of winter mirrors their sadness and loneliness.
Silence
We remember nations and communities where people long to be free from the darkness of poverty, and injustice.
Silence
We remember those who long to see your word of truth and light and hope made flesh in their midst.
Silence
Help us to recognise your presence, not only in what is good and beautiful and hopeful and creative.
Help us to see your activity in the painful complicated struggle for fairness and justice for others.
Help us to join forces with you as you bring faith and hope to fulfilment in the lives of those who are drawn to the light.
Amen.

Year C   EPIPHANY 1

Isaiah 43.1–7; Psalm 29; Acts 8.14–17;
Luke 3.15–17, 21–22 *You are my Son, the Beloved;
with you I am well pleased.*

Call to worship

North, south, east, west,
wherever we go, wherever we are,
the Lord is near.
Night, day, morning, noon,
whatever the time, whatever the season,
the Lord is near.
Darkness, light, joy, despair,
whatever the day, whatever the moment,
the Lord is near.
Near to help, near to care,
near to shelter, near to comfort,
praise the Lord who is with us.

A prayer of confession for all ages

For the times when we meant to help somebody,
but forgot:
we are sorry, Lord.
For the ways in which we have not shared good
things with others:
we are sorry, Lord.
For the bad habits that we don't really try to give up:
we are sorry, Lord.
For the chances we miss to tell other people about
Jesus:
we are sorry, Lord.
For the times when we forget to read our Bibles or
say our prayers:
we are sorry, Lord.
We thank you, that even if we break our resolutions,
you never break your promise to forgive us if we are
truly sorry.
Amen.

A prayer of approach

Loving Lord, we praise you
for you have created us and redeemed us.
You know each one of us and care for us.
You call us by name to come and worship you.
You draw your people together to be with you.
As a mother bird gathers her young to herself,
draw us near to you, Lord Jesus.
Hide us under your wings of love,
and keep us secure in your care.
Tell us once more that we are precious in your sight,
and that in all things you are there with us.
Make us aware of your presence now,
that we might give ourselves in worship to you.
Amen.

A responsorial prayer of praise

We are precious to God,
who knows us and loves us.
Lord, we praise you for your love and care.
The Lord created and formed us,
the Lord knows us by name.
Lord, we praise you for your love and care.
The Lord is with us,
and promises never to leave nor abandon us.
Lord, we praise you for your love and care.
The Lord is with us in adversity,
and will help us in times of need.
Lord, we praise you for your love and care.
The Lord is our Saviour,
who gave Jesus that we might know life.
Lord, we praise you for your love and care.
The Lord is faithful,
and overcomes our fear with hope.
Lord, we praise you for your love and care.
Amen.

Meditation or prayer of assurance *based on Isaiah 43.1–7*

*Focus on the words 'I have called you by name –
you are mine' (Isaiah 43.1). Suggest that people
personalize this prayer by inserting their own name,
so as to hear God speaking directly to them:*
N, before I formed you in the womb I knew you.
N, do not be afraid. I am with you.
I have called you by name, N, you are mine.
Should you walk through the waters, N, I will be
with you.
They will not swallow you up.
Should you walk through the fire, N, you will not
be scorched
and the flames will not burn you.
N, you are precious in my eyes.

A prayer activity

*Give everyone a small card and ask them to write
their name on it. Help younger children. Collect the
cards and shuffle them. Deal them out and check that
no one has their own (arrange a swap if necessary).
Encourage everyone to say a prayer, out loud or in
their heart, for the person whose card they have,
asking God to be with that person and help them in
the coming week.*

A prayer of petition

*Gather together around a display of items from
around the world (or pictures, guidebooks, etc.). Pray:*
Lord God,
you are always with us,
you call us by name,
you call us to work for you in your world.
Help us to listen and respond.
Amen.

Year C   EPIPHANY 2

Isaiah 62.1–5; Psalm 36.5–10; 1 Corinthians 12.1–11;
John 2.1–11 *On the third day there was a wedding in Cana of Galilee, and the mother of Jesus was there.*

Call to worship

Spirit of God, inspire our worship and praise,
lead us to Jesus.
Spirit of God, teach us the way of Jesus,
make us like Jesus.
Spirit of God, help us to forgive and love one another,
make us one body.
Spirit of God, reveal to us the wonder of God's love,
make us ever grateful.
Spirit of God, fall upon your Church,
make us new.

Prayer for transformation

Lord Jesus Christ,
You took ordinary water and changed it into wine.
As you did so, you revealed your glory.
We are ordinary people.
Take our ordinary lives:
Change them so that they reveal your glory.
Take our ordinary actions:
Change them so that they reveal your glory.
Take our ordinary words:
Change them so that they reveal your glory.
We are ordinary people. Take us and change us so that we reveal your glory.
Amen.

A prayer of confession

Lord, you are so generous to us,
but we do not always reflect your
generosity to others.
For the times we have been self-centred
and mean-minded, we are sorry.
For the times we have placed ourselves
above others, we are sorry.
For the times we have not been witnesses
of your abundant generosity, we are sorry.
Silence
Because of the generosity of a loving God,
and the willingness of a loving Son,
our sins are forgiven.
Amen. Thanks be to God.

A prayer of thanksgiving

Before the service begins, ask people what they want to say thank you to God for, and note down the responses:
Lord God, we know that you are a generous God,
whose love overflows into this world.
You pour out on us wonderful gifts and we have so much to thank you for.
Read the list of thank yous collected earlier
But most of all we thank you for the amazing gift of Jesus, your most generous gift of all time.

He showed us clearly the depth of your love,
as he walked to his death in Jerusalem to bring the gift of new life to us.
Amen.

A prayer activity

Prepare a gift-voucher slip for each person present. Invite them to write on a voucher the gifts they would like to give to God, then seal it in an envelope. Individuals can come forward in turn to place their gift before a candle or cross.

A prayer of intercession

Lord, help us to remember that there are a variety of ways to serve you. You give different gifts to your people, and different skills to achieve your purpose. You inspire many and various acts of service, so may all our serving, all our ministering be led by Jesus, through the outpouring of the Holy Spirit.
Help us not to be envious of each other, but to delight in the richness of our diversity, to recognize that a variety of gifts is needed, as are many ways of serving one another and a world in need.
Help us to remember that it is you who gives the gift according to your grace and not through our own merit. Save us from the sin of pride or false modesty, and with humility help us to offer our gift in love. May we accept the ministry of others without resentment. Enable us all to use the gifts you give and the activities you empower to serve and encourage each other, to deepen faith in you and to show your power at work in your world. So may we proclaim that Jesus is our Lord and be a sign of your coming kingdom, for your own name's sake.
Amen.

A prayer for all ages

To be said slowly and thoughtfully:
Over heart and home,
Jesus, be Lord.
Over work and play,
Jesus, be Lord.
Over actions and words,
Jesus, be Lord.
Over money and possessions,
Jesus, be Lord.
Over church and people,
Jesus, be Lord.
Over time and talent,
Jesus, be Lord.
Over today and tomorrow,
Jesus, be Lord. Amen.

A sending out prayer

There are three things that last: faith, hope and love;
and the greatest of these is love.
Enable us, Lord, in love, to accept your promised gifts.
Amen.

Year C   EPIPHANY 3

Nehemiah 8.1–3, 5–6, 8–10; Psalm 19; 1 Corinthians 12.12–31a; **Luke 4.14–21** *The Spirit of the Lord is upon me, because he has anointed me to bring good news to the poor.*

Call to worship

Creator God,
Every part of creation declares your glory,
we come into your presence with praise and wonder.
Your word is sure and revives our soul,
we seek your wisdom for our lives and our communities.
Your commands are clear, your way is just,
we come that we might walk in your light.
Your plans for our lives are righteous and enduring,
**we desire your way more than gold,
you are our strength and our redeemer.**

A prayer of thanksgiving

For angels and archangels,
for biographers and broadcasters,
for composers and choirs,
for dramatists and diarists,
for essayists and epigramists,
for graphic designers and Gospel writers,
for humorists and hymn writers,
hallelujah!
For informers and interrogators,
for jesters and jokers,
for kissograms and keeners,
for lecturers and lyricists,
for messengers and mystery writers,
for novelists and newsreaders,
for opera singers and orators,
for poets and preachers,
praise be!
For quiz setters and Quakers,
for rock stars and rhymers,
for storytellers and singers,
for teachers and toastmasters,
for ululators and upbraiders,
for valedictorians and verbalists,
for writers and website designers,
for xenoglossists, yarn-spinners
and zany prayer writers,
thanks be to God.
Amen.

A prayer of supplication

Lord of the Church,
We recognize that you have given each one of us a part to play in your body.
We thank you that you believe in us and have a vision for your Church.
Strengthen us where we are weak, guard us where we are strong, give us humility where we are proud, and in your patient love continue to call us to serve you in the places of your choice.

Give us grace to grow in faith, that we might step into new situations with joy.
Give us courage to use our gifts, that others may hear the good news of the kingdom of our Lord Jesus Christ.
Amen.

A prayer activity

Invite the group to try out different positions for prayer (sitting, kneeling, standing, prostrate). Discuss how posture affects how we pray. Invite each person in the group to choose their own position for prayer. Then pray the Lord's Prayer together.

A prayer of intercession

You could use the Taizé response, 'O Lord, hear my prayer'
Pray for those whose words are not heard,
whose pleas for help are unanswered,
and whose requests for aid are ignored.
Pray for those who control the media,
who edit newspapers, or television and radio programmes, or who censor films.
Pray for those who cannot speak or who are inarticulate,
who depend on others to speak for them.
Pray for those who are illiterate and depend on others to write for them.
Pray for wisdom to use words
to promote truth and understanding,
to encourage and affirm
rather than destroy and debase.
Pray for those whose words carry influence,
who can change government policy,
affect the stock markets, inspire commitment,
or instigate violence.
Amen.

A prayer for all ages

Lord Jesus, you speak to us through the words in the Bible:
Help us to listen to your good news.
Lord Jesus, you speak to us through the words of other Christians:
Help us to listen to your good news.
Lord Jesus, you speak to us through the words of songs and hymns:
Help us to listen to your good news.
Lord Jesus, you speak to us through the words of our prayers:
Help us to listen to your good news.
Lord Jesus, you speak to us in so many different ways:
Help us to listen to your good news.
Amen.

Year C   EPIPHANY 4

Jeremiah 1.4–10; Psalm 71.1–6; 1 Corinthians 13.1–13; **Luke 4.21–30** *Today this scripture has been fulfilled in your hearing.*

Call to worship

Today we arise: **Christ is beside us,**
who walks through the night **to scatter new light.**
Yes, Christ is alive, **and beckons God's people**
to hope and to heal, **resist and invite.**

A prayer of confession

When we realize that we are the ones who are blocking the way forward,
God, strengthen our will to change.
When we know that it is our hardness of heart that prevents progress,
God, increase our compassion.
When we hear ourselves justifying the indefensible,
God, encourage our confession.
When the cause is just,
God, strengthen our will to make change.
When the images of suffering become familiar,
God, sharpen our compassion.
When the injustice lies with us,
God, encourage us to change.
Amen.

A prayer for forgiveness

Loving God, maker of all things,
we come before you knowing our failings.
We have closed our ears to your word.
We have closed our eyes to suffering in the world.
Forgive us our failings.
Loving God, sustainer of all things,
we come before you knowing our wilfulness.
We have turned away from your face.
We have chosen to act against your will.
Forgive us our wilfulness.
Give us grace to see as you see,
so that we may do your work of love in the world.
Give us strength to stand alongside the outsider,
so that we may do your work of justice in the world.
Give us steady hearts to carry your peace to unquiet places, through Jesus Christ, our Lord.
Amen.

A prayer of thanksgiving

Light candles for everyone to see:
Enlightening God, as the flame gives light:
We thank you for the light of your Holy Spirit.
As the flame moves, we thank you for the life your Spirit brings.
We thank you for the light of your Holy Spirit.
As the flame burns, we thank you for the warmth of your love.
We thank you for the light of your Holy Spirit.
As the flame shines, we thank you for the glory of your kingdom.
We thank you for the light of your Holy Spirit.

As the flame glows, we thank you for the friendship of your presence.
We thank you for the light of your Holy Spirit.
As the flame flickers, we remember that your light is eternal.
No darkness can overcome your light; with you we will never be lost in night.
We thank you for the light of your Holy Spirit.
Amen.

A prayer activity

Prepare some cut-out footprints of different sizes. Place these in a circle around the room. Invite the children to follow the prints as you play some quiet reflective music. Then stand still to pray the following prayer:
Lord God, we know you are with us wherever we go, no matter how old we are. We ask you to bless all babies and toddlers, children and teenagers, college students, mums and dads,
carers and friends, aunts, uncles and grandparents. Help us to follow you wherever you call us to live and work in your service.
Amen.

A prayer of intercession

Loving God, make our church a loving family, where everyone feels valued as a much-loved child of God.
Lord of love, **hear our prayer.**
May each one of us recognize with confidence your call in our lives and give us courage to speak out for you in all situations.
Lord of love, **hear our prayer.**
May we be a people who wait in humility for your guidance, obedient to your will for our lives and for our church.
Lord of love, **hear our prayer.**
May we be a church that serves where you send us, ready to go to the needy wherever they are.
Lord of love, **hear our prayer.**
May we be a church ready to take your healing love to those who are sick or sad, that you may touch and heal them at their place of need.
Lord of love, **hear our prayer.**
Loving God, we long to grow to maturity in Christ. We ask this in the name of Jesus who loved us and gave himself for us.
Amen.

A prayer for all ages

Loving God, we ask you to make us into people who show your love consistently to our families, friends and everyone we meet. Give us patience and kindness, help us to be happy with the truth and help us to believe, to have hope and to trust you in everything. Teach us not to be jealous or short-tempered, not to bear grudges or do wrong. Help us throughout our lives to continue to grow to maturity in Christ.
Amen.

Year C EPIPHANY 5

Isaiah 6.1–8 (9–13); Psalm 138; 1 Corinthians
15.1–11; **Luke 5.1–11** *Do not be afraid, from now on
you will be catching people.*

Call to worship *based on Psalm 138*

As we stand in your holy presence, we acknowledge
your love and faithfulness to us, opening our hearts
before you.
We give you thanks and praise.
O Lord God, you have answered our prayers and you
have given us strength.
We give you thanks and praise.
O Lord God, we come to hear your words to us, to
sing of your wonderful ways and to see your glory.
We give you thanks and praise.
O Lord God, we come in humility from our untidy
lives, knowing you will save us.
We give you thanks and praise.
O Lord God, we come to seek your purpose, for we
know you have not finished your work of love in us.
We give you thanks and praise.
O Lord, with our whole heart we will sing your praise.

A prayer of adoration

Lord God, as I think of the mighty rolling sea in all
its power,
I think of you.
As I think of your call to the disciples and your help
and strength,
I think of you.
As I think of the tiny baby in a manger whose love
spreads out to all the world,
I think of you.
As I think of friends and families and loving
relationships,
I think of you.
As I think of my life and work and hard tasks ahead,
I think of you.
Amen.

A fisherman's prayer for protection

Dear God,
Be good to me.
The sea is so wide
and my boat is so small.
Amen.

A prayer activity

*Invite people to put a floating candle into a bowl of
water and light it using a taper. A leader prays:*
Lord Jesus, help us to know that you are with us
when things are difficult.
Help us to work together in whatever you call us to do,
to obey you and know your strength and joy and help.
May your love ripple out from each one of us and
bring people into your kingdom.
Amen.

A prayer of intercession

Move us to action, loving God,
so that we do not avoid the pain of the world by
escapism, but engage in work for justice and peace.
Move us to action, compassionate God,
so that we do not care only for ourselves or our own,
but care for all those in need, friends and stranger
alike.
Move us to action, healing God,
so that we do not aim simply for our own health, but
share our resources with all who are diseased.
Move us to action, friendly God,
so that we do not exclude those different from us, but
welcome with generous hospitality those in need.
Move us to action, wonderful God,
so that we do not lie lukewarm in apathy, but give
ourselves in courage and daring for your cause.
In the power and grace of the Spirit of Christ,
we offer ourselves and our prayer, for you to make us
your wonder.
Amen.

A prayer for all ages

Loving God, you are holy, full of compassion and
grace towards your children, and we long to share
your love with the people we meet.
Make us brave to speak when we feel you nudging us.
Help us to trust the words you give us.
May we fulfil your plan for our lives, wherever you
send us, and bring glory to your holy name
through Jesus Christ, our Lord.
Amen.

A prayer of praise

Open my eyes to your glory, O God.
When I do not see you in the world,
blaze before me, shine your light upon me.
Spirit of God, fill me with praise.
Open my ears to your cries, O God.
When I do not hear the pleading of the weak,
sing freedom songs to summon me.
Spirit of God, fill me with praise.
Open my mind to your mystery, O God.
When I try to over-explain,
still me with your quietness.
Spirit of God, fill me with praise.
Open my heart to your will, O God.
Set my hand to work for your kingdom,
my tongue to speak for you.
Spirit of God, fill me with praise.
**Let me join with the song of the angels
this day and for ever.**
Amen.

Year C   EPIPHANY 6

Jeremiah 17.5–10; Psalm 1; 1 Corinthians 15.12–20;
Luke 6.17–26 *Blessed are you who are poor, for*
yours is the kingdom of God.

Call to worship *based on Psalm 1 and Jeremiah 17.5–10*

Happy are those who walk with God,
their delight is the law of the Lord.
Blessed are those who trust in God,
they are like trees planted by water.
The Lord knows the way of the righteous,
and gives to all according to their ways and the
fruit of their doings.
Let us worship God who knows us and loves us.
We praise and worship God.

A prayer of approach *based on Jeremiah 17.5–10 and Corinthians 15.12–20*

Creator God, we worship you, the source of all life,
the creator of the world and all that is seen and
unseen. You are the source of our life and we praise
you for the promise of life eternal.
Gracious God, we gather to celebrate our lives in
you, rooted and grounded in your love, the love that
we see in Jesus Christ, who lived among us, knowing
our humanity in its fullness.
Loving God, we worship you in the power of the
Spirit, rooting us in your presence, filling us with your
love, showering us with many blessings.
Be with us now as we worship you, God, our life.
Amen.

A prayer of confession

Merciful God, when we are enticed by the ways of the
world, forgetting you, denying your love,
forgive us.
When we fail to keep our roots in your life-giving
water, giving in to the negativity and pessimism of
much of the world,
forgive us.
When our trust in your grace and love is lacking,
preventing us from leaving our comfort zone and
serving you,
forgive us.
When we turn away from your promise of eternal life,
having no hope beyond this life,
forgive us.
When our hearts prompt us to act in devious ways,
forgetting your knowledge of us,
forgive us.
Generous God, you know our hearts better than we
know ourselves. You deal with us justly; grant us
your forgiveness and by the power of your Spirit,
strengthen and empower us to follow your way.
Amen.

A prayer activity

Encourage the group to choose somebody to swap
a prayer with. Each person then writes a prayer and
swaps it with their partner. Suggest they take the
prayers away and pray them during the following
week.

A prayer of thanksgiving and intercession

Ask four people to bring forward simple items of
food and water, clothing, medical supplies, and a
Bible, and put them on a table (in front of a globe,
if available). As each person places their symbol
in view, they say the appropriate sentence of this
prayer:
All four voices: We are members of the family of
God. But many of our sisters and brothers live lives
that are different from ours.
Voice 1: We have food to eat and fresh water to
drink, yet for many in the world these are not freely
available.
Voice 2: We have shelter and clothing, yet for many
in the world these are in short supply.
Voice 3: We have access to medical care, yet
for many in the world, clinics and hospitals are
overcrowded and understaffed, or are far away.
Voice 4: We are able to meet freely to worship God,
yet many Christians suffer persecution for their
beliefs.
All four voices: We are members together of the
family of God.
Loving God, help us to be generous and selfless with
all that you have given to us. Teach us to share so
that others may benefit. Help us to be thankful and
not to take your gifts for granted. Grant us the grace
to offer ourselves in service to others, for the sake of
your Son who offered his life for us.
Amen.

A prayer for all ages

Lord Jesus,
As we travel along our own road of life,
whether it is bumpy, smooth, steep or flat,
help us to choose the right way to travel.
Help us to share our prayers, money, time and love
with others,
in this country, and in the world,
who may find their road difficult, steep and bumpy at
this time.
Help us to take the hard road when we need to.
Amen.

A blessing

Blessed are those who call on the name of the Lord.
Blessed are those who walk in the way of the Lord.
Blessed are those who live in the strength of the Lord.
They shall be like trees planted by streams of water
that bear fruit and evergreen leaves,
and their lives shall give worship and praise.
Amen.

Year C EPIPHANY 7

Genesis 45.3–11, 15; Psalm 37.1–11, 39–40;
1 Corinthians 15.35–38, 42–50; **Luke 6.27–38**
*Jesus said, 'Do to others as you would have them
do to you.'*

Call to worship

Let us worship God,
whose love is unconditional,
whose mercy is unending,
who accepts us as we are.

A prayer of supplication

Lord, forgive our lack of forgiveness;
we are inclined to hold a grudge.
Help us to love those who have wronged us,
and let us be forgiven in turn.
Father, let us do as we would be done by.

Lord, help us to turn the other cheek;
not smarting at the injury to our pride, our ego.
Disperse our thoughts of retaliation,
that peace may reign in place of anger.
Father, let us do as we would be done by.
Amen.

A personal prayer of confession

Lord, I find it so hard to let go of anger.
It must have an outlet, must have a target.
If I've been wronged, I want revenge.
Help me to hand it all over to you.
To turn the other cheek, to forgive, and move on.
Amen.

A prayer for all ages

When someone hurts us, *(Mime flinching)*
and makes us sad, *(Pull a sad face)*
and we feel angry, *(Shake fist)* and very bad.
Stop and think! *(Scratch head)*
We needn't row and fight all day, *(Put up fists)*
because God *(Point up)* will hear us *(Cup ear)*
when we pray. *(Make praying hands)*
Stop and think! *(Scratch head)*
If we can learn to forgive,
to say, 'OK, live and let live.' *(Shrug)*
If we can learn to stop and think, *(Scratch head)*
the row will be over in a wink! *(Wink)*
Amen.

A prayer of intercession

We pray for a world of warfare and strife,
Where nation rises against nation;
Lord, let there be forgiveness.

We pray for countries torn apart,
Where tribe rises against tribe;
Lord, let there be forgiveness.

We pray for families at war,
Where brother rises against brother;
Lord, let there be forgiveness.

We pray for the conflict in ourselves,
Where anger and hatred sway our judgement;
Lord, let there be forgiveness.

Help us to forgive,
And to live in the light of your love.
Amen.

A prayer activity

*Give everyone a balloon. Ask them to picture in their
minds someone who has upset them at some time
or another. Perhaps they have never quite forgiven
them. Invite people to blow all their anger into the
balloons. At the end of the service, release them
outside the church as a symbolic 'letting go' of angry
feelings. Let forgiveness flood in to replace them.*

A blessing

May we live to forgive,
And forgive to live.
May we trust in God's grace,
To bless this place.
Amen.

A sending out prayer

Empowered by God's unconditional love,
Walk through the world with mercy in your hearts.
Let your lips speak forgiveness,
And your hands be ready to bless.
Amen.

Year C   EPIPHANY 8

Sirach 27.4–7, or Isaiah 55.10–13; Psalm 92.1–4, 12–15; 1 Corinthians 15.51–58; **Luke 6.39–49** *Jesus said, 'Why do you see the speck in your neighbour's eye, but do not notice the log in your own eye?'*

Call to worship

Aware of our faults and failings,
yet trusting in the mercy of God,
we gather in humility to offer our worship.

A prayer of confession

Lord, we are the blind leading the blind;
so quick to condemn, we don't see the fault in ourselves.
Father, as you have forgiven us, so let us forgive.

Lord, we like to think we know it all;
we counsel others, yet sin is deeply embedded in ourselves.
Father, as you have forgiven us, so let us forgive.

Lord, we think we are all goodness and light;
we are ignorant of the darkness within us.
Father, as you have forgiven us, so let us forgive.
Amen.

A prayer activity

Hand out small pieces of paper. Invite people to think about what the 'log in their own eye' might be. Ask them to write it down and fold the piece of paper. Gather all the papers in, and offer them to God with the following words:
Lord God, we have looked deep within ourselves, and we bring before you the failings we have found there. We repent, and ask your forgiveness, so may we forgive others, as you forgive us.
Amen.

A prayer of intercession

We pray for all who judge and condemn;
May they know your forgiveness, so that they will learn to forgive.

We pray for all who are spiritually blind;
May their eyes be opened, so that they will see with your eyes of mercy and compassion.

We pray for all who find fault in others;
May they look first within themselves, and deal with the sin there.

We pray for all who speak evil from the heart;
May they know repentance deep within, so good words will pour from their lips.

We pray for all whose lives have no foundation in you;
May they dig deep in the bedrock of your love and compassion, to withstand the rising tide.

We pray for ourselves, for we are guilty of all these things;
May we be forgiven, just as we hope to forgive one another.
Amen.

A prayer for all ages

Let us dig deep *(Mime digging)* into the love of God,
and build our house *(Mime building fist over fist)* on the rock.
When the river rises, *(Make waves with arm)* we will not be shaken, *(Shake)*
because God *(Point up)* is our strength, *(Show muscles)* and our foundation.
Amen.

A meditation

Repeat three times, dwelling on each word:
Love,
Forgive,
Live and let live;
In the image of your Son,
May your will be done.
Amen.

A sending out prayer

Eyes wide open, we seek your grace,
'specks' and 'logs' to find and erase.
God, who sees our innermost heart,
help us now to make a fresh start;
seeking what's good and true in each other,
aiming to love each sister and brother.
We go now into the world today,
to follow Christ, and live his way.
Amen.

If Easter falls late, Proper 4 on page 149 may be used as Epiphany 9.

Year C   LAST SUNDAY AFTER EPIPHANY/ TRANSFIGURATION

Exodus 34.29–35; Psalm 99; 2 Corinthians 3.1–4.2; **Luke 9.28–36 (37–43)** *This is my Son, my Chosen; listen to him!*

Call to worship *based on Psalm 99.5, 9 and 2 Corinthians 3.17*

Proclaim the greatness of the Lord our God.
We fall at the feet of God, who is the holy one.
The Lord our God, the holy one is Spirit.
**Where the Spirit of the Lord is,
there is freedom.**
Proclaim the glory of the Lord.
**We worship the Lord our God,
the holy one.**

A prayer of confession

When we cannot read the signs,
when we fail to wake up,
when we are lost in our own dreaming,
God, forgive us.
When the old is too comfortable,
when we'd rather not be challenged,
when we grow weary of the Gospel demands,
God, forgive us.
When we follow the rules and not your voice,
when we crush freedom in favour of safety,
when we think there are no more surprises,
God, forgive us.
When we carefully plan the future without you,
when we sit surrounded by comfort,
when we turn away from other people,
God, forgive us.
Take us to the top of the hill,
to the dizzy heights of insecurity,
to the place where earth stretches below
and sky reaches above,
and give us wings to fly in faith and trust
as your saints did before us,
full of light and truth,
and the love of God,
Creator, Son and Holy Spirit.
Amen.

A prayer of adoration

Gracious God, your glory fills the universe: we see it in the sun, moon and stars.
Your glory is all around us:
we see it in majestic trees, delicate flowers, tumbling streams and cascading waterfalls.
Your glory is in us, created in your image.
And so we praise you.
Gracious God, your glory was seen in Jesus Christ, your Son, who lived among us and loved us to the end.
Your glory is seen in those who follow Jesus, loving as he loved, caring as he cared.
And so we praise you.
Gracious God, your glory was seen in the Holy Spirit, brooding over the waters of chaos, sweeping down in tongues of flame.

Your glory is seen in those filled by the Spirit, inspiring us, challenging us, enabling us.
**And so we praise you.
Amen.**

A prayer activity

Create a mountain by draping a dark cloth over a box. It needs a safe, flat surface at the top. Place three lit tealights on top of the mountain. Encourage the group to sit in a circle, with the display in the centre. Pray:
Jesus, you climbed a mountain and changed into glory. May we come to know and understand your special love and power.
Just as God said, we need to listen to you.
Help us to obey the things we hear you say.
Amen.

A prayer of intercession for all ages

Glorious God, we bring you our prayers for peace in the world; for ....
May your peace and glory transform the world.
We bring you our prayers for leaders whose decisions affect people's lives; for ....
May your love and Spirit guide their actions and transform the world.
We bring you our prayers for the Church, especially where there is persecution; for ....
May your peace, glory and love transform the world.
We bring you our prayers for those who are bereaved, and those who are the victims of injustice; for ....
May they know your peace and love and be transformed.
We bring you our prayers for those in need of healing; for ....
May they know your glory and healing power and be transformed.
We bring you our prayers for ourselves, for your Spirit to fill us and enable us to see your glory in our lives.
Silence
**May we know your love and peace, that they may transform your world in the name of Christ.
Amen.**

A personal prayer

Lord God,
You chose to reveal your glory to me
through the life and death of your Son, Jesus.
Help me to live my life in the light of that glory.
Lord, let my life reflect you in everything I do.
Amen.

A sending out prayer

Lord, your transforming presence is in our lives.
Help us to recognize it as we journey through the high points and low points.
Amen.

Year C   LENT 1

Deuteronomy 26.1–11; Psalm 91.1–2, 9–16; Romans 10.8b–13; **Luke 4.1–13** *Jesus returned from Jordan and was led by the Spirit in the wilderness.*

Call to worship

Come, let us worship God.
We worship the Lord God.
Come, let us serve God.
We serve the Lord God only.
Come, let us call on the name of God.
We call on the name of God, who is Lord of all and who saves us.

A prayer of approach

In the desert, flowers grow.
In the wilderness, life flourishes.
In a thirsty land, water flows,
for the word of the Lord has been spoken,
and all people have heard it
and come to worship God together.
Amen.

A prayer of confession

Forgiving God, at this Lenten time we seek your forgiveness.
Forgive us, we pray, for the lack of self-knowledge that prevents us from knowing you and hinders our understanding of the choices and temptations we face.
Forgive us our lack of love, our desire to be in control and in charge, our wish to live our way rather than yours.
Forgive us our concern with material things for ourselves, rather than being willing to share your gifts with all people.
Forgive us that so often we worship other gods, that keep us from serving you alone.
Forgiving God, your heart is full of mercy. Hear our confessions, and in your mercy grant us forgiveness, peace and your Spirit to strengthen and enable us to truly be your people.
Amen.

A prayer of intercession

Living God, as we think of Jesus in the wilderness, we pray for those who are in the wilderness today, those excluded from society because of their colour, race or creed.
Lord, in your mercy, **hear our prayer.**

We pray for those excluded from society because of illness, disability, unemployment.
Lord, in your mercy, **hear our prayer.**

As we think of Jesus' temptations, we pray for those who exercise power, the leaders of the nations, directors of multinational companies. May they act for the benefit of all.
Lord, in your mercy, **hear our prayer.**

We pray for those we know who hold power in our communities, in our churches, in our families. May they use that power following the way of Jesus.
Lord, in your mercy, **hear our prayer.**

We pray for those who are powerless, the homeless, refugees, asylum seekers.
Lord, in your mercy, **hear our prayer.**

We pray for those obsessed with materialism, those for whom people and relationships are unimportant.
Lord, in your mercy, **hear our prayer.**

We pray for ourselves, for strength to face the choices and temptations of today and the wisdom to discern your will in our lives.
Lord, in your mercy, **hear our prayer.**
Gracious God, hear our prayers, asked in faith and trust.
Amen.

A prayer for all ages

When we're tempted, Lord,
help us stay strong.
When we're weak, Lord,
help us stay strong.
When we're uncertain, Lord,
help us stay strong.
When we're under pressure, Lord,
help us stay strong.
Amen.

A prayer activity

Give each child an angel outline cut out from card. Remind them that the Bible tells us that angels will help to look after us if we need to be protected. Invite them to write or draw on their angel what they would like to be protected from. Provide coloured or glitter glue pens for them to decorate their angel. Arrange the angels on the floor and explain that together you are going to ask God to look after you all. Then pray:
Creator God,
Thank you that you are always ready to help us.
Keep us safe when we are scared, and guide us when we don't know what to do.
Help us to remember to ask you for help each day.
Amen.

A sending out prayer

God of plenty,
Be with us as we journey in the world.
Sustain us, that we may always walk in your way and follow your example of justice, peace and love for all.
We ask this through your Son, who resisted the temptations of the world.
Amen.

Year C   LENT 2

Genesis 15.1–12, 17–18; Psalm 27; Philippians
3.17–4.1; Luke 9.28–36, or **Luke 13.31–35**
*Jesus said, 'O Jerusalem…, how I have desired
to gather your children together as a hen gathers
her brood under her wings.'*

Call to worship

We come to worship God, knowing that God will
always be with us.
**Loving God, help us to worship you, especially
when you seem distant from us.**
We remember how Jesus journeyed to Jerusalem,
and that the journey ended on a cross.
**Understanding God, be with us when our journey
is testing and painful.**
Jesus said, 'Jerusalem, Jerusalem, the city that kills
the prophets and stones those who are sent to it!'
**Caring God, help us to empathize with those in
difficulty.**
And we remember that Jesus' death was transformed
by resurrection.
**Risen Christ, we praise you that you are with
us now.**

A prayer of confession

Jesus wept over Jerusalem.
Forgiving God,
You must also weep over the things we do
that make the lives of others more difficult.
Forgive us for the times
we have wanted you to stop and do our bidding,
when we have not seen the needs of those
around us, when our desire for wealth,
or recognition, or status
has inadvertently led to others having less.
Open our eyes; help us, like you,
to empathize with those around us.
Amen.

A prayer of thanksgiving

Loving Lord Jesus,
In this season of Lent we give you thanks
that you set your eyes and heart on the journey
to Jerusalem, even though you knew where it
would lead.
We thank you that through this journey
you showed us the true path of servanthood.
We thank you that we, too, can journey with you
during this time of Lent, to Jerusalem,
there to see the lengths to which you went
to enable all humanity to be reconciled
with God and with each other.
Amen.

A prayer of intercession

In the shadow of the cross, let us pray for the healing
of the Church, and the world.
We look forward to the coming of the one
who can transform our situations.

Jesus, we look to you for help:
blessed is he who comes in the name of the Lord.
We pray for nations that wrestle with hard choices…
As Jesus embraced Jerusalem, we pray that leaders
of nations might repent and seek help.
Jesus, we look to you for help:
blessed is he who comes in the name of the Lord.
We pray for those in need, sickness or other difficulty,
and those close to death…
As a hen gathers her chicks, so we ask for Christ's
protection for those who need it now…
Jesus, we look to you for help:
blessed is he who comes in the name of the Lord.
Amen.

A prayer for all ages *based on Psalm 27*

The Lord is my light.
The torch that shines upon my path.
The bike light that enables me to be seen.
The Lord is my salvation.
God saves me from myself, protects me from danger
and guides me when things are tough.
The Lord will hide me in his shelter.
In God I am safe, I feel secure. I know I am treasured.
I will sing and make melody to the Lord.
Praise God, who guides me, protects me, shelters me.
Hear my prayer,
for those who are alone, those who are frightened,
those who are in danger.
God is good.
God loves his children and comforts those who are
sad. God gives hope to those who feel lost.
I will wait for the Lord.
God, give me patience,
God give me strength. God give me courage.
The Lord is my light and my salvation.
I have nothing to fear.
Amen.

A prayer activity

*Make or give out pictures of hens and chicks. Each
child holds theirs as you say the prayer:*
When I'm afraid and don't know where to turn,
Jesus, shelter me under your wings.
When it's dark and I can't see the way,
Jesus, shelter me under your wings.
When I have something hard to do,
Jesus, shelter me under your wings.
When I'm sorry for something I've done wrong,
Jesus, shelter me under your wings.

A sending out prayer

Lord of light, may your brightness guide and
protect us so that we always know that you are
with us and we feel safe.
Amen.

Year C   LENT 3

Isaiah 55.1–9; Psalm 63.1–8; 1 Corinthians 10.1–13;
Luke 13.1–9 *Let the fig tree alone for one more year.*
If it bears fruit, well and good. If not, cut it down.

Call to worship *based on Psalm 63.1–4*

You are our God,
we come earnestly seeking you.
Our souls thirst for you,
with our whole being we long for you.
We come that we might gaze on you,
that we might behold your power.
Your loving kindness is better than life itself,
our lips shall give you praise.
We will bless you, O God, as long as we live,
we will lift up our hands in praise to your name.
Let us worship God,
let us sing praise to his name.

A prayer of confession

Caring God,
You gave the fruitless fig tree another
chance to grow fruit;
forgive us when we have not given
another chance to those who needed it.
Forgive us when we have forgotten you.
Merciful God, we are sorry and
we praise you, loving God,
that you do not leave us bowed down
with a weight of sin and remorse.
You promised that if we repent, you will
show mercy, you will forgive us.
Thanks be to you, God.
Amen.

A prayer of praise

Loving, gentle God,
We praise you that you are always there,
walking alongside us, even when we forget your
presence.
You don't force yourself into our lives,
but you are always there when we need you
and even when we don't.
You encourage us to care for others
and to say sorry when we have hurt others and
you. You are even prepared to give us chance after
chance to come back to you again.
Loving, gentle God, thank you for your support
when we go through desert times in our lives,
and when our lives are enriching and full.
Loving, gentle God, we praise you.
Amen.

A prayer of intercession

Loving Lord, in the days when you walked upon earth
life was hard and people suffered.
Your land was occupied, you knew about trouble.
So, Lord, we bring our troubled world to you now.
You are the Lord of all, the gardener of creation.

Teach the world's leaders how they best may tend
the trees of healing and righteousness.
Creator God, great gardener of earth and heaven,
restore your creation to wholeness.
We have made our world a garden of damaged trees
and bitter fruit.
Lord, we pray for those places where there is hurt,
anger and war, for lands where children have never
known peace, for those brutalized by suffering.
Creator God, great gardener of earth and heaven,
restore your creation to wholeness.
We pray for those who are dying, or are recently
bereaved: may they know you are with them on their
journey.
Comfort all those who are frightened or lonely:
may their sadness give way to joy as they feel the
warmth of your love.
Creator God, great gardener of earth and heaven,
restore your creation to wholeness.
God of all things, we pray for the ravaged earth.
We ask your forgiveness for our carelessness with
your gifts. We ask you to show us how to be better
gardeners, better stewards of the world.
Creator God, great gardener of earth and heaven,
restore your creation to wholeness.
Amen.

A prayer for all ages *based on*
Isaiah 55.1–9

God our heavenly Father, we thank you for all the
good things you give us. Help us to listen more
closely to you and to understand that our ways
are not your ways, and our thoughts are not your
thoughts. We ask this through your Son, our Saviour
Jesus Christ.
Amen.

A prayer activity

Put a green plant in the centre as a prayer focus.
Read out the parable again, and be silent. Think
about the times when we have been fruitful…
and about the times when we have not looked after
others, only ourselves…
Lord, you know us completely.
You know when we are being kind or selfish.
You know when we are being helpful or cruel.
You know when we are thinking of others or
ourselves.
Help us always to look outwards,
to bear fruit for other people.
Amen.

A sending out prayer

Go in the love of God; be generous as God is
generous to you. May God the Father bless us.
May God the Son be deep within us.
May the Holy Spirit guide us and give us life.
Amen.

Year C   LENT 4

Joshua 5.9–12; Psalm 32; 2 Corinthians 5.16–21;
Luke 15.1–3, 11b–32 *This son of mine was dead and is alive again; he was lost and is found.*

Call to worship

Loving God, always there for us,
we come into your presence
to worship and praise you.
Loving God, always calling us,
we come into your presence
to listen for your voice.
Loving God, always ready to forgive,
we come into your presence
to know your forgiving love.
Loving God, always ready to receive us,
we come into your presence to be sent out again
to share your love with others.
Loving God, always there for us,
we come to worship and praise you.

A prayer of confession

Understanding God,
Like the father who ran to welcome his
estranged and prodigal son,
forgive us for the times that we have
deliberately run away from your patient care.
Forgive us for the times
when we have been so busy enjoying
ourselves, or been so involved in our work or our
families, that we have forgotten that you were there.
Forgive us when we have withheld love
and forgiveness from those around us;
for the times that we have sulked because
we did not get our own way.
Teach us generosity of spirit to others,
since in loving and forgiving others
we can better love you.
Amen.

A prayer of thanksgiving

Lord, when we are like the prodigal son,
careless, selfish, wasteful,
you go on loving us.
Thank you, loving God.
Thank you, loving God.
Lord, when we are far away,
lost and lonely, frightened and confused,
you don't forget us.
Thank you, loving God.
Thank you, loving God.
Lord, when we turn towards you,
no matter how far we've travelled,
no matter how unworthy we feel,
you welcome us with love.
Thank you, loving God.
Thank you, loving God.

Lord, when we feel
proud and resentful like the older brother,
you speak to us gently.
Thank you, loving God.
Thank you, loving God.
You bring us back to the centre with you.
Surround us with your love
and pour your grace upon us.
Thank you, loving God.
Thank you, loving God.
Amen.

A prayer of intercession

Gracious God, the prodigal son came to that point in
his life where he had to make a difficult decision.
So, loving God, we pray for all who are facing a time
of decision, a time of being at a crossroads,
a fork in the road of life.
May they know your guiding hand in the decisions
they make.
May they find your love and strength as they
encounter friends along their path,
whether old or new.
May they know your arms enfolding them, that they
may go forward, confident that all life finds its true
path with you and in your presence.
Amen.

A prayer for all ages

Dear God,
Help me to realize that with you I am never alone.
Let me think of others, who need your love too,
those who do not have enough to eat, or a safe
place to stay – children in this country and in other
countries.
Your love surrounds everyone.
Amen.

A prayer activity

*Prayer pigs. Give each child a large picture of a pig.
This may symbolize a piggy bank to some. Each child
can attach 'savings' to the pig; their savings could
be prayers attached to their pigs or pictures of things
they value. This helps them to remember that Jesus
and prayer are richer than just money. The son also
prayed when he was at his lowest point, feeding pigs.*

A sending out prayer

God, our loving parent, help us to accept the love that
is offered to us and to show it to others.
May we never be jealous, always grateful and ever
willing to share.
Amen.

Year C LENT 5

Isaiah 43.16–21; Psalm 126; Philippians 3.4b–14;
John 12.1–8 *Mary took a pound of costly perfume, anointed Jesus' feet and wiped them with her hair.*

Call to worship

Jesus calls us to journey with him,
to journey with him to a woman pouring
perfume in a house at Bethany,
to journey with him to a man pouring
water, cleaning up after the devastation of war,
to journey with him to a woman pouring
lotion on the bruises of a husband's violence.
Jesus calls us to speak out with him,
to speak out for the beauty of a woman's
extravagance,
to speak out for the unveiling of rules that deny
people's existence,
to speak out for justice for the poorest of the poor.
And Jesus calls us to celebrate in the dance of
liberation.
Jesus calls us to celebrate love wherever it is found.
Jesus calls us to celebrate the many gifts offered by
women and men.
Jesus calls us to celebrate the dignity and worth of all
people.

A prayer of confession

Jesus, you walked among us as one of us: you gave
up everything for us.
**We are sorry for the times we have been unwilling
to give to others.**
Mary gave her gift of precious perfume in loving
response to you.
**Forgive us when we do not respond to your love
for us.**
Judas said the right thing but his heart was full of
selfish motivation.
**We are sorry when our selfish desires mean that
we aren't motivated to love or care for others.**
We are sorry, Lord, and ask for your forgiveness;
hear us and bless us we pray.
**Take our sins from us and fill us with your love.
Amen.**

A prayer of intercession

Lord Jesus Christ, we give you thanks that you came
and walked in our shoes as one of us,
that we might know you as our friend and saviour.
God of all, you reach out to us in love.
We, your children, respond in love.
Lord, we pray for those who have suffered at the
hands of others because of their faith in you.
God of all, you reach out to us in love.
We, your children, respond in love.

Lord Jesus, you rose from the tomb and brought new
life to us:
teach us to bring new life to our community.
May we be willing to speak out for those who have
no voice,
to hear the cries of the poor and the weak.
God of all, you reach out to us in love.
We, your children, respond in love.
Lord God, you call us onwards in this life and will
eventually call us home.
We pray for all those who mourn the death of a
loved one.
God of all, you reach out to us in love.
We, your children, respond in love.
We lift these prayers to you
in the name of our Lord and Saviour Jesus Christ.
Amen.

A prayer of thanksgiving for all ages

Extravagant God,
We praise you for the rich diversity of life,
for the many colours and fragrances,
textures and flavours that we see, smell, touch, taste,
and enjoy.
And we think of the woman at Bethany,
who was not afraid to show her love and concern,
not afraid to touch another's pain
and be accepted in return.
Help us to appreciate the beauty of life,
and to share our sense of wonder with others.
Help us to feel loved,
to love ourselves,
and to share your love with those around us.
Amen.

A prayer activity

*Cover surfaces and provide aprons. Put A4 sheets of
sugar paper on the floor and ask each child to stand
on one. Draw around each foot and help the children
to cut them out. Encourage the children to paint
inside the outlines of their feet. Sprinkle salt or glitter
over the paint as it dries and the feet will sparkle. Ask
each child to come forward and lay their sparkling
feet in a circle with the toes pointing inwards. Say:*
Jesus,
Mary showed how much she loved you
by pouring oil onto your feet.
Help us to find ways to show our love for you
and words to tell you how much we love you.
Amen.

A sending out prayer

As you have called us here today, Spirit of Love,
now send us on our way to fill the world with the rich
perfume of your presence and by our silent actions
tell the world of the extravagant love of God.
Amen.

Year C   LENT 6/PALM SUNDAY

Palms: Psalm 118.1–2, 19–29; **Luke 19.28–40** *Jesus went on ahead going up to Jerusalem.*
Passion: Isaiah 50.4–9a; Psalm 31.9–16; Philippians 2.5–11; Luke 22.14–23.56, or Luke 23.1–49

Call to worship

Jesus is coming, riding on a donkey.
Hosanna!
Fling wide the doors, make room.
Hosanna!
Wave the branches, wave your arms,
shout in welcome.
Hosanna!
Let us greet Jesus and pray that all people meet him.
Hosanna!

A prayer of thanksgiving for Palm Sunday

As we celebrate this day,
we thank God for the coming of Jesus.
As he follows the hard road into Jerusalem,
we thank God for his strength and courage in
pursuing the journey.
In the light of the events of the week ahead,
the loneliness that Jesus will face, despite the
crowds, we thank God for his commitment and
dedication.
As we journey on as a church family,
towards the heart-rending events of Good Friday,
we thank God for such forgiving love.
As we shout our 'Hosannas' with the crowd,
we thank God for all the years of praise and worship
that have brought us thus far and will carry us on into
the future.
On this celebration day, we thank you, God, for Jesus.
Amen.

A prayer of confession

Lord Jesus, you wept over the city that greeted you
as King and then crucified you. We are sorry for the
times when we have turned our backs on you by
simply following the crowd.
God of all, who created the universe and sent your
Son to reach out in love: we are sorry for the times
we have not listened to that call of love and have
thought only of ourselves.
Holy Spirit, who moves in our hears to stir us to
praise, worship and service: for all that we have done
wrong, we are sorry and ask for your forgiveness.
Amen.

A prayer of intercession

God of the palms,
We give you praise and thanks
for the work of Jesus in our world and in our lives.
We pray for those in our church family,
especially our children and young people.
**Lord of all hope,
be with us, we pray.**

God of Bethany,
You spent time with your friends and disciples
in the household of Lazarus who died and was raised:
we pray for those who find themselves alone
and for those who mourn the death of a loved one.
May the fragrance of your loving presence
be made real to them this week.
**Lord of all hope,
be with us, we pray.**

God of the seekers,
During your ministry there were many who came to
you to seek for answers and comfort in their lives:
we pray for all those who are seeking and searching
this day,
for all who are troubled and need answers and
comfort.
Be with them this day and give them strength for their
search.
**Lord of all hope,
be with us, we pray.
Amen.**

A prayer for all ages

Dear Lord Jesus,
I would have liked to have been there
on that wonderful day,
when everyone shouted and cheered,
and welcomed you into Jerusalem.

I would not have liked to have been there
on that terrible day,
when everyone shouted and jeered,
wanting you to be crucified.

I love to be here, now,
on this wonderful day,
when you are here with everyone and me,
because you came alive again.
Amen.

A prayer activity

*When each child is holding a palm cross, ask them
to think about people and places they would like to
remember in their prayers. Each child can then write
this on their own cross (biro works well, or fibre-tipped
pen). The cross can be taken home, placed where it
can be seen, and act as a reminder to pray.*

A sending out prayer

Step lightly into this Holy Week. Be ready to find
holiness in unexpected places, and walk lovingly:
for the love of our crucified Saviour opens the door to
all things on earth and in heaven.
Amen.

Year C   EASTER DAY

Isaiah 65.17–25, or Acts 10.34–43; Psalm 118.1–2, 14–24; 1 Corinthians 15.19–26, or Acts 10.34–43; John 20.1–18, or **Luke 24.1–12** *Two men in dazzling white said to the women, 'Why do you look for the living among the dead? He is not here, but has risen.'*

Call to worship

In the rising of the Easter dawn,
Christ is risen.
In the laughter of children at play during a ceasefire,
Christ is risen.
Where the hungry celebrate with feasting,
Christ is risen.
Where people find their voices and sing their songs,
Christ is risen.
When enemies give up violence and become friends,
Christ is risen.
When love is allowed to flourish and grow into community,
Christ is risen.
We welcome you, our crucified and risen Christ,
Christ is risen, Alleluia.

A prayer of confession

God our Father, for the times when we have failed to live as Easter people, in your mercy,
Lord forgive us.
For the times when we have doubted, and acted as though there was no good news, in your mercy,
Lord forgive us.
For this morning above all mornings, we claim for ourselves Jesus' promise that in him sins are forgiven.
Thanks be to God.
Amen.

A prayer of adoration

God and Father of our Lord Jesus Christ, on this Easter morning we adore you. We praise you for the good news of the resurrection, for the way it spread to the first disciples and now to us. Help us to hear it afresh today as though we were those first disciples, and to understand the difference it made to their lives. And help us to live today, and always, as resurrection people who tell good news to those around us.
Amen.

A prayer of intercession

Risen, living Lord, **come, make all things new.**
Throughout the Church, across the world, may the joyful message of this resurrection day break through barriers of complacency and disinterest, that human spirits may be enriched and strengthened.

Risen, living Lord, **come, make all things new.**
We pray for leaders and thinkers:
that they may focus on the greatest good for those for whom they carry responsibility.
Risen, living Lord, **come, make all things new.**
We pray for those broken in mind or body:
for victims of war; for grieving families and communities displaced; for those without food and water, the essentials of life;
where there is no hope, and daily struggles bring despair.
Risen, living Lord, **come, make all things new.**
We pray for the people closest to us:
those of our church family who are unwell, in hospital or at home; for those in our wider community; for our own families and friends.
Lord, come among us with your grace that shows its perfection in human weakness.
Risen, living Lord, **come, make all things new.**
Alleluia! Christ is risen!
He is risen indeed. Alleluia!

A responsive prayer for all ages

Lord Jesus, when you rose from the dead, the disciples didn't understand what had happened.
Sometimes I'm confused too.
Help me, Lord Jesus.
When Mary thought someone had stolen the body, she was in despair.
Sometimes I'm distressed too.
Help me, Lord Jesus.
Whenever life is hard.
Help me, Lord Jesus.
Amen.

A prayer activity

Give everyone a hollow plastic or cardboard egg (undecorated), or a flat egg shape cut from card, and invite them to decorate it with coloured pens, items to stick on, etc. Invite people to write prayers, to thank God for the clues they see to the risen Christ, or asking for help to show others the clues. If you are using hollow eggs the prayers can go inside, or they can be stuck onto flat card eggs. Hang the prayers on an Easter tree made from a tree branch in a pot, or drawn onto a large sheet of paper. Spend a few quiet moments offering the prayers to God.

A sending out prayer

Risen Lord Jesus, help us to tell the story of the first Easter to those we know, as the women who went to the tomb told the disciples: that the story may be heard just as fresh and exciting in our day and as good news for people everywhere and always.
Amen.

Year C   EASTER 2

Acts 5.27–32; Psalm 118.14–29, or Psalm 150; Revelation 1.4–8; **John 20.19–31** *Thomas said, 'My Lord and my God.'*

Call to worship

Thomas knelt before the risen Christ and
said, 'My Lord and my God.'
Through doubt he came to faith,
through disbelief he came to know the
glory of the risen Christ.
With Thomas we come to worship – just as
we are – full of questions and contradictions,
offering our faith and our doubts,
offering our whole selves.
My Lord and my God.
Like Thomas, we long for the presence of
Christ in our lives.
Like Thomas, we acknowledge the mystery
of the resurrection,
the mystery of Christ present with us now.
My Lord and my God.

A prayer of confession

Jesus said to Thomas, 'Do not doubt but believe.'
Lord, bring us your forgiveness and healing today,
for we have been like Thomas. Forgive us and bring
us your peace, that we might live in the joy of your
resurrection.
Amen.

A prayer of intercession

Glorious risen Lord,
We pray for your Church,
inheritors of the resurrection witness.
Give to all Christians the strength and conviction
to tell of your life-changing love.
Jesus, the Alpha and the Omega,
hear our prayer.

We pray for the world.
Give to its rulers the wisdom
to lead with compassion and love.
Jesus, the Alpha and the Omega,
hear our prayer.

We pray for this community of ………….
May it be a place where fear is vanquished by love
and people work together for a better world.
Jesus, the Alpha and the Omega,
hear our prayer.
Amen.

A responsive prayer

*Give everyone a small card cross that they can hold
in the palm of their hand. Ask them to write their
name on the cross and hold it in their hand. As you
pray they can then join in the response.*

Faithful God,
Sometimes we are a bit like Thomas, not quite sure
what's happening. At these times,
help us to trust in you.
Sometimes we find it hard to believe in all that you
have promised us. At these times,
help us to trust in you.
There are times when, like Thomas, we demand to
see the evidence. At these times,
help us to trust in you.
There are times when we are not sure of the truths
others tell about you. At these times,
help us to trust in you.
Thank you that your cross reminds us that you are
always there for us. When things are difficult, help us
to hold on to the truth that you died for each of us.
Amen.

A prayer of reflection for all ages

Today is another day on our journey together as
pilgrims of God. Each of us needs support, whether
old or young, new to church, or a member for many
years, for the journey will sometimes be hard.
There may be times when we are like the disciples,
frightened and behind locked doors.
There may be things that we find difficult to do on our
own and we need the help of others.
There may be times when we can't find God in our
lives and need others to help show us that God is
always with us.
There may be times when we can't pray and we need
others to pray for us.
There may be times when we don't know where to go
on our journey and we need others who will help to
show us the way.
There will be times when we can pray together.
There will be times when we can learn together.
There will be times when we can worship together.
There will be times when the Spirit comes – and we
will come home rejoicing.
Amen.

A prayer activity

*Ask the children to think about a place or situation
where they find peace and to write or draw it. If they
haven't got a place, ask them to write or draw what
or where they feel peace could be created for them
in their daily lives. At the end all say together Jesus'
words, 'Peace be with you.'*

A sending out prayer *based on Revelation 1.4–8*

Creator God, be at the beginning and be at the end
of my coming week. Help me to recognize you in
everything, so that others may recognize you in me
and that every eye may see you. Alpha and Omega,
you are the God that was and is and is to come.
The Almighty.
Amen.

Year C   EASTER 3

Acts 9.1–6 (7–20); Psalm 30; Revelation 5.11–14;
John 21.1–19 *Jesus said, 'Do you love me?'*

Call to worship

In the middle of the busyness of life,
you call us.
When work and leisure, joy and sorrow
make us close our eyes to you,
you call us.
Through all the living world, through
seasons' change, through wind and weather,
you call us.
Through human creativity, through all our skills as
makers and shapers, through everything we build,
we echo your creative power. Through all of this,
you call us.
Through everyone we meet, through family
and friends, through strangers, through
those we care for and through those who
care for us,
you call us.
Through all that is, you call us to
relationship, to reconciliation and to peace,
you call us.

A prayer of praise *based on Revelation 5.11–14*

Christ is our bright morning star, who rises in our
hearts. **Alleluia!**
Christ is the lamb who was slain, whom all creation
praises. **Alleluia!**
Christ is our risen Lord, whom we are called to follow.
Alleluia!
To him who sits on the throne and to the lamb, be
blessing and honour, thanksgiving and praise, now
and for ever. **Alleluia! Alleluia! Alleluia!**

A prayer of confession

*The responses can be sung to any setting of the
Kyrie (Lord, have mercy)*
Jesus said: 'Do you love me?'
Lord, there are times when we forget to love you.
Help us to set aside those things that we place before
you, and give us the heart to worship you alone.
Lord, have mercy.
Lord, have mercy.
Jesus said: 'Do you love me?'
Lord, there are times when we forget to love our
neighbours. Help us to remember that we are called
to serve our sisters and brothers, and give us the
mind to be open to the cries of those in need.
Christ, have mercy.
Christ, have mercy.
Jesus said: 'Do you love me?'
Lord, there are times when we forget to love
ourselves. Help us to remember that we are made in
your image, and give us your Spirit to be temples of
your holiness.
Lord, have mercy.
Lord, have mercy.
Amen.

A prayer of intercession

Lord, we come before you aware of the poverty of
our worship.
You are enthroned in glory:
show us how to bow down in true worship.
Lord, **hear us and help us.**

Lord, we want to be your people,
to be worthy of receiving your blessing and coming
into your presence, to be robed in white.
Lord, **hear us and help us.**

Lord, we want to bring with us all people and
creatures of the earth.
Give us faith and courage, that we may boldly speak
out and share the good news,
that others may see you in your glory.
Lord, **hear us and help us.**

Lord, there are many who face tribulations,
those far away and those close to us.
Show us how we can be your hands and voices to
bring strength and help,
that they may persevere and win the victory,
taking their place in your kingdom.
Lord, **hear us and help us.**
Amen.

A prayer for all ages

Crescendo prayer *(Start quietly and build up to a loud
shout at the end)*
In sad times, in bad times, in worry and confusion,
Jesus is always there!
In good times, in great times, in joy and excitement,
Jesus is always there!
In special times, in boring times,
in 'let's just praise' times,
Jesus is always there!
Jesus is alive and here with me,
NOW!

A prayer activity

*Give each child a fish shape on thin card. Ask them to
think of someone they want to tell Jesus about and to
write the person's name or draw a picture of them on
the fish. Use a green net made of garden netting and
let the children put their fish in the net. Pray for all the
people whose names are in there.*

A sending out prayer

Go out and sing praise to God, at all times and in
all places, that others may see him through your
worship. In Jesus' name,
Amen.

Year C   EASTER 4

Acts 9.36–43; Psalm 23; Revelation 7.9–17;
John 10.22–30 *Jesus said, 'My sheep hear my voice.
I know them and they follow me.'*

Call to worship

O come, let us worship and bow down, and kneel
before the Lord our maker!
**You, Lord, are our God, and we are the people of
your pasture, the sheep of your hand.**
O come, let us worship and listen to the voice of the
Lord!
**You, Lord, are our God, and we are the people of
your pasture, the sheep of your hand.**

A prayer of approach *based on Psalm 23*

Good Shepherd, you have called us into your fold
and, hearing your voice, we have come to worship
you. Anoint us with your presence, comfort us and
guide us, even when we walk in the valley of the
shadow of death, that our voices may join with those
who dwell in your house for ever and ever.
Amen.

A prayer of confession *based on Psalm 23*

Lord, where the waters of our life have been troubled,
you still our hearts and minds.
In your mercy, **restore our souls.**
Where we have walked in strange and difficult ways,
you guide us in the right paths.
In your mercy, **restore our souls.**
Where we have walked even through the valley of
death, you have been beside us.
In your mercy, **restore our souls.**
May our sins be forgiven and our souls restored,
through the name of Christ our Saviour.
Amen.

A prayer of intercession

God of love, we pray for healing for your Church.
For unity between all Christian people; that our
divisions may be set aside so that we work together
for the furtherance of your kingdom.
Hear our prayer, **loving God.**

God of love, we pray for healing for our world.
For people of every race and language to recognize
that we discover your will for us through justice,
reconciliation and peace.
Hear our prayer, **loving God.**

God of love, we pray for healing within our
community. That all may be joined together
regardless of background, culture or age.
Hear our prayer, **loving God.**

God of love, we pray for healing within our homes.
That wherever families are divided you will mend
broken relationships so that your love will be
experienced by all.
Hear our prayer, **loving God.**

God of love, we pray for healing among the sick.
That they will feel your presence, and their lives be
transformed.
Hear our prayer, **loving God.**

God of love, we pray for those who are bereaved.
That your grace will bring them comfort in their need
and sorrow.
Hear our prayer, **loving God.**

We ask these prayers through Christ, our faithful
Shepherd.
Amen.

A prayer for all ages

Dear God, help us to hear your voice every day.
To hear your voice in the words and stories of the
Bible.
Child opens up a Bible. Pause
To hear your voice in the songs of worship we sing.
Child opens up a songbook. Pause
To hear your voice in silent prayer.
Leader lights a candle. Pause
To hear your voice in the advice of good friends.
Everyone holds hands. Pause
To hear your voice through the world around us and
the things we see each day.
Pass globe around. Pause
Help us to hear your voice and so be part of your
special people each and every day.
Amen.

A prayer activity *based on Revelation 7.9–17*

*Remind the children that in Revelation 7.17 it says,
'and God will wipe away every tear from their eyes'.
Give each child a teardrop shape cut from paper or
card. Invite them to write a prayer on their teardrop
for someone who has a problem or who is sad at the
moment. It might be someone they know or it might
be about a global issue. Prayers could start with
'Loving Lord, please help ....'.
Younger children could draw and colour a picture.
Hang the teardrop prayers from an umbrella.*

A sending out prayer *based on Revelation 7.9–17*

We join with all the living creatures around the throne
in saying: **praise and glory and wisdom and thanks
and honour and power and strength be to our
God for ever and ever. Amen!**

Year C   EASTER 5

Acts 11.1–18; Psalm 148; Revelation 21.1–6;
John 13.31–35 *Jesus said, 'Just as I have loved you, you should love one another.'*

Call to worship

This is the message you have heard from the beginning, that we should love one another.
Let us live in love, as Christ loved us.
We know love by this, that he laid down his life for us.
Let us live in love, as Christ loved us.
This is my commandment, that you love one another as I have loved you.
Let us live in love, as Christ loved us.

A responsive prayer of confession

God, you love us without condition or limit, but often we reject your love and that of our friends and neighbours.
Lord, have mercy.
We hide from those who demand more of our care and compassion than we are willing to give.
Lord, have mercy.
We nurse grievances and refuse to forgive those who have hurt us.
We hurt others by our words, by our actions and by our silence.
Lord, have mercy.
We are greedy for your gifts and refuse to share them with those in need.
We turn away from images of poverty, and shut our ears to the cries of the poor.
Lord, have mercy.
God, teach us to love as you love.
Lord, have mercy.
Amen.

A prayer of thanksgiving

Lord God, we thank you for those who care for us day by day, and show us love's tenderness.
We thank you for those you have given us to love, in our families and our friends, who show us love's gratitude.
We thank you for those who help us when we are unable to help ourselves, who show us love's kindness.
We thank you for those who know all our faults, who show us love's patience.
We thank you for those we have grieved and hurt, who repeatedly forgive us, and show us love's generosity.
We thank you for your love which sustains us, and shows us that love has no end.
Amen.

A prayer of intercession

Lord, we pray for those who need a special sense of your love today.
We pray for those who struggle with changes and new beginnings,
especially in their family lives.
You have given us a new hope.
You will make all things new.
You are the Alpha and Omega.
You are the Beginning and the End
and that hope will not disappoint us.
Accept these prayers in the name of
Jesus Christ our Saviour.
Amen.

A prayer for all ages

Glory – Thank you, Lord Jesus, that you said 'yes' to God's way of saving the world even though it was hard.
Love – Thank you, Lord Jesus, that you showed us how to love by the life you lived on earth with your friends, strangers and enemies.
Glory – Please help us, Lord Jesus, to see how you can bring glory through all the things that happen to us, as we trust in you.
Love – Please help us, Lord Jesus, to love others just as you did, to show the world that you are living in us.
Glory – Forgive us, Lord Jesus, that we have looked for God in the wrong places and missed seeing your way of glory in this world.
Love – Forgive us, Lord Jesus, that we have not opened our eyes to see your love in the lives and faces of other people each day.
Glory – May glory shine into us and through us, Lord God.
Love – May your love fill our lives and make us more like you, Lord God.
Amen.

A prayer activity

Give each person a plain postcard. Using pens, glitter and so on, ask each person to make a 'love one another' postcard using words and images. Ask each member to self-address an envelope, then swap it with someone else's. The postcards should then be placed in the envelopes, and in a couple of weeks' time the leader posts them as a prayer reminder of Jesus' second commandment.

A sending out prayer

Lord, you are grace for our needs, strength for our weakness, love for our loneliness, word for our deafness, rest for our weariness, peace for our anxiousness.
Be with us as we go from this place and throughout the coming days.
Amen.

Year C   EASTER 6

Acts 16.9–15; Psalm 67; Revelation 21.10, 22–22.5;
John 14.23–29, or **John 5.1–9** *Jesus said to the man,
'Do you want to be healed?'*

A prayer of approach

Christ, be with us as our pilgrimage of faith continues
in this place.
Your gospel was proclaimed by apostle and friend
and spread to the ends of the earth.
We are your witnesses to this great tradition
as we gather again to hear your word.
Make us a people eager to listen to you.
May your word be a living word, inspiring us in our
fellowship with one another to be a community of
hope in a world of great need.
Help the worship we celebrate today become food for
our continuing pilgrimage journey.
Amen.

A prayer of confession

Jesus, you ask, 'Do you want to be healed?'
Oh yes, Lord, we want to be healed.
From our self-preoccupation and self-pity, and our
indifference to those in need, from our greed for
material things and our wasting of the gifts we have
been given:
Oh yes, Lord, we want to be healed.
From our reluctance to let go of hurts, and our pursuit
of petty revenge, from our fear and anxiety, and our
inability to trust you or others:
Oh yes, Lord, we want to be healed.
From our lethargy and cynicism in the face of the
need to change and be changed, from our
narrow-mindedness and prejudice:
Oh yes, Lord, we want to be healed.
Amen.

A prayer of praise *based on Psalm 67*

God, come to us and shine upon us.
Let our actions be your actions.
**May all the ends of the earth stand in awe
before God.**
We tell of your wonders, we sing of your praise.
You watch over us with justice and fairness, O Lord.
We seek your guidance and wisdom in all things.
**May all the ends of the earth stand in awe
before God.**
Bless us, God, and bless all our loved ones.
And let that blessing reach out to all people and
places.
**May all the ends of the earth stand in awe
before God.**
We praise you, God! We sing of your praise.
**May all the ends of the earth stand in awe
before God.**
Amen.

A prayer of intercession

Jesus, you saw a helpless man alone in a crowd
and chose to heal him.
We bring before you all those who are alone and
have no one to help or befriend them.
Those who are housebound through disability,
sickness, or fear.
Lord, draw near.
Lord, draw near, draw near and stay.
We bring before you those excluded from society by
crime or addiction. Those whose faith, culture, race or
language sets them apart from others.
Lord, draw near.
Lord, draw near, draw near and stay.
We bring before you those cut off from their families
because of old quarrels and grievances.
Lord, draw near.
Lord, draw near, draw near and stay.
We bring before you those who isolate themselves
through guilt, pride or fear of rejection.
Lord, draw near.
Lord, draw near, draw near and stay.
Amen.

A prayer for all ages

Lord God, you are in our world.
Lord God, you are in our land.
You fill them through and through.
Your living water offers peace.
Lord God, you are in our church.
Lord God, you are in our homes.
You fill them through and through.
Your living water offers peace.
Lord God, you are in our lives.
You fill them through and through.
Your living water offers peace.
Amen.

A prayer activity

*Ask everyone to light a candle for those who are
alone or in need. Or give cards for everyone to write
to God about someone who is treated as an outsider.
Pray for them and each other:*
Dear Jesus,
You looked after the man who was lonely.
You made him better when he was sick.
Please look after us when we are lonely.
Please make us better when we are sick.
Amen.

A sending out prayer *based on
Revelation 21.10, 22–22.5*

Dear Lord, Creator God, the tree of life,
help us to be seeds in the world,
shining with the light of the morning star
and standing tall as the tree of life itself.
Thank you for all you do.
Amen.

Year C EASTER 7

Acts 16.16–34; Psalm 97; Revelation 22.12–14, 16–17, 20–21; **John 17.20–26** *Jesus prayed, 'May they all be one. As you, Father, are in me and I am in you.'*

Call to worship

Come to the Lord of freedom!
We gather in your name, O Lord.
Acknowledge your need for God's mercy.
We seek your forgiveness and justice, O Lord.
Cast aside your doubts and fears.
We trust in you, O Lord.
Open your hearts to listen to God.
We are eager to hear your word, O Lord.
Bring your thoughts and prayers before God's holy throne.
We seek your protection and inspiration, O Lord.
Come to the Lord of freedom!
We gather in your name, O Lord.

A prayer of confession *based on Acts 16.16–34*

God of compassion and mercy, we lay at your feet the times when we have been imprisoned by words of anger and hatred rather than liberated by words of gentleness and peace.
Set us free, Lord Jesus!

God of compassion and mercy, we lay at your feet the times when we have been imprisoned by thoughts of jealousy and bitterness rather than liberated by thoughts of understanding and acceptance.
Set us free, Lord Jesus!

God of compassion and mercy, we lay at your feet the times when we have been imprisoned by selfishness and thoughtless actions rather than liberated by actions of friendship and love.
Set us free, Lord Jesus!
Grant us your forgiveness, and change our hearts, that we might dare to be more like you.
Amen.

A prayer of adoration

We are fed at your table.
We are redeemed by your passion.
We adore you, faithful God!

We are set free by your cross.
We are renewed in the resurrection of your Son.
We adore you, faithful God!

We are an Easter people.
We are open to your Spirit of truth.
We adore you, faithful God!

We are disciples, called to mission.
We are a community of hope.
We adore you, faithful God!

We are called to share your good news.
We are witnesses of the gospel.
We adore you, faithful God!
Amen.

A prayer of intercession for prisoners of conscience

Liberating God,
We bring before you all those unjustly imprisoned.
We enjoy the freedom of expression, of belief, of rights and responsibilities, and yet so many face persecution and injustice.
We pray for those who struggle to make their voice heard, and for those who live in daily fear.
We ask you, Lord, to release those held captive, and to bring liberty to places of oppression.
We ask you to strengthen the family, friends and companions of those who are imprisoned.
Grant them perseverance and hope,
and encourage their resolve to bring release to their loved ones.
We pray, too, for the aggressors, that they may share our longing for human rights and come to realize the hurt and pain they cause to others.
Bring freedom to your people, Lord, and teach us to be a community set free from tyranny.
Amen.

A prayer for all ages

God our heavenly Father,
we thank you that we are all different;
we are different ages,
we have different abilities,
we have different appearances, likes and dislikes.
Help us to remember that our whole world belongs to you, and we are your children, brothers and sisters in your love.
Thank you for sending Jesus Christ your only Son to help us believe in you, love you and trust you.
Please help us to show your love in our lives so that others may know and believe in you too.
Glory be to you, our wonderful, loving God,
for ever and ever.
Amen.

A prayer activity

Ask the children to think quietly of one person to pray for. Play some music and light a variety of different-coloured candles – stubby, tall, new, old and bent. Remind everyone that we are together in the love of God and Jesus and of Jesus' prayer that we might be one.

A sending out prayer

May God the Father, who is one with the Lord Jesus, hold us in tender unity with himself and with each other: now, as we wait for the gift of the Spirit, and in all eternity.
Amen.

Year C PENTECOST

Acts 2.1–21, or Genesis 11.1–9; Psalm 104.24–34, 35b; Romans 8.14–17, or Acts 2.1–21; **John 14.8–17 (25–27)** *Jesus said, 'The Holy Spirit whom the Father will send in my name will teach you everything.'*

Call to worship

We come to celebrate God's gift today!

While he was with his disciples Jesus said, 'I will ask the Father, and he will give you another Advocate, to be with you for ever'.
We come to celebrate God's gift today!

This gift is the Spirit of truth; the one who teaches us; who communicates God's love.
We come to celebrate God's gift today!

This gift is the Spirit of power; the one who creates and renews; the one who empowers and inspires.
We come to celebrate God's gift today!

A prayer of confession

Spirit of God,
who strengthens our weakness and guides us in prayer: you give light, but we prefer darkness; you give wisdom, but we listen to foolishness. Hear us as we confess our failure to listen and to act, our lack of trust in your power and our unwillingness to be empowered by you. Nevertheless, we are bold to claim your promise for ourselves today: the promise that in Jesus our sins are forgiven.
Amen. Thanks be to God.

A prayer of petition

Holy Spirit, who created the world,
help us to know your life and love and power.

Holy Spirit, who came to the disciples at Pentecost,
help us to know your life and love and power.

Holy Spirit, who came in rushing wind and tongues of fire,
help us to know your life and love and power.

Holy Spirit, who fills us with joy and truth and peace,
help us to know your life and love and power.

Holy Spirit, who pours out yourself to everyone,
help us to know your life and love and power.
Amen.

A prayer of intercession

Come, Holy Spirit.
We pray today for our homes and families, for love and peace:
come, Holy Spirit.
We pray today for our schools and our friends:
come, Holy Spirit.
We pray today for our community:
come, Holy Spirit.
We pray for Christians in the world who are frightened of persecution when they follow Jesus:
come, Holy Spirit.
We pray for Christians who are working for peace and justice in the world:
come, Holy Spirit.
We pray for each one of us, that we will know how much we are loved by God:
come, Holy Spirit.
Amen.

A prayer for all ages

At Pentecost the Holy Spirit came to the disciples.
Thank you for the gift of the Holy Spirit.

The disciples spread the good news of Jesus to all the crowd.
Thank you for the gift of the Holy Spirit.

Starting with a small group of disciples,
there are now billions of Christians in the world.
Thank you for the gift of the Holy Spirit.

Help me to accept your gift of the Holy Spirit and to play my part in sharing the good news of Jesus.
Thank you for the gift of the Holy Spirit.
Amen.

A prayer activity

Give everyone a party popper and a sticky note. Ask them to write a short prayer on the note that shows that the Holy Spirit is inclusive, and that his power 'explodes' everywhere. Attach the prayer to the popper, and encourage everyone to pull the cord and make a bang with their prayer! Perhaps ask everyone to stand in the middle and direct their party poppers in all directions as a symbol of the far-reaching nature of God and the Spirit. Say together:
Lord, unite people from every corner and every language through your gift of the Holy Spirit. Send this Spirit into all our hearts.
Amen.

A sending out prayer

The God of Pentecost fill you with the knowledge of his power, lead you into the possibilities he is opening up for you, and bless you with joy and hope and peace, today and every day.
Amen.

Year C   TRINITY SUNDAY

Proverbs 8.1–4, 22–31; Psalm 8; Romans 5.1–5;
John 16.12–15 *Jesus said, 'When the Spirit of truth comes he will guide you into all truth.'*

Call to worship *based on Proverbs 8*

At the beginning of the cosmos you breathed order out of empty chaos.
Come Creator, Wisdom, Word.
At the beginning of the Church you breathed courage into fearful hearts.
Come Creator, Wisdom, Word.
At the beginning of this service may you breathe into all that is said and done and sung.
Come Creator, Wisdom, Word.

A prayer of confession

Father, Son, Holy Spirit,
Living in harmony as one, we confess to you the ways in which we refuse community,
by blaming others for conflict rather than examining ourselves, by cherishing our isolation, and hoarding our privileges,
by believing that we are better than others,
by looking down on people who are different.
Christ, have mercy:
Lord, have mercy.
We open to you the ways in which we resist your call to change and grow, clinging to the past,
letting self-pity and anxiety rule our lives.
Christ, have mercy:
Lord, have mercy.
Father, Son, and Holy Spirit,
Your work together is always for our reconciliation.
As you now receive us, so we too receive in our hearts those we have injured or been injured by,
asking you to weave community between us
and to lead us into the future that you have prepared for us, so that your work in creation may continue to flow without impediment.
Amen.

A prayer of adoration

God the Holy Trinity, we praise you.
We praise you as Father and creator.
We praise you as Son and redeemer.
We praise you as Lord and giver of life.
Guide us now and always as we praise you, that our praise may be worthy of you and true to ourselves.
And give us a sense of your glory, that we may sing with the angels: 'Holy, holy, holy.'
Amen.

A prayer of intercession

Trinitarian God, we bless you for the Church.
We thank you for theologians and biblical scholars and for those who interpret their work so that we can understand your story.
Here in this church may we have open minds and clear voices as we seek to communicate your good news by what we say and by who we are.

God in three persons,
We bless you for diversity in our society; for differences in sex and age, colour and culture, talent and interest.
We pray that appreciation of diversity may be reflected in equality so that, in all our variety, we may become one world.

Father, Son and Holy Spirit,
We bless you for setting us in community,
for those who are closest to us.
We pray for their needs,
in a few moments' silence bringing to you any particular sources of trouble or joy, illness, loss …

We pray for ourselves,
asking that our lives may become full of the harmony and power of the Trinity, and that our joy in you may flow out, bringing others to share your life.
Father, Son and Holy Spirit.
Amen.

A prayer for all ages

We thank you, God, for giving us many things in threes – parents and child,
triangles and pyramids,
stools and corner cupboards,
plaiting and clover leaves,
three meals a day.
We thank you that you give yourself to us in three ways; Father, Son, and Spirit. The One who made us, the One who came to be our friend, who lived and laughed and loved, our Lord Jesus Christ, and the One who helps us become the people you want us to be, your Holy Spirit, who softens our hearts to love you and makes us understand your ways.
Three-in-One, strong and beautiful God.
We love you!
Amen.

A prayer activity

Prayer triplets. In threes, think together of people and places and events to pray or give thanks for, each one of the three taking God or Jesus or Holy Spirit as a basis for their prayers. Stand in a triangle shape, holding hands to pray:
Please, Father God, help …………,
Thank you, Jesus, for …………,
Holy Spirit, please bring …………
Amen.

A sending out prayer

As we leave this place:
God our Father, protect us.
Lord Jesus, teach us and lead us.
Holy Spirit, guide and inspire us, so that we can live the life you want us to live.
Amen.

Year C   PROPER 4

1 Kings 8.22–23, 41–43; Psalm 96.1–9; Galatians 1.1–12; **Luke 7.1–10** *When Jesus heard this he was amazed at him, and turning to the crowd that followed him, he said, 'I tell you, not even in Israel have I found such faith.'*

Call to worship *based on Psalm 96*

Ascribe to the Lord the glory due his name;
bring an offering, and come into his courts.
Worship the Lord in holy splendour;
tremble before him, all the earth.

A prayer of confession

Lord, we confess our lack of faith;
believing in you, we yet doubt what you can do.
Half-heartedly, we bow our heads and pray in your name,
not fully believing that anything will come to pass.
We hope, we hesitate, we fear, we doubt;
the spectrum of emotion betrays our faltering faith.
Forgive us, Lord, and help us to seek you as the centurion did, with humility in place of doubt,
and faith in place of fear.
Amen.

A prayer of thanksgiving

Thank you, Lord, for the centurion,
and for people like him;
for men and women who have blessed your children;
for people who are good to others, no matter their rank or creed;
for those who respect and honour you, Lord, with all due humility;
for those special people whose faith is a beacon of light, and whose stories live on
as an example to us all.
Amen.

A prayer for all ages *based on Psalm 96 and the Gospel*

O sing *(Mime singing)* to the Lord *(Point up)* a new song;
Sing *(Mime singing)* to the Lord, *(Point up)* all the earth. *(Make a circle with your arms)*
Sing *(Mime singing)* to the Lord, *(Point up)* bless *(Raise hands in blessing)* his name;
Tell of his salvation from day to day.

The centurion *(Salute)* sang *(Mime singing)* a new song of faith;
He believed Jesus *(Point up)* could heal from afar.
Jesus *(Point up)* was amazed *(Mime wow!)*,
And the servant *(Bow)* of the centurion *(Salute)* was healed *(Mime hooray!)*.

For great is the Lord, *(Point up)* and greatly to be praised.
Amen.

A prayer of intercession

We pray for all who are afflicted in body;
Lord, speak the word, and let them be healed.
We pray for all who are afflicted in mind;
Lord, speak the word, and let them be healed.
We pray for all who are afflicted in spirit;
Lord, speak the word, and let them be healed.
Amen.

A prayer activity

While the congregation sings 'We cannot measure how you heal and answer every sufferer's prayer', invite people to come forward and light candles for those known to them who are in need of healing.

A personal prayer

Help me to sing a new song, Lord,
a song of faith in you;
disperse the clouds of disbelief
that hide you from my view.
I cannot see you here, my Lord,
but yet, by faith, I know;
you hold me in the tides of life,
and will never let me go.
Amen.

A sending out prayer *based on Psalm 96*

God's honour and majesty are before him;
strength and beauty are in his sanctuary.
Go now and declare his glory among the nations,
his marvellous works among all the peoples.
For great is the Lord, and greatly to be praised.
Amen.

Year C PROPER 5

Sunday between June 5 and June 11 inclusive

1 Kings 17.17–24; Psalm 30; Galatians 1.11–24;
Luke 7.11–17 *God has looked favourably on his
people!*

Call to worship

Welcoming God,
we come from our different spaces.
Welcoming God,
we gather in your space.
Welcoming God,
we are home.
We come
and find you reaching out to us
in poverty and lowliness.
We come and find you already here.

A prayer of confession

Welcoming God,
Forgive us when we fail to be welcoming;
when we show others the door or make excuses not
to open our arms;
when we fail to feed the hungry,
visit those who are at a distance from us,
or re-clothe those who live naked lives.
Forgiving God, forgive our selfishness and greed,
our inhospitality.
Forgive us; forgive the fear of the stranger in us;
the fear of intimacy, and of rejection.
Take from our mouths all untruths, all gossip and
unkind words.
Forgive us when we fail to recognize you in those
we meet.
You persist in forgiving us, you melt our hearts,
encountering us in strangeness and poverty.
We are forgiven because you forgive … even us.
Amen.

A prayer of thanksgiving

Lord, thank you for being with us
even when we seem to face disaster:
when we have lost a job, had things stolen,
when the freezer dies.
When the week is dreadful: if we are depressed,
angry or sad; when we are irritated with the kids;
mistrustful of a partner; when we feel abandoned by
those we expect to spend time with.
You are there, reaching out to us, welcoming and
caring, soothing and pacifying.
You, mother and father God,
accept us even as we are.
You love us still, and your love transforms everything.
Your love changes me and changes everyone.
You are our rock, our foundation,
our ever-comforting God.
Amen.

A prayer of intercession *based on Galatians 1.11–24*

**God who changes not,
we trust in you for our todays and tomorrows.**
We pray for those with responsibility for making key
decisions that might change the direction of world or
local events. *(Name particular situations)*
**God who changes not,
we trust in you for our todays and tomorrows.**
We pray for those affected by the decisions of others,
but who feel powerless in the face of the forces of
change. *(Name particular situations, if appropriate)*
**God who changes not,
we trust in you for our todays and tomorrows.**
We commend to you the decisions that have to be
made in our own lives and in the lives of those close
to us. *(Leave an appropriate time for silent prayer)*
**God who changes not,
we trust in you for our todays and tomorrows.**
You have not failed us in the past, and so with
confidence we thank you that you have heard us
and will answer our prayers,
through Jesus Christ our Lord.
Amen.

A prayer activity

*Give each child a colourful heart shape with the
words 'Lord, help me to have a change of heart' on
one side. Invite each child to write something they
would like help with, or a habit they would like to
break, on the other side. Ask the group to stand and
hold their prayer hearts while a leader prays:*
Lord God, you know all our hearts and minds.
Help us to rely on you more and follow your guidance
in our decisions.
Help us to be true to you always and work on the
things we need to change.
Amen.

A prayer for all ages

Lord, there are times when it is easier to avoid telling
the truth than stand up for what I know is right.
Help me to speak the truth in love.

Lord, when I know there are things I ought to say but
am afraid that I will look foolish in front of others:
Help me to speak the truth in love.

Lord, when I think no one is watching, I sometimes do
not act as you want me to.
Help me to speak the truth in love.

Lord, help me to listen to your guiding Spirit of truth
when I am not sure what to do or say.
Help me to speak the truth in love.
Amen.

Year C   PROPER 6

Sunday between June 12 and June 18 inclusive

2 Samuel 11.26–12.10, 13–15; Psalm 32; Galatians 2.15–21; **Luke 7.36–8.3** *And he said to the woman, 'Your faith has saved you; go in peace.'*

Call to worship

Before we loved God, God loved us.
Lord God, we love you.
Before we came to Christ, Christ came to us.
Jesus Christ, we come to you.
Before we took our first breath, the Spirit breathed across the face of the deep.
Holy Spirit, breathe on us again.

A prayer of praise

Loving God,
You have known me from before the beginning of time,
from before I knew myself.
You saw my foot fall before I decided to take each step.
You saw the misdeeds and mistakes mixed into my life,
and in your gracious love,
you took my life in your hands and mended it,
before it even began.
You love me in all my imperfections,
because I am your child.
Loving God, I love you.
Amen.

A prayer of intercession

Loving God, three in one, one in three, be eternally united, yet distinct.
We remember before you those who are different from us:
those of other cultures and creeds,
those of different political and theological perspectives,
those of different generations, different gender or different sexual orientation.
You look on all with the same loving eyes.
May we look at others with acceptance as you do.
Lord of all,
hear our prayer.

We pray for those in communities and countries where difference and division have spilled over into confrontation and conflict.
Mention different current situations, allowing a pause for reflection
Only you know the rights and wrongs,
victims and perpetrators.
Bring healing to those who hurt,
protection to the innocent,
and stay the hands of those who would use violence to further their cause.
Lord of all,
hear our prayer.

We pray for conflicts closer to home, tensions in the family, in our neighbourhoods, at work or school or here at church, poisoning relationships and creating stress.
Forgive us for our part in such conflicts and help us to deal with difference more constructively.
Make us peacemakers rather than merely peace lovers, offering reconciliation, not recrimination.
Lord of all,
hear our prayer.

Lord, we pray that this church and we its members may be open to all, seeking to share your love with all who need it.
Lord of all,
hear our prayer
in Jesus' name.
Amen.

A prayer activity

Jesus said, 'Whatever we do to or for one another, we do to or for him.' Put the children in pairs and give each pair a turn with a bowl of water and a towel, and let them wash one another's feet. As they wash, they could imagine that they are washing the feet of Jesus, as a way of saying sorry for their sins. Then say:
Amen.

A prayer for all ages

Dear God, we love you because you love us.
Nothing we can do can make you love us more;
nothing we can do can make you love us less.
We often make you sad,
but we want to make you glad.
So forgive us and help us to do what is right,
in Jesus' name.
Amen.

A sending out prayer

Constant God,
you are with us as we leave.
Constant God,
you inspire us through worship.
Constant God,
as we step out into the future, you are with us.
May God's blessing, and imagination, and passion inspire us as we travel through the coming week.
Amen.

Year C   PROPER 7

Sunday between June 19 and June 25 inclusive

Isaiah 65.1–9; Psalm 22.19–28; Galatians 3.23–29;
Luke 8.26–39 *Return to your home, and declare how much God has done for you.*

A prayer of approach

Faithful God,
To an earth where deserts are spreading and waters rising, you declare your intention of a new, renewed earth.
To those who forget to look for you, who follow their own way, you continually hold out your hand.
To those who suffer hunger, persecution or injustice, you promise your new reign of plenty, compassion and justice.
To those who commit themselves to you, you say, 'Take up your cross daily and follow me'.
Fill us with the strength and compassion we need as we play a part in the coming of your new reign.
Amen.

A prayer of thanksgiving

God of generous provision, for the great variety of clothes we have – clothes for work or school, for play or parties and for special times – we say:
**Thank you that we have enough
and to spare.**

For the homes where we find shelter, food, fun, company and love, we say:
**Thank you that we have enough
and to spare.**

For the friends we have and the scope to meet new people and to socialize, we say:
**Thank you that we have enough
and to spare.**

For all that this community provides, a place to belong and the opportunity to do our bit, we say:
**Thank you that we have enough
and to spare.**

For your love shown to us through Jesus, we say:
**Thank you that we have enough
and to spare.**

Help us to share generously from all that we have.
In Jesus' name.
Amen.

A prayer of praise

Where are you, God?
Are you there in splendour?
As a king, as a slave girl, as a child?
Where are you, God?
We dance in delight; we sing in surprise;
we clap our hands.
We praise you, mystical God.
We want to see you, hear you, touch you.
We want to dance, sing and celebrate with you.
You are great!

All power and strength and grace and truth are yours today, as always.
You are our constant foundation and courage
and we praise you.
Amen.

Prayer of intercession

O God, help those who feel uncomfortable in their present situation, job or church.
Help them discern when it's time to stick at it,
and when it's time to get out,
when to wait and when to act.
Show them what they can do to make their current situation more bearable.
Turn a restless experience into a creative one.
Guide those who are contemplating a career change, or are being forced into one by poor health or redundancy.
Be their inspiration in making a good change, giving them courage in the face of the unknown.
And turn even their unfortunate choices to good ends.
Amen.

A prayer activity

Give each person a stone, asking them to consider silently when they or people they know have been absorbed in activities that have led them away from God. When everyone is ready, invite them to place their stone on a table. In the process, ask them to offer a prayer for themselves and others for freedom from all that stops them being close to God.

A prayer for all ages

God of power, you are with us
at all times and in all places.
In times of darkness, encircle us with light.
In times of despair, encircle us with hope.
In times of sorrow, encircle us with compassion.
In times of anxiety, encircle us with calm.
In times of doubt, encircle us with faith.
In times of sadness, encircle us with joy.
You are with us at all times and in all places.
Amen.

A sending out prayer

From the mountain top we leave in hope.
Having known the presence of God, we go with determination, charged with our ministry, and seeking God's will in our world.
Amen.

Year C   PROPER 8

1 Kings 19.15–16, 19–21; Psalm 16; Galatians 5.1, 13–25; **Luke 9.51–62** *Foxes have holes, and birds of the air have nests; but the Son of Man has nowhere to lay his head.*

Call to worship *based on Galatians 5 and Psalm 16*

For freedom Christ has set us free:
we are called to freedom.
I will bless the Lord who gives me counsel;
my heart teaches me, night after night.
I have set the Lord always before me;
because he is at my right hand I shall not fall.
Let us worship the living God who has set us free.
Alleluia! Let us bless the Lord.

A prayer of adoration and thanksgiving

O loving God, as we come into your presence,
we come to worship and adore you;
we come to declare, with our lives and our lips,
the psalmist's belief: 'You are my Lord, I have no good apart from you.'
We thank you that in your loving kindness you have blessed us with the gift of freedom:
freedom to think,
freedom to act,
freedom to be still,
freedom to choose –
even freedom to make mistakes.
Thank you for believing in us, loving God.

We thank you that even when we make mistakes,
even when our failures and our sins entangle us by their vicious power, your love for us is so great that you gave Jesus to us to set us free; for to freedom we were called.
Thank you for believing in us, loving God.

As we worship you today, may your freedom fill our lives and thrill our hearts. And when we leave this holy space may the freedom you have given us be lived in your name and to your praise and glory.
Amen.

A prayer of intercession *based on Martin Luther King's famous speech*

We have a dream
that all people might be free and equal,
that race and gender might count for nothing.
Let freedom ring.
We have a dream
that slaves and victims of persecution will rise against their oppressors and all people will be free.
Let freedom ring.
We have a dream
that our children may grow in a land of tolerance and justice for all.
Let freedom ring.
We have a dream
that one day every valley shall be exalted,
every hill and mountain laid low,
the rough places will be made smooth,
the crooked places made straight,
and the glory of the Lord shall be revealed
and all flesh shall see it together.
This is our hope.
This is our faith.
Let freedom ring!

A personal prayer

Lord Jesus, from those things that bind me close,
set me free.
Lord Jesus, from those things that hem me in,
set me free.
Lord Jesus, from those sins that hold me in their grip,
set me free.
Holy Spirit, for the life you want me to lead,
set me free.
Holy Spirit, to be the person you want me to be,
set me free.
Holy Spirit, for a desire to do your will,
set me free.
So shall I be your child, O God.
So shall I reflect your face, O Creator.
So shall I be free indeed, O Companion on my way.
Amen.

A prayer activity

Cut out fruit shapes and invite the young people to write prayers on them. Encourage them to ask God to help them develop the aspects of the fruit of the Spirit that they find hard.
Amen.

A sending out prayer

May the God who created you,
set you free.
May the Son who cut the chains,
set you free.
May the Spirit who longs to fill your life,
set you free.
And the blessing of God, Creator, Son and Spirit,
free you and fill you now and always,
that you may walk as children of God.
Amen.

Year C   PROPER 9

Sunday between July 3 and July 9 inclusive

Isaiah 66.10–14; Psalm 66.1–9; Galatians 6.(1–6), 7–16; **Luke 10.1–11, 16–20** *See, I am sending you out like lambs into the midst of wolves.*

Call to worship

Are you ready?
Are you ready to go on an adventure?
Are you ready for your life to be changed?
Are you ready to meet with the living God?
A different person could read each line,
from a different part of the church:
Almighty God is calling us to rejoice:
we rejoice in God's presence.
Jesus Christ is calling us to be his people:
we come together as Christ's people.
The Holy Spirit is calling us to celebrate the love of God:
we celebrate God's love, held by the Holy Spirit.

A prayer of confession

Forgive our frail faithfulness,
content with comfort,
saved from testing and trying.
Forgive our desire for safe havens,
happy with quiet,
secure from worldly challenge.
Forgive our timidity in the task
of telling out and living out the gospel,
and fire us, instead,
with courage to speak
and compassion to act,
in the name of Jesus.
Amen.

A prayer of dedication

Take, bless and use all the gifts we bring,
loving God:
offered as they are in the name
of your gift above all gifts to us all –
Jesus Christ, our Redeemer.
Use our money gifts,
our time and our talents
in the way you will,
for the work of your kingdom,
for the sake of the world,
in the name of the same
Jesus Christ, your Son our Saviour.
Amen.

A personal prayer

Gracious God,
Help us as we try to follow you.
Help us to hear the deep rhythm of your love,
pulsating through your world.
When we face challenges,
help us not to draw back defeated,
but to give our all,
trusting that you will surprise us and strengthen us.

In our lives
and in our world,
let your kingdom come
and your will be done.
Amen.

A prayer activity

Do some research into the role of an ambassador. With the group, talk them through some of your discoveries about the work, status, authority, respect, etc., that an ambassador commands. Then pray for God's help to be ambassadors for Jesus. Invite everyone to feel the honour and privilege of this as well as the responsibility.

A prayer for all ages

Circle me, O God, with your love.
Keep fear without, keep peace within.
Don't let my circle be a force-field.
May your love always reach in to me,
and may my love reach out to others,
that all may be embraced by your love.

Circle me, O God, with your love.
Keep fear without, keep peace within.
Let the circle be tough enough
to keep the fears outside.
And let the circle be strong enough to stop me from bringing the fears back in.

Circle me, O God, with your love.
Keep fear without, keep peace within.

A sending out prayer

We're leaving our worship,
but we're not leaving God behind.
We're saying 'goodbye' to each other,
but we're not leaving God behind.
We're going to different places and meeting different people,
but we're not leaving God behind.
We're not sure what the week will hold,
but we're not leaving God behind.
We'll be having good moments and bad moments,
but we're not leaving God behind.
We want to live life to the full,
but we're not leaving God behind.
Encourage the congregation to make the responses as emphatically as they dare!

Year C   PROPER 10

Sunday between July 10 and July 16 inclusive

Deuteronomy 30.9–14; Psalm 25.1–10; Colossians 1.1–14; **Luke 10.25–37** *You shall love the Lord your God with all your heart, and with all your soul, and with all your strength, and with all your mind.*

Call to worship

Look around you.
Here are the children of God.
See your neighbours,
each different from each other
and made in the image of God.
Think of our world
and its millions of people.
They are our neighbours,
each different from each other
and made in the image of God.
Open your hearts
to meet with the creator of us all.
Offer your praise as we come together,
each different from each other
and made in the image of God.

A prayer of confession

Forgive us for walking by on the other side:
**when need was before us
and skills were ours to share.**
Forgive us for walking by on the other side:
**when pain was apparent
and healing was ours to give.**
Forgive us for walking by on the other side:
**when loneliness was near
and rich time was ours to spend.**
Forgive us for walking by on the other side:
**when fear was present
and compassion was ours to offer.
Amen.**

A prayer of praise

Praise be to you, loving God,
for you lavish care on creation:
bring order to chaos,
light to darkness,
life to emptiness.
Praise be to you, redeeming God,
for you lavish love on all people:
bringing forgiveness for sin,
belief for doubt,
wisdom for uncertainty.
Praise be to you, inspiring God,
for you lavish breath on all beings:
bringing hope to the dispirited,
trust to the despairing,
faith to the fearful.
Amen.

A prayer of thanksgiving

At the beginning of time your love touched the void,
bringing order out of chaos
and creating a world that gave you joy.
God of love,
we thank you for your priceless gifts.

In Jesus Christ love was poured out without limit,
challenging, caressing and captivating human hearts
and minds,
and never being defeated.
God of love,
we thank you for your priceless gifts.

Your Spirit's boundless love moves us ever onwards,
revealing how the world can be changed by your
invigorating love,
giving strength and offering hope.
God of love,
we thank you for your priceless gifts.

In our lives your love goes deep,
beyond words or explanation,
into darkness and into light,
present for us now and in all our tomorrows,
shaping us into your image.
God of love,
**we thank you for your priceless gifts.
Amen.**

A prayer of intercession

We pray for those whom we pass by each day,
who are part of the backdrop of our lives,
and whose needs never seem pressing or important.
Loving Christ, as you have reached out to us,
help us to reach out to others.

We pray for those whom our community passes by:
difficult or threatening people,
adults or children vulnerable to neglect.
Loving Christ, as you have reached out to us,
help us to reach out to others.

We pray for those whom our world passes by,
whose oppression is timeless,
the poor, the frightened, the refugee.
Loving Christ, as you have reached out to us,
**help us to reach out to others.
Amen.**

A prayer activity

On blank postcards, each person writes the words from verse 27, starting, 'I will love the Lord my God …' In silence, they add words or symbols to remind them of the challenge of these words. The cards are to act as prayer reminders over coming days.

Year C PROPER 11

Sunday between July 17 and July 23 inclusive

Genesis 18.1–10a; Psalm 15; Colossians 1.15–28;
Luke 10.38–42 *Now as they went on their way, he entered a certain village, where a woman named Martha welcomed him into her home.*

Call to worship

Stop!
Now is the time to be still.
Now is the time to listen.
Now is the time to learn.
God is waiting.
Let us turn to worship.

A prayer of confession

O God, you do not have to shout to make
yourself heard.
You speak in a still small voice.
There are glimpses of your glory to be seen every day,
if only we take time to look.
Forgive us when we would rather keep busy than
make time to be still,
when we assume that rushing must always be
the norm.
Help us when our good intentions are squeezed
out by everyday life,
or when we cannot listen for you because of the
clamour that fills our mind.
Teach us the language of the Spirit and the
language of the heart,
so that even when life is full, we can cultivate
moments of calm,
and relax in your strengthening presence.
Amen.

A personal prayer

Jesus, today I stopped rushing around and stopped
being busy.
Then I saw.
I SAW the sky.
It was SO blue and SO grey.
I NOTICED the pavements.
The wild flowers – now not weeds – forcing their way
through the cracks
were SO green.
Then I saw faces.
Faces that looked out on the world
were filled with SO MUCH care,
with SO MANY questions,
with both laughter and pain…
SO…
Jesus, stop me from being busy again and again.
Let me SEE and NOTICE SO MUCH.
Amen.

A prayer of intercession

God of the field and river,
of the desert and oasis,
of the plain and steppe,
of the town and city:
Lord of all,
we ask your blessing.

For people who are waiting for food,
for people who are waiting for water,
for people who are waiting for shelter,
for people working to relieve want and need,
wherever they are, whoever they work with:
Lord of all,
we ask your blessing.

For children and young people,
for their families and friends,
for the old and infirm,
for the childless and the bereaved,
for those working to bring communities together:
God of all,
we ask your blessing.

For each Christian community meeting today,
for our leaders and all committed to their care,
for our missionaries, teachers and administrators,
our worship leaders and worshippers,
for all those working to forward your kingdom:
God of all,
we ask your blessing on this world.
Amen.

A prayer activity

Becoming pregnant seemed laughable to Sarah, yet it was clearly not impossible for God, who doesn't have our limitations – anything is possible for God. Hand out paper and pens, and give the group time to write a prayer asking for God's help in a situation or scenario, even if it seems impossible!

A prayer for all ages

Lord Jesus, if you came to my house today,
would I be ready for you?
Would I recognize you?
Lord, this idea of you coming again,
I find it hard to understand.
It's exciting, but a bit scary too.
Lord, I know you come to me every day.
You can be happy with me in the good times;
you can help me through the hard times.
Lord, I won't hang around just waiting for you to
come again.
Help me to remember at the beginning of each day to
invite you to share my life.
Show me how you want me to live.
Help me to recognize you in other people.
Then I'll always be ready for you.
Amen.

Year C   PROPER 12

Genesis 18.20–32; Psalm 138; Colossians 2.6–15
(16–19); **Luke 11.1–13** *When you pray, say, Father,
hallowed be your name.*

Call to worship

Abba, Father, as we gather for worship,
hallowed be your name.
Let your kingdom come!
Give us our daily bread.
**Forgive us our sins as we forgive those
who sin against us.**
**Do not bring us to the time of trial,
but set us free in our praise.**

Lord, teach us to pray.
Lord, teach us to pray as you prayed.
Teach us to pray early in the morning and during the
watches of the night.
Teach us to pray in times of elation and in times of
deepest anguish.
Teach us to pray in desert places and in holy places.
Teach us to pray patiently and persistently.
Teach us to pray humbly and graciously.
Teach us to pray with a childlike spirit,
in love and trust.
Teach us to pray 'Let your will be done' with courage
and faith.
Lord, teach us to pray.
For your name's sake.
Amen.

A prayer of confession

'Forgive us our sins', you taught us to pray.
And so, Lord, we seek your forgiveness for the sins of
our hearts and minds and bodies,
for the sins of pride and selfishness and
unforgiveness,
for the sins we have repeated and the sins we have
regretted.
'As we forgive those who sin against us', you went on
to say.
And so we seek your forgiveness
for those who have lied to us and hurt us,
for those who have taken advantage of us and
denied us,
for those we struggle to forgive.
Your cross speaks of the power of your forgiving love.
As we receive this afresh for ourselves,
help us to offer it to others.
For your name's sake we pray.
Amen.

A prayer of intercession

Today we hold before our gracious God:
all those who are asking and those who do not know
what to ask for.
May they be given all they need and may they
recognize truth when they meet it.

Today we hold before our gracious God:
all those who are searching
and those who do not know what to search for.
May they find all that they seek
and may they recognize their discovery.
Today we hold before our gracious God:
all those who are knocking
and those who knock but do not recognize the door.
May the door be opened to them and may they be
greeted by the God who loves them and created
them.
Amen.

A prayer for children

Our Father, we know that the Lord's Prayer is a
special prayer:
Thank you that you taught us how to pray.
We know that it comes from you:
Thank you that you taught us how to pray.
Help us to think about the words as we say them:
Thank you that you taught us how to pray.
Help us to do the things you ask us – to give you
honour, and to forgive those who are unkind to us:
Thank you that you taught us how to pray.
And one day, Father, the world will live as you want
it to live:
Thank you that you taught us how to pray.
Amen.

A prayer activity

*Give everyone paper and a pen and ask them
to rewrite the Lord's Prayer in their own words.
Encourage them to be creative, using text-speak,
a rap, a poem. Listen to each other's prayers. Ask
the group to share their experiences of learning the
Lord's Prayer. What does the prayer mean to them
today?*

A prayer for all ages

*Ask everyone to stand up and hold hands so that the
whole congregation is linked:*
We stand before you, our Father God,
and we ask you to bless all those
families that we represent here today,
wherever and whoever they are.
Be with them in their work and in their play,
in their waking and in their sleeping.
May they know your love and your peace today.
Amen.

A sending out prayer

Go now, with the love of God within you,
the peace of God around you,
and the wisdom of God within your hearts.
For when I called, you answered me.
You have increased your strength within me.
We go now in the love of God.
Amen.

Year C PROPER 13

Sunday between July 31 and August 6 inclusive

Ecclesiastes 1.2, 12–14, 2.18–23; Psalm 49.1–12; Colossians 3.1–11; **Luke 12.13–21** *Be on your guard against all kinds of greed; for one's life does not consist in the abundance of possessions.*

Call to worship *based on Psalm 49.1 and Colossians 3.1*

Hear this, all you peoples,
hearken all you who dwell in the land,
you of high degree and low,
rich and poor together.
If you have been raised with Christ,
seek the things that are above.
When Christ who is your life is revealed
you also will be revealed with him in glory.
O Lord, open our lips:
and our mouths shall praise you.
O Lord, open our ears:
that we may hear you.
O Lord, open our hearts:
that we may worship you
in Spirit and in truth.

A prayer of confession

Invite people to hold something familiar to them: keys, bank card, ring, mobile, etc., as a personal focus during this guided meditation:
Creating One, as we choose to renew our relationship with you, forgive us;
work with us as we choose what to hold on to and what to let go.
Help us to choose those things we need for life and those things that bring life to others.
Guide us, as we choose what is important in our living and what to spend energy on achieving.
Renew us, as we choose to live into your future and build the kingdom community.
Lead us, as we choose to treasure the abundance and generosity of your gifts.
Heal us, as we choose to let go of what corrupts and to share what brings life.
Creating One, hear us.
Amen.

A prayer of thanksgiving

We look at our hands,
at the lines running through them,
each one unique,
each one special to God:
and we thank our Creator for life.
We look at our bodies,
at the differences between us,
each one unique,
each one special to God:
and we thank our Creator for life.

We look at our church,
this body of people,
each one unique,
each one special to God:
and we thank our Creator for life.
Amen.

A prayer of intercession

Gracious God,
In a world where the rich build ever bigger barns and banks
and millions live in shanty towns and slums,
let there be justice, let there be peace.
In a world where many eat and drink to excess
and millions more simply long for clean water,
let there be justice, let there be peace.
In a world where many make merry
and millions grieve,
let there be justice, let there be peace.
In a world where many join health clubs
and millions long for basic health care,
let there be justice, let there be peace.
In a world where many are stressed out with work
and millions feel their labour is in vain or unwanted,
let there be justice, let there be peace.
In a world where many are materially poor and yet
spiritually rich, and millions are materially rich and yet
spiritually poor,
let there be justice, let there be peace.
Amen.

A prayer activity

Ask each person to think about how they would like to be remembered, or to write their own epitaph. Use the epitaphs as a focus for personal prayer about their own hopes and dreams.

A prayer for all ages

Invite different members of the congregation to proclaim the adverbs:
May we live
abundantly.
May we live
generously.
May we live
for others.
May we live
caringly.
May we live
lovingly.
May we live richly for you.
Amen.

Year C   PROPER 14

Sunday between August 7 and August 13 inclusive

Genesis 15.1–6; Psalm 33.12–22; Hebrews 11.1–3, 8–16; **Luke 12.32–40** *Do not be afraid, little flock, for it is your Father's good pleasure to give you the kingdom.*

Call to worship

Happy are the people God has chosen to be his own!
Our soul waits for the Lord; he is our help and our shield.
The Lord sees and understands all the people in the world.
Our soul waits for the Lord; he is our help and our shield.
It is God who gives us life and who feeds us; our heart rejoices in him, and in his holy name we put our trust.
Our soul waits for the Lord; he is our help and our shield.
Amen.

A prayer of confession

As we confess, O God,
may we be ready for your forgiveness.
As we confess those times we have failed to serve and failed to be served:
may we be ready for your forgiveness.
As we confess those treasures we have stored up that have tarnished and spoiled:
may we be ready for your forgiveness.
As we confess those times when our lamps have dulled and us with them:
may we be ready for your forgiveness.
Yet you call us once more to be renewed, to set our lamps alight, focus our minds and to be servants again. You forgive us and transform us:
may we be ready for your renewal.
Amen.

A prayer of commitment

Generous God, help us to learn that our treasure is found not in gold or silver or bronze,
but in giving away;
not in banks or coins or wealth,
but in serving each other;
not in paintings or houses or cars,
but in caring for one another.
Show us how to find treasure
in the simple things in life.
In being with each other –
that is where our treasure is found.
Amen.

A prayer of supplication

Lord, we lay our fears at your feet.
Our fears that we are not good enough and that we cannot cope,
our fears of failure and ridicule,
our fears for our health, our wealth and our future.
We lay at your feet our fears for those close to our hearts,
our fears for those who are sick, or anxious, grieving or lonely,
our fears for our children growing up in a world full of pressures and temptations,
our fears for those who worry about growing old.
Lord, we lay our fears at your feet.
'Do not be afraid,' you say.
Grant us your peace, we pray,
and let your peace fall afresh upon your anxious world, for your name's sake.
Amen.

A prayer of intercession

We pray for those who always live in tents: the nomads, wanderers, those with no settled home.
Lord, bring them comfort, bring them protection.
We pray for travellers, those who face hostility and rejection; and for those who minister to them and offer them acceptance.
Lord, bring them comfort, bring them protection.
We pray for our transient people, for those coming to our shores and finding no welcome, those forced to move from place to place in search of livelihood, those with no security, no home – finding food and shelter where they can.
Lord, bring them comfort, bring them protection.
We are all travellers, Lord, serving you in a world that is often indifferent or hostile to your message.
We travel on, in our fragile tents of faith,
looking to the place which is in you and for you.
Lord, our hearts are restless till they find their rest in you.
Amen.

A prayer activity

Younger children will love to shout 'YES!' as the response to each line of this prayer:
Are you ready to pray? **Yes!**
Are you ready to welcome Jesus? **Yes!**
Are you ready to love God? **Yes!**
Are you ready to love your neighbour? **Yes!**
Are you ready to party with God? **Yes!**
Are you ready to shout AMEN? **Yes!**
Amen!

A sending out prayer

May we go into the world and
share the treasure of justice.
May we unfold the treasure of service.
May we proclaim the treasure of love
and may we be held by the treasure of grace.
Amen.

Year C   PROPER 15

Sunday between August 14 and August 20 inclusive

Jeremiah 23.23–29; Psalm 82; Hebrews 11.29–12.2;
Luke 12.49–56 *Do you think that I have come to bring peace to the earth?*

Call to worship

God saw all that had been made.
And behold it was very good.
Mighty God, your majesty fills the earth.
All you have created displays your glory.
You have gathered us here as your people
in this place,
to reflect your glory and to echo creation's praise.
Enable us by your Spirit to offer our worship
in spirit and in truth,
and our witness in generosity and faithfulness.
Empower us and equip us to fulfil the promise
made to us and in us.
Help us to walk in your ways and to bless you.
God saw all that had been made.
And behold it was very good.

A prayer of thanksgiving and supplication

Gracious God,
We thank you for all that enriches our lives and
makes life exciting and challenging.
We thank you for opportunities to question and to
challenge, to search and to explore.
When there are no simple answers,
help us to keep our minds open.
When others bring us face to face with our prejudices
and preconceptions,
help us to keep our hearts open.
We thank you that there is no part of our lives that is
untouched by your Spirit.
Bless all we would touch and hold;
help us to keep our hands open to receive from you
and from others.
Bless us in the hospitality we offer to those the same
as ourselves and those different from ourselves.
Help us to keep our doors open in Jesus' name.
Amen.

A prayer of praise

Creator God, the universe in which we live echoes
the sound of your praise. From the farthest star to the
smallest fleck of dust, you reveal yourself. From the
wonder of ocean depths to the majesty of mountain
peaks, the world is alive with your music. Even in
the very depths of our being, you are present, close
to the core of our nature, one with us through Jesus
Christ your Son. We worship and adore you. We
celebrate the love and grace that binds us to you and
to one another.
Amen.

A prayer for all ages *based on Hebrews 11.29–12.2*

When we think the race is over:
Help us to remember you.

When we're lagging far behind:
Help us to remember you.

When we're running out of steam:
Help us to remember you.

When we reach the goals we set:
Help us to remember you.

When we worry about success:
Help us to remember you.

When we are trying to keep on running:
Help us to remember you.
Amen.

A prayer of confession and intercession

When we are divided between those who
eat and those who starve,
may we share a banquet together.
When we are divided between those of one
denomination and those of another,
may we share bread and wine together.
When we are divided between those who have
homes and those who are strangers,
may we play the Samaritan to each other.
When we are divided between those with Paul and
those with Apollos,
may we follow Christ together.
When we are divided between left or right,
may we share our humanity together.
When we are divided between the past and the future,
may we share the present with each other.
Amen.

A prayer activity

*Sit the children in a circle on the floor around a
large selection of pictures (slightly more than one
per child). These can include pictures of candles,
crosses, creation, etc. Encourage the children to look
at all the pictures and then choose one that helps
them to think about God. Have a period of silence,
introduced and concluded with your own brief prayer,
when the children can say thank you to God for the
picture they are holding.*

A sending out prayer

The God who fills heaven and earth,
fill our lives with love for the truth.
The pioneer and perfecter of our faith,
energize our lives to achieve the goals we are called
to aim for.
The Spirit of fire, keep our hearts loving,
strong and ready to endure.
Amen.

Year C   PROPER 16

Sunday between August 21 and August 27 inclusive

Isaiah 58.9b–14; Psalm 103.1–8; Hebrews 12.18–29;
Luke 13.10–17 *When Jesus saw her, he called her over and said, 'Woman, you are set free from your ailment.'*

Call to worship

You shall call, and the Lord will answer:
Here I am.
You shall cry for help, and God will say:
Here I am.
Whenever we act justly, God says:
Here I am.
Whenever we honour God with our
hearts, God says:
Here I am.
We hear the call of God to us as we come
to worship, and we ourselves respond:
Here I am.
Today, God, when you say to us, 'Whom
shall I send?' make us ready to reply:
Here I am. Send me.

A prayer for all ages

Life-changing God, we thank you that you have given
us important rules to live our lives by:
the rules of peace, love, respect, justice and equality.
We thank you for the way Jesus challenged things he
saw and knew to be wrong.
We thank you that his special rule – 'love one
another' – was first shown in all that he did and said,
and for how it challenged people's ideas, words and
actions.
We thank you for the ways Jesus changed people's
understanding of rules, making them think about care
and compassion.
Help us to remember to put loving you and loving our
neighbour first in our lives.
Help us to replace the words and actions we know to
be unfair and unkind with love.
We ask our prayer in the name of the one whose love
for everyone changed things so much.
Amen.

A prayer of praise

Jesus, you call us and unbind us.
You whisper our names and set us free.
You know our souls and let them live.
You hold our lives and grant them purpose.
You renew our dreams and make them our future.
You transform our living and make us belong.
Loving God of transformations,
with justice you serve us,
and with grace you give us life.
May our turning towards you
be our praise and thanksgiving.
Amen.

A prayer of intercession

We pray for those in need of healing,
whose lives are confined by pain and frustration;
whose relationships are marred by the experience of
disappointment and betrayal.
Touch their lives with your grace,
to bring freedom and forgiveness,
renewal and reconciliation.
Amen.

A prayer activity

*Spread out a world map on the floor. Talk with the
children about the kind of place God intended the
world to be. Encourage words such as 'peaceful',
'fair', 'loving'. Write some of these words on pieces
of paper and place them around the outside of the
map. Put tealights on different places around the
world where children know there is war, famine or
natural disaster. Ensure the tealights have suitable
heat-proof bases. Pray for each place in turn and
light the candles as you do so. Focus on the fact that
ordinary people suffer because of the things that
are happening around the world. Pray for the love of
Jesus to transform things, just as it did for the woman
who was healed.*

A prayer when children are present

Lord Jesus, you know how much we love journeys.
It is exciting to go somewhere new and to travel by
car or train or aeroplane.
We get impatient to arrive!
On our life's journey
we know we are travelling with you.
Thank you for the adventure we are on.
Today, teach us something new about yourself
and help us to be happy with you, with each other,
with our families.
Amen.

A prayer of affirmation

God who crosses all boundaries in the gift of justice,
may we meet you in reconciliation and renewal.
In breaking the rules that prevent full living,
may we hear your call to accompany the process
of heaven.
As lives are set free by your reckless grace,
may we be set free to live for you in this world.
God who crosses even the boundary of death,
may we meet you on the side of eternity.
Amen.

Year C   PROPER 17

Sirach 10.12–18, or Proverbs 25.6–7; Psalm 112;
Hebrews 13.1–8, 15–16; **Luke 14.1, 7–14** *For all who
exalt themselves will be humbled, and those who
humble themselves will be exalted.*

Call to worship

The banquet is ready! The table is set!
The food is prepared! The wine is poured!
Come into the Lord's presence.
Come and celebrate.
Come and worship.
All are invited.
All are welcome.
God's time is now and all time.
God's place is here and everywhere.
Come at this special time to this special place.
Come, for you, too, are special.
You are invited.
You are welcome.
You are accepted, cherished and chosen.
God delights in your company.
Make yourself at home.
You are God's guest.
The God and creator of us all,
the God and Father of our
Lord Jesus Christ,
the God, from whom all life and being
flows in the gift of the Spirit,
loves and accepts those who recognize
their need,
who come to open their lives in humility
and in faith.

A prayer of confession

When plates are unfilled,
forgive us.
When tables are unset,
forgive us.
When justice is undone,
forgive us.
When neighbours are unwelcome,
forgive us.
When people are uninvited,
forgive us.
When the lost are unfound,
forgive us.
May our table be un-closed,
our community undivided,
our grace unselfish,
and our anger unspoken.
When the bread is unbroken,
may we break it with the world.
Amen.

A prayer of intercession *based on Hebrews 13*

The Lord is my helper;
I will not be afraid.
What can anyone do to me?
Lord, make us sensitive, yet brave
so that we may entertain angels unawares.
We pray for prisoners and those who have
experienced prison life,
especially those who are rootless and homeless.
Lord, make us sensitive, yet brave
so that we may entertain angels unawares.
We pray for leaders in all walks of life: for people in
government; for those in service organizations; for
religious leaders in all the faiths.
Lord, make them sensitive, yet brave
so that they may entertain angels unawares.
We pray for all concerned to encourage and support
marriage and family life.
We pray for strong commitment and generosity to
those seeking a place to call home.
Lord, make us sensitive, yet brave
so that we may entertain angels unawares.
Help us to do good and to share what we have.
Lord, make us sensitive, yet brave
so that we may entertain angels unawares.
Let us continually offer a sacrifice of praise to God,
through Jesus Christ our Lord.
Amen.

A prayer activity

*With the children, make a list of groups of people who
can feel lonely and left out, like those who live alone.
Try to work it so that each child has a person or group
of people to pray for. Children write prayers and then
read them out. If your church has a list of prayer
requests somewhere, use these suggestions too in
your prayers.*

A prayer for all ages

Lord God,
You have promised that you will never leave us.
We thank you for all the people who spend time with
us and remind us that you are with us.
We thank you for people who sit next to us and talk to
us, or play games with us and share jokes with us.
Be with us when we want to be noisy together and
when we want to be quiet together.
Be with us when we want to share our happiness and
when we need to share our sadness.
Be with us when we have done something well and
when we could have done something better.
Be with us when we are angry with other people and
when other people are angry with us.
May Jesus be our friend today and always.
Amen.

Year C   PROPER 18

Deuteronomy 30.15–20; Psalm 1; Philemon 1–21;
Luke 14.25–33 *Whoever does not carry the cross
and follow me cannot be my disciple.*

Call to worship

*Divide the congregation into two (perhaps
side A and side B) for the responses:*
God of majesty and might,
A: All we are is in your hands.
B: We come to worship.
God of faithfulness and justice,
B: All we have been is in your hands.
A: We come to seek forgiveness.
God of truth and love,
**All: All we shall be is in your hands;
we come to be renewed.**
God of mystery and miracle,
A: Create in us a sense of wonder.
God of grace and glory,
**B: Share our life in our frailty and
weakness.**
God of power and peace,
All: Set us free to praise and adore.

A prayer of invocation

Merciful God,
Give us the determination to speak out for your values,
even when those closest to us disapprove.
Give us the courage to face up to inhuman social
structures,
so that we might create your kingdom in our everyday
lives.
Make us bold to challenge oppressive systems, and
to confess your name and your good news.
Give us the inspiration to show the joy that comes
through living in your love.
God of choice, thank you that you go on calling us.
May our willingness to be called into the unknown be
our gift to your world.
Amen.

A personal prayer

Almighty God, you brought the universe into being.
You breathed life into your world.
All time is in your hands.
You bless our lives with change.
Help us to choose change and not to be afraid of
consequences.
Set us free from the desire to hold everything under
our control.
When change threatens to overwhelm us, and we are
reluctant to take risks, hold us close and remind us
that you enfold us with your love.
Set us free to live as your people and be with us
as we respond to the call and the challenge
to set others free.
In Jesus' name.
Amen.

A responsive prayer of intercession

Warm Spirit of God,
there are times when we want only the security of
saying nothing,
when we want to curl up in a safe corner of life and
take no risks, make no decisions,
when we want to stay in the places we know and do
things in the way that we've always done them.
But we sense that you are calling us.
Warm Spirit of God – awaken us.
Show us how to walk in ways that lead to justice.
Make us honest enough to tell you if we fail or are
afraid.
Give us the courage to take risks.
Reassure us when we are hurt.
We don't know where this new life will lead us,
but we will let ourselves be carried along.
Warm Spirit of God – walk with us.
Help us to be brave enough to face the pain of the
world's indifference.
Give us the confidence to smile when people find us
amusing and strange.
Hold us firm so that we do not stumble or turn back
when the way seems too difficult.
Help us to face honestly the terrors of the world, and
to walk with Christ, in wisdom and bravery.
Warm Spirit of God – inspire and protect us.
Amen.

A prayer activity

*Sing a quiet worship song together or listen together
to some quiet Taizé music. Ask the children to think
about all the things they enjoy in life and to thank God
for them.*

A prayer for all ages

Lord God,
*Each of the following lines may be read by
a different voice from the congregation:*
Be with us when we want change.
Be with us when we do not want change.
Be with us when we enjoy change.
Be with us when we dislike change.
Be with us when we find change exciting.
Be with us when we find change frightening.
Be with us when we encourage change.
Be with us when we prevent change.
Be with us when change comes too slowly.
Be with us when change comes too quickly.
Father, Son and Spirit,
enfold us in your love and be with us now and always.
Amen.

Year C   PROPER 19

Sunday between September 11 and September 17 inclusive

Exodus 32.7–14; Psalm 51.1–10; 1 Timothy 1.12–17;
Luke 15.1–10 *Just so, I tell you, there is joy in the presence of the angels of God over one sinner who repents.*

Call to worship

God of words, **we offer our words.**
God of silence, **we offer our silence.**
God of beginnings, **we offer our beginning.**
God of endings, **we offer our ending.**
God of moving, **we offer our moving.**
God of being, **we offer our being.**
God of our minds, **create within us.**
God of our bodies, **create through us.**
God of our spirits, **create among us.**
For your kingdom's sake.

A prayer of invocation

Loving God,
Draw us together and make us one,
as we sing with the whole of creation in praise of you,
as a new day unfolds its infinite potential.
Help us never to lose our sense of wonder,
as we see, hear, taste and touch the beauty of this world.
Inspire us with the energy to put right all that is bruised or broken.
Show us that we are all linked in one humanity.
Amen.

A prayer for all ages

God, our loving Father,
We live in the world you gave us,
but we do not always understand it.
We want to worship you
but we do not always feel like worship.
We want to reach to you
but sometimes we are afraid.
As we learn about Jesus,
remind us of your promise
that you will never leave us.
Help us to be honest with you
and with one another.
Help us to speak to you
and to listen to you, day by day.
Amen.

A prayer of confession

Almighty God,
When we rebel against your righteousness,
forgive us and heal us.

When we injure one another through ignorance,
forgive us and heal us.

When we forget your faithfulness,
forgive us and heal us.

When we neglect each other's needs,
forgive us and heal us.

When we justify injustice,
forgive us and heal us.

When we search only for ourselves,
forgive us and heal us.

For your Son, Jesus Christ's sake,
forgive us and heal us.
Amen.

A prayer of intercession

When we are rejected and yearn to belong,
when we are isolated and long for company,
when we are lonely and miss our family,
Spirit of love, breathe on us.

When we are abused as children,
when we are despised as outsiders,
when we are exhausted by shame and guilt,
Spirit of healing, breathe on us.

When we are underpaid workers,
when we are tortured victims,
when we are hungry refugees,
Spirit of justice, breathe on us.

When we speak peace but act with violence,
when we preach love but practise hate,
when we shout liberation but live oppression,
Spirit of forgiveness, breathe on us.
Amen.

A prayer of petition

Jesus Christ,
strong and loving shepherd,
who seeks the lost
and welcomes the stranger,
may we know your presence in our lives.
Help us to pass on your love to the unloved,
that they may shine with happiness;
your peace to the troubled,
that they may be quiet and still;
your joy to those who are sad or in darkness,
that they may sparkle and rejoice.
Please guide and protect all your sheep,
and carry us home safely
when we stray and fall.
Amen.

A prayer activity

Invite the young people to pray together or join in with the response:
Help us, Lord,
to look to you.
In the times when things get lost…
In the times when we feel lost…
In the times when we forget your love…
In the times when we can't see your presence…
Help us, Lord,
to look to you.
Amen.

Year C   PROPER 20

Amos 8.4–7; Psalm 113; 1 Timothy 2.1–7;
Luke 16.1–13 *No slave can serve two masters; for a slave will either hate the one and love the other or be devoted to the one and despise the other.*

Call to worship

God of parables,
you teach by examples
drawn from everyday life,
from the worlds of finance,
trade and business, and the realities
of debt and money lending.
God of parables, teach us,
through the experiences of our lives,
to take up the challenges of discipleship,
to respond to the unexpected,
and to weigh up decisions of justice.

A prayer of praise and thanksgiving

Generous God,
You gave us everything.
You embraced the limitations of the human condition.
You felt the pain of love.
You took the risks.
Help us not to turn you away.
Help us not to crucify your love,
even though sometimes the scale and perfection of
your love is too much to grasp.
We thank you for that love.
Pour it into our lives,
so that we may give all that we have and are, for you,
for each other and for the world.
In Jesus' name,
Amen.

A prayer focusing on Jesus as
the Light of the World

Light a candle
Illuminating God,
You are the light in whom there is no darkness.
In Jesus we see your radiance.
We believe that no one will be turned away from
this light.
We believe that this light shines for everyone in
the world.
Light of liberation and love,
shine in the darkness of debt and desperation.
Light of the world,
lead us where you want us to go.
Lead us on the path to your kingdom.
Light of the world,
even when we face the unexpected,
light our way with the promise that we are not alone.
Amen.

A prayer of intercession

God of justice,
We pray for people who have too little because other
people want too much.
We pray for people who have no freedom because
other people want slaves.
We pray for people who lose out because other
people cheat.
Please help us to pray fairly and buy fairly and do
fairly.
Amen.

A prayer activity

*Write short prayers on the inside of a wrapper of
Fairtrade chocolate, then read them out in turn.
Encourage the children to write about issues related
to this week's readings. Share the chocolate.*

A prayer for all ages

Lord Jesus, light of the world,
we know that you long for justice, truth and love –
for all your people.
Help us to love you more than wealth,
serve you more than ourselves,
trust you more than anything else,
and follow you to the end.
Help us to use all our senses
and all our gifts
as we seek to serve you.
Amen.

A sending out prayer

God who set the earth spinning
and set life in a finely tuned balance,
go with us as we seek to live lives
that are environmentally sustainable.

God who taught using everyday stories,
highlighting the imbalance of power and ownership,
go with us as we seek to make decisions
according to your measure of justice.

God who speaks through the people we meet,
pricking our conscience to nudge us to action,
go with us as we seek to tip the scales,
so all can share in your 'kin-dom' of justice
and of peace.
Amen.

Year C   PROPER 21

Amos 6.1a, 4–7; Psalm 146; 1 Timothy 6.6–19;
Luke 16.19–31 *He said to him, 'If they do not listen to Moses and the prophets, neither will they be convinced if someone rises from the dead.'*

Call to worship *based on Psalm 146*

Let us praise the Lord as long as we live;
let us sing praises to God all life long.
Praise the Lord!
Praise the Lord, O my soul!

Happy are those whose hope is in God
who made heaven and earth,
and keeps faith for ever.
Praise the Lord!
Praise the Lord, O my soul!

The Lord executes justice for the oppressed
and gives food to the hungry.
Praise the Lord!
Praise the Lord, O my soul!

The Lord sets the prisoners free
and lifts up those who are bowed down.
Praise the Lord!
Praise the Lord, O my soul!

The Lord will reign for ever,
our God for all eternity.
Praise the Lord!
Praise the Lord, O my soul!

A prayer of confession

God of forgiveness,
You never forget us but we often forget you.
We place before you the times we have gone our own way and forgotten your love.
Lord, in your mercy,
forgive us and heal us.

We place before you the times we have overeaten
and forgotten the hunger of others.
Lord, in your mercy,
forgive us and heal us.

We place before you the times we have spent beyond
our means and forgotten the poverty of others.
Lord, in your mercy,
forgive us and heal us.

We place before you the times we have been idle
and forgotten the needs of others.
Lord, in your mercy,
forgive us and heal us.

Help us to remember you and remember our
neighbours –
the people you have given us to love –
for the sake of your Son who died for us.
Amen.

A prayer of reflection

How easy it is for us to say:
'I am not rich'; 'I have no need to worry that my riches
are getting in the way of my relationships'.
How easy it is for us to say:
'I am quite poor really',
as we look at the glossy magazines and drool over
celebrity lifestyles.
Yes, it is easy.
Loving God, help us to look with a different eye.
Not to look at what we aspire to
and to see only what we have not got,
but to look at the life you have given us
and see just what we have, in you.
Amen.

A short prayer of intercession

O God, who is always on the side of the poor, keep
your Church alert to hear the message of salvation,
eager to preach it, and compassionate to those in
need of it.
Amen.

A prayer activity

*Invite each person to hold a stone in their hand while
thinking of a situation or wrong attitude that they want
to hand over to God. Place the stones at the foot of
a cross. Then each light a candle symbolizing prayer
for change.*

A prayer of thanksgiving for all ages

God of love:
you have made a beautiful world for us to live in.
Thank you,
and teach us to care.
Your world is filled with all sorts of people.
Thank you,
and teach us to care.
We have friends nearby and friends far away.
Thank you,
and teach us to care.
We have things we can share with one another.
Thank you,
and teach us to care.
Your love is always in our hearts.
Thank you,
and teach us to care.
Amen.

Year C PROPER 22

Habakkuk 1.1–4, 2.1–4; Psalm 37.1–9; 2 Timothy 1.1–14; **Luke 17.5–10** *If you had faith the size of a mustard seed, you could say to this mulberry tree, 'Be uprooted and planted in the sea,' and it would obey you.*

Call to worship *based on Psalm 37*

With trust and delight,
we wait for the Lord.

With desire and commitment,
we wait for the Lord.

With patience and stillness,
we wait for the Lord.

With hope in God's promises,
we wait for the Lord.

A prayer of confession

Creator God,
We thank you for the beauty of the world you created and we confess before you our failures of stewardship.
Forgive our greed and selfishness, our concern for our own economic security at the expense of others, and our ignorance of the plight of those who suffer as a result of our choices and actions.
Turn our hearts, that we may heed the warnings of the environment,
the voices of those who see the bigger picture,
and the poverty and hunger of those who grow the food we eat.
Fit us to serve you and to inherit the land you have prepared for us.
In the name of Christ.
Amen.

A responsive prayer

All-giving God,
Source of our being and the whole creation,
bless the earth and bless our use of the earth.
Be with us in our care of this planet.
Lord, open our eyes to see
and open our hearts to love.

All-loving Jesus,
Our guide and our teacher,
bless all people and bless our relationships.
Be with us in our care for one another.
Lord, open our eyes to see
and open our hearts to love.

All-embracing Spirit,
Our inspiration and our joy,
bless our work and bless our rest.
Be with us in our care of our time.
Lord, open our eyes to see
and open our hearts to love.
Amen.

A prayer of intercession for all ages

Lord of all,
With thanksgiving we pray for your world,
and for the power and beauty of your creation.
We pray for the part of the world in which we live.
Help us to look after the streets and the parks so that everyone can enjoy using them.
Help us to look after the countryside and the animals so that they may flourish.
We pray for those parts of the world that are far away.
Help us to care about the people who live there even though we don't know them.
Help us to learn about the changes to their land so that we may help.
Lord of all,
with thanksgiving we pray for your world.
Amen.

A prayer activity

Sing or play quietly a song that emphasizes God's power around us – such as 'Be still for the presence of the Lord' or 'Father we place into your hands'.

A prayer of stillness

Lord Jesus,
still my restlessness
that I may find true rest in you;
still my anxieties
that I may find reassurance in you;
still my anger
that I may find healing in you;
still my fretting
that I may find peace in you;
still the voices that clamour within me
that I may hear your still, quiet voice of love.
Amen.

A sending out prayer

Lord Jesus, my faith is small; help it to grow.
Lord Jesus, my faith is weak; strengthen it.
Lord Jesus, my faith stumbles when I meet obstacles;
make it determined to follow you,
all the days of my life.
Amen.

Year C PROPER 23

2 Kings 5.1–3, 7–15c; Psalm 111; 2 Timothy 2.8–15;
Luke 17.11–19 *Then he said to him, 'Get up and go on your way; your faith has made you well.'*

Call to worship

Come, meet with Christ.
We come.
Come from the centre and from the margins.
We come.
Come with people of all cultures, all ages,
all interests.
We come.
Come to receive the gifts of God.
We come.
Come, worship.
We come.

A prayer of confession

When we think more of ourselves than others,
forgive us, Lord.
When we reject people because they are different
from us,
forgive us, Lord.
When we fail to meet others where they are,
forgive us, Lord.
When we talk the talk, but don't walk the walk,
forgive us, Lord.
When we forget to be grateful to you and to others,
forgive us, Lord.
Amen.

A prayer of petition

O loving and inclusive God,
we pray for all who are prevented from exercising
their gifts and skills,
and from taking their full place in our world
because of what others regard as disablement or
disfigurement.
Open our eyes to see as you see;
look not on the outward appearance,
but on the heart.
Amen.

A prayer of intercession

Loving God,
There are still people today who, like the lepers in the
Bible story, live on the very edge of our society.
We pray for homeless people who take shelter in
shop doorways and sleep rough.
We ask your particular care and protection for young
people who have run away from their homes and
families and now face the world alone.
We think of old people who, though they live in our
neighbourhoods, feel isolated and abandoned.
We pray for refugees and asylum seekers.

We pray for people of whom we are frightened or
wary because they are sick, and for strangers who
have different customs and who we find hard to
understand because they are not like us.
Sometimes we judge other people on what they look
like on the outside.
We turn away from them because they are different
from us.
Sometimes we shun them because we don't
understand them or because we fear them.
Make us more like Jesus, who did not see only the
outside of a person.
Heavenly God, thank you for seeing me, and not just
looking at me.
Amen.

A prayer activity

*Cover a large die or square cardboard box with a
different colour on each face. The children take it
in turns to throw the die into the centre of the room.
When the die lands, the leader says:* 'Thank you,
God, for …………', *and the children complete the
sentence with something in whichever colour comes
up (such as red apples, yellow bananas, oranges,
green grass, blue sky, white snow, and so on).*

A prayer of praise for all ages *based loosely on Psalm 111*

Whenever we get together in church with God's
people it's good to tell God how great he is.
Wow, God, you're amazing!

You've done great things all through history so we
can see how great you are.
Wow, God, you're amazing!

You give us fantastic food of every kind – lots of
things to choose from, and lots of things that are
good for us.
Wow, God, you're amazing!

You work in this country, and all over the world.
You look after your people wherever we are, and
never let us down.
Wow, God, you're amazing!

You are so big, so great that we can't really get our
heads round it.
Help us to remember to respect your greatness, as
well as love your kindness.
Wow, God, you're amazing!

You always keep your promises; you're always there
for us when we need you.
Thank you that we can trust you always and for ever.
Wow, God, you're amazing!
Amen.

Year C   PROPER 24

Genesis 32.22–31; Psalm 121; 2 Timothy 3.14–4.5;
Luke 18.1–8 *When the Son of Man comes, will he find faith on earth?*

Call to worship

'Ask and it shall be given to you, search and you will find, knock and the door will be opened for you. For everyone who asks receives, and everyone who searches finds, and for everyone who knocks, the door will be opened' (Matthew 7.7–8).
'Rejoice always, pray without ceasing, give thanks in all circumstances, for this is the will of God in Christ Jesus for you' (1 Thessalonians 5.16–18).
'Confess your sins to one another, and pray for one another, so that you may be healed. The prayer of the righteous is powerful and effective' (James 5.16).
Come, let us worship and pray for God's grace.
We'll keep praying – may we never lose heart.
In our worship, may God build up our faith
and strengthen our resolve to pray and to wait for the answer.

A prayer of approach

We come before you, mighty God;
with awe and with wonder,
with thanksgiving and with reverence.
Thank you, almighty God,
for welcoming us into your presence today.
Amen.

A prayer of confession

We have no time, no time, no time,
and in rushing here and there
we easily forget you, gracious God.
Too readily we treat others badly
in what we do and say.
Then too often we do nothing
when others need our love, our help, our hope.
It is the busy bustle that brings us to our knees,
instead of to you.
Yet you, in still, small ways,
call us to pray, and pray, and pray again.
Forgive us, loving God, for being centred on ourselves.
Remind us of your love for us,
and as we mark the path to your kingdom,
make us more than mere flickering lights,
in Jesus Christ who loves us.
Amen.

A prayer of praise

God, you are mighty:
we see your handiwork in all the beauty of creation:
the crashing seas speak of your power,
the beautiful skies speak of your peace,
the stunning sunrise speaks of your hope.

God, you are with us:
we see your face in the faces around us:
the face of a friend speaks of your humanity,
the tears on a face speak of your compassion,
the laughter of a child speaks of your joy.
We praise you that you are great,
and yet you share yourself with us:
you reveal yourself to us in the beauty of the world,
you come close to us through the people we meet.
Thank you, almighty and incarnate God.
Amen.

A prayer of intercession

God of justice, God of love,
We keep praying for peace,
while harbouring resentment in our hearts.
Have mercy upon us.
Help us live what we pray.
We keep praying for an end to the world's hunger,
while enjoying the comfort of more than we need.
Have mercy upon us.
Help us live what we pray.
We keep praying for suffering people,
forgetting that we could be sharing their load.
Have mercy upon us.
Help us live what we pray.
And teach us again to keep praying,
not only with words,
but in all that we say and all that we do,
that your love and your justice
may be known on the earth
in each generation.
Amen.

A prayer activity

Spend some time deciding on one particular issue of justice that the whole group wants to pray about. In groups, prepare different ways to pray about this: quiet, noisy, visual, song and so on, then come together and do the praying.

A prayer for all ages

God of hope,
We thank you for promising to listen to our prayers.
Help us to keep practising until we are praying all the time.
Give us hope and courage so that we do not lose heart.
Help us to listen when you answer our prayers.
Amen.

Year C   PROPER 25

Sirach 35.12–17, or Jeremiah 14.7–10, 19–22; Psalm 84.1–7; 2 Timothy 4.6–8, 16–18; **Luke 18.9–14** *God, be merciful to me, a sinner!*

Call to worship

We meet to celebrate the presence of God,
who creates us in love,
redeems us through faith,
and sustains us with hope.
We come with joy and we come with sorrow,
sad at our failings, grateful for God's acceptance.
May God stir among us now, as we join in worship.

A prayer of confession

When I feel thankful, God,
it is easy to forget my need of you.
Too quickly I remember my achievements
and my successes in doing what I ought to have
done anyway.
Too slowly I call to mind the times I got it wrong,
and so often pride gets in the way.
Take me by the hand again,
and help me walk with you,
for you love me despite the things I do,
not because of them.
Teach me to watch and listen,
and so to learn of you,
that I may reflect a little of your glory in the world,
though I may never know it.
For your love's sake.
Amen.

A prayer of praise

We praise you, Lord God,
for all you are and all you do.
For your faithfulness,
for being there when we need you:
we praise you, Lord.
For standing with us when times are hard,
for being there when we feel deserted:
we praise you, Lord.
For giving us the strength we need,
and rescuing us from evil attack:
we praise you, Lord.
For giving us the hope of heaven,
and the crown of righteousness:
we praise you, Lord.
Amen.

A prayer of adoration and thanksgiving

Creator, we thank you for the world you have given us,
for the opportunities we have to live full lives,
and the bountiful earth that we share.
Redeemer, we thank you for calling us to follow,
forgiving us when we get things wrong,
and still helping us to make new starts.

Spirit of holiness, we thank you for stirring among us,
energizing our faith, inflaming our hope and leading
us to do new things by your power.
Great trinity of love, we praise you.
You transcend our understanding,
yet we know you go beside us,
eternal and beyond our grasp,
yet familiar, deep within us.
We praise you, Living God.
Amen.

An intercessory prayer of repentance and submission

Lord, we praise you and you alone.
You are the one true God,
the Almighty, our creator.
We thank you that you reach down to us.
Lord, **we bow before you.**
We ask that you forgive our unholy ways.
We ask that you forgive the things we do that give no
honour to you.
We ask that you forgive our readiness to ignore you
and our weakness of placing our faith in people
instead of you.
Lord, **we bow before you.**
We accept that we are not worthy of honour.
We accept that we are nothing compared with you.
We accept that we need you.
Lord, **we bow before you.**
Teach us, we pray, how to walk the path of humility
and holiness.
Amen.

A prayer activity

What posture would express each person's relationship with God now? (Curled up, dancing, clenched fists, kneeling, etc.) Try them, if the group is brave enough. Pray anyway, inviting each person to offer themselves to God, inside and out.

A prayer for all ages

Dear Jesus,
Please help us be true to you.
Please help us to be brave and strong when others
say things against our faith.
Help us to fight the good fight.
Please help us to keep going as Christians when we
feel like giving up.
Help us to finish the race.
Please help us to think about how you want us to live,
all the time.
Help us to keep the faith.
Thank you for giving us the help we need.
Help us to be strong for you.
Amen.

Year C   PROPER 26

Isaiah 1.10–18; Psalm 32.1–7; 2 Thessalonians 1.1–4, 11–12; **Luke 19.1–10** *For the Son of Man came to seek out and to save the lost.*

Call to worship

Come and see Jesus!
Climb above the crowded thoughts that block your gaze.
Come as you are,
ready to spread the truth about yourself at his feet.
He offers forgiveness, salvation is granted. Come!

A prayer of confession

God of mercy, forgive us, we pray,
for the times when we have wronged others,
defrauding them of their integrity, judging them by
high standards that we cannot keep ourselves.
Take from us the stinging memory of what we have
failed to do, and how we have succeeded in offending
our neighbours.
God of love, come, stay with us today.
Hear our longing to put things right,
to give and not to grasp,
to care and not to criticize.
Help us to stand out from the crowd,
not because of false piety,
but because we truly follow Jesus,
in whose name we ask our prayer.
Amen.

A prayer of thanksgiving

Thank you, Jesus, for coming down the road to
meet us, and for looking around you to find us.
Thank you for hearing when we call out to you
and for agreeing to come and stay with us.
Thank you for forgiving us, despite our wanton
wilfulness, and our readiness to put ourselves
before the needs of others.
Thank you for helping us to start again with a clean
sheet, and for seeking and saving us when we
were lost.
Thank you, Jesus, for accepting us, with all our
complexities, and for offering us life and hope
and love.
Amen.

A prayer of intercession

O God, we pray for Christians across the world,
that together we may help people caught in life's
ruts to see Jesus over the heads of the crowd.
God of hope, you call us by name.
We are yours; help us serve you.
For countless communities suffering injustice,
for the victims of hunger, disease and neglect,
we pray to you, O God.
God of hope, you call us by name.
We are yours; help us serve you.

In our own small corners of the world,
come as our friend, and give comfort to the
neighbours who have no peace, the lonely,
the lost and the broken.
God of hope, you call us by name.
We are yours; help us serve you.
Come, God of life's fullness and care,
for the sick and the troubled,
for those who are dying.
Grant them peace and your courage
in their time of need.
God of hope, you call us by name.
We are yours; help us serve you.
Amen.

A prayer activity

*Many churches 'pass the peace' during worship,
often by shaking hands and saying 'Peace be with
you'. One of the functions of this is to demonstrate
acceptance. Explain this, then ask everyone to
exchange the peace with everybody else.*

A prayer for all ages

Jesus, you loved Zacchaeus.
You wanted to be his friend.
You called him to be with you.
You stayed in his home.
You love each and every one of us.
You want to be our friend.
You call us to be with you.
You are with us wherever we go.
When he met you, Zacchaeus knew that he needed
to change.
Help us to know when we need to change.
Zacchaeus found out what was really important.
Help us to understand what matters to you.
You love each and every one of us.
You want to be our friend.
You call us to be with you.
You are with us wherever we go.
Thank you.
Amen.

A sending out prayer

In the bustle of our lives
and the longing to claim some celebrity as our own,
help us, Jesus, to see you,
to meet and welcome you.
You call us as we are,
and give us the quiet strength to become the people
we are meant to be.
As we make ready to turn our backs on past
shortcomings,
inspire us with the courage and confidence
to mould our tomorrows into new opportunities to
witness to your love.
To the glory of your name.
Amen.

Year C PROPER 27

Job 19.23–27a; Psalm 17.1–9; 2 Thessalonians 2.1–5, 13–17; **Luke 20.27–38** *Now he is God not of the dead, but of the living; for to him all of them are alive.*

Call to worship

Gathered here for the Lord's Day,
we know he is already here.
With us – **Christ!**
In us – **Christ!**
Behind us – **Christ!**
Before us – **Christ!**
Beside us – **Christ!**
Beneath us – **Christ!**
Above us – **Christ!**
Winning and restoring Christ;
quiet and confirming Christ.
In hearts – **Christ!**
In mouths – **Christ!**

A prayer of confession

Lord Jesus Christ, you came to us,
warning and pleading,
living the good life, living the word.
We doubted you.
We rejected you.
We argued against you.
We nailed you to the cross.
We denied you.
Lord Jesus Christ, you still come to us,
warning and pleading.
You are the living word,
you show us how to live the good life.
Still we doubt you.
Still we reject you.
Still we argue against you.
Still we nail you to the cross.
Still we deny you.
Forgive us, we pray.
Open our hearts and minds and spirits,
not only to the warning and the pleading,
but to the truth of who you are.
Forgive us and lead us to faith in you,
and the vibrant life you offer
in resurrection power.
Amen.

A prayer of intercession

Lord, we know that everyone is special and precious in your sight.
We pray that we might live in a way that affirms this.
We pray for those who know they are different, for people who think differently, behave differently, move differently, react differently.
Lord, may they know that everyone is special and precious in your sight.
We pray for families and others with responsibilities and concerns for those with special needs.
Lord, may they know that everyone is special and precious in your sight.

We pray for churches and communities that have the opportunity to welcome those with special needs.
Lord, may they know that everyone is special and precious in your sight.
We pray for institutions of education, that they might be open to fresh understanding,
flexible in their interpretations and willing to change.
May they use their powers wisely and without discrimination.
Lord, may they know that everyone is special and precious in your sight.
Living Lord, in and through Jesus we see your resurrection power.
By the power of the Holy Spirit we receive inspiration and encouragement to live lives that are vibrant with joy and hope.
Hear our prayer this day and grant that as we engage with each other in our daily lives we may know that everyone is special and precious in your sight.
Amen.

A prayer activity

Talk about how much we have to give thanks for, for our lives now and for the life to come. Give older children a party popper each, and ensure they know how to pull them safely (pointing upwards, away from faces). Take turns to thank God for something, ending with the prayer below. Pull the party poppers with the Amen.

Lord God, loving God,
we thank you today for all that you give us,
and the life that you have given us.
Help us to follow you always,
until we come to be your children in heaven,
where we will be with you for ever.
Amen.

A prayer for all ages

Why not put each phrase on a flash card and ask individuals to hold them up, act them, or call them out?
Drum roll, cymbal clash, crowd cheer,
belly laugh, heartbeat, hand clap, foot tap.
Blazing fire, howling gale, banging door,
roaring sea, buzzing bee, blinding sun.
Cows lowing, lions roaring, sparrows chirping, friends chatting, kids laughing.
Vibrant life!
The life of God's world.
Rejoice! Be glad! Sing praise!
Live it!
And give God the glory.
Amen.

Year C   PROPER 28

Malachi 4.1–2a; Psalm 98; 2 Thessalonians 3.6–13;
Luke 21.5–19 *They asked him, 'Teacher, when will this be, and what will be the sign that this is about to take place?'*

Call to worship

This is the Lord's day.
Every day belongs to the eternal God.
This is the place of worship.
**In every place we can worship
the ever-present God.**
You are God's people.
**We are together the people of God,
disciples of Jesus, empowered by his
Holy Spirit.**
Thanks be to God.
Let us worship God.
**Let us worship together, witness
together, work together.**

A prayer of thanksgiving

Great God, your glory hovers over the face of our
earth and we catch glimpses of it in creation's
colours.
You are the God who involves us in your grace-full
purposes, calling us to share in your love for the
world and its people;
enabling us to do great things that enhance the living
of our neighbours.
This day, we declare that as your children,
following in the footsteps of Jesus of Nazareth,
we shall endeavour, in the strength of your Spirit,
to make the kingdom more visible around us,
to speak with the tongue of a prophet,
to caress a weary world with our enthusiasm.
Amen.

A prayer of praise *based on Psalm 98.4–9*

*You may want to accompany this prayer with photos
of different parts of creation that praise God with us:*
We praise you, God, with the whole earth.
We shout and sing and praise you:
we remain silent and still you are praised.
Everything that can make a sound can praise you:
the sea, the rivers, the trees.
Every creature can praise you:
birds, animals, bugs and mini-beasts.
As we add the sounds we make to these others, we
wait expectantly for your just rule to cover the earth.
Amen.

A prayer of intercession *based on
2 Thessalonians 3.6–13*

Merciful God, silence the voice of your Church when
it preaches without mercy.
Those who come bowed down need no reminder that
they are sinners:
every movement of their body expresses that, every
experience of life has branded them worthless.
Rather may your Church encourage, not condemn:
and reach out hands that say, 'You are forgiven, you
are loved.'
For that is what we all need reminding of time after
time, day after day, failure after failure;
until at last we believe it, and look up at one another,
at Christ our peace, and at your great heart which
grieves with those who judge and reject, but weeps
with joy every time guilt is lifted, a soul is set free and
individuals become a community.
Amen.

A prayer activity

*Pray for the people in your church who take on roles
and responsibilities. Then ask the children to pray for
them in turn. This could be done in smaller groups if
time is short, each group praying for just one or two
people. If the children don't want to pray aloud, ask
them to think of the person and then, in their head,
ask God to love and help him or her. If you have
photographs of these people place them on to a large
heart-shaped piece of card with the words 'God loves
you' written on it.*

A prayer for children

Dear Jesus,
Sometimes it's fun following you
and we have a wonderful time.
Sometimes it's hard following you
especially when people are unkind to us.
Please help us to be brave
and to tell you all about it.
Amen.

A prayer of petition

Give us the words, Companion Christ, to tell it
like it is.
To tell others what discipleship is really like;
the highs and lows, the mundane days and the
exciting ones;
to tell the stories of your involvement in the world;
to motivate people to act justly and peacefully;
when we know the needs of the world;
to communicate hope when despair creeps in,
and to stand firm in our faith in you.
Amen.

Year C PROPER 29/CHRIST THE KING

Sunday between November 20 and November 26 inclusive

Jeremiah 23.1–16; Psalm 46; Colossians 1.11–20;
Luke 23.33–43 *Truly I tell you, today you will be with
me in Paradise.*

Call to worship *based on Psalm 97 and Jeremiah 23*

The Lord is King!
Let the earth rejoice;
let the many coastlands be glad!
Clouds and thick darkness are all around him;
righteousness and justice
are the foundation of his throne.

A prayer of confession

In daily events, the rush to work,
getting the kids to school, meeting deadlines,
getting to appointments in time, making ends meet,
it's so easy to pass you by and never even see you.
Forgive us for crowding you out.
In our times alone, cooking, watching TV,
at the gym, out on a drive, sitting at the computer,
reading the paper, walking the dog,
it's so easy to ignore you, cut you out,
delete the message, switch off from you.
Forgive us for crowding you out.
In the social round of church life,
in its committees and meetings,
in all the little jobs and rotas and routines,
in the pressure to fundraise and keep things going,
it's so easy to forget you, to sideline you,
to worship what we believe rather than you.
Forgive us for crowding you out.
Amen.

A prayer of praise for all ages *based on Psalm 46*

God is in our city (town/village/place).
See what God is doing here.
God settles disputes and makes right our
relationships.
We can find a home in God.
God is always ready to help us.
We can put our fears aside if we trust God:
even when the world around is changing quickly.
We can find a home in God.
The things God does are amazing.
With our city (town/village/place) founded on God we
will not be afraid.
We will be full of joy and celebrate in this community.
We have a home in God, our refuge and strength.
Amen.

A prayer of intercession

King of love, you are our strength and refuge
in the midst of life.
**Help us to turn to you and be subject to
your wisdom and guidance.**
We pray for people who are subject to undue
pressures in their lives at this time…
King of love, you are our strength and refuge
in the midst of life.
**Help us to turn to you and be subject to
your wisdom and guidance.**
We pray for people who are subject to
injustice and the breakdown of
right relationships…
those who are persecuted because of their
race, gender, sexuality, or faith…
King of love, you are our strength and refuge
in the midst of life.
**Help us to turn to you and be subject to
your wisdom and guidance.**
We pray for our church here, locally, nationally and
worldwide.
We pray for those who give their time and talents
joyfully and generously,
those who go out with the good news,
those who lead, support and encourage.
King of love, you are our strength and refuge
in the midst of life.
**Help us to turn to you and be subject to
your wisdom and guidance.**
Amen.

A prayer activity

*At the end of this church year, invite those present
to reflect on all that has passed, to entrust to God all
that is to come and to light a candle in the name of
peace. Play music as people come forward to light
candles. Pray:*
We light our candles in longing for that peace: may
their light disarm the darkness of war, may their
flames be symbols of hope, and their burning, a sign
of self-giving love.
We light our candles for peace at the ending of one
year and on the threshold of another.
We light our candles for peace.
There is hope in lighting a candle.
There is hope and healing, there is the past, the
present, the future.
There is mystery. There is peace.
Let us rejoice in the light of that hope.
Let us rejoice in the light of Christ.

A sending out prayer

Almighty God, as we go out today to be
your kingdom builders,
we pray for the grace to grow in your love and
friendship, so that we can truly be your very own
people.
Amen.

Seasons and Festivals

Epiphany

A prayer of approach *based on Psalm 72*

We welcome the King:
may he judge his people with righteousness.
We receive the King:
may he defend the cause of the poor and needy.
We honour the King:
may our lives reflect his glory.
We worship the King:
may he reign for ever and ever,
Amen.

A prayer of confession

Loving God, we come before you with open hearts
to ask your forgiveness for our failure
to live as your children.
Together we say:
Loving God, giver of all good gifts,
you give us ears and we do not listen;
eyes, and we do not see.
You fill our lives with love
and we do not return it.
You fill us with your life
and we do not share it.
You give us each other
and we refuse the gift.
Forgive us our blindness,
our deafness and our ignorance;
forgive us our narrowness
and our smallness.
Help us to grow in the gift of your love
and fulfil the promise
you have set within us.
Amen.

A prayer of praise

As gold is presented
Praise and glory to God our king!
As myrrh is presented (or a suitable substitute)
Praise and glory to Christ our Saviour.
As incense is presented (or a suitable substitute)
Praise and glory to the Spirit,
our mediator and advocate.
Praise and glory to God,
Father, Son and Holy Spirit.
Amen.

A prayer of wonder

Creator God, over millions of years and through
billions of selections your earth has evolved on a truly
amazing journey.
Our own personal development is also amazing to us.
May your eternal wisdom guide us as we seek
constructive ways to develop your kingdom for all
creation.
Amen.

A prayer for all ages

God of all daily journeys,
may we know that you are always with us
even though we can't see you.
Help us to recognize
that sometimes we have to risk
getting things wrong or being foolish.
Give us the courage sometimes
to choose to risk making mistakes
for the sake of trying to do
something good and worthwhile for you.
Help us to learn well
from all our experiences.
Amen.

A prayer of intercession

We pray for our world.
We pray that Christ will be revealed
to the whole world through his Church.
We pray for our community, our
workplaces, schools and colleges.
We pray that we will be
Christ's representatives in those places.
We pray for our church.
We pray that we will worship Christ
in spirit and in truth,
giving of ourselves and loving our neighbours.
We pray for our homes and families.
We pray that our lives
will be a true reflection of Christ's love.
We pray for ourselves.
Lord Christ, reveal yourself to each one of us.
We pray all these things in the name
of Christ.
Amen.

A prayer activity

*Sit in a circle around a large five-pointed star made
from silver card. Each arm of the star represents a
different aspect of our concerns as we come close
to God in prayer. Label or put a symbol at each point
to represent five things, e.g. family, friends, school,
church, and world. From a box passed around the
circle, invite the children to place small stars onto the
points representing the areas for which they want to
say either a silent or a spoken prayer.*

A sending out prayer

Dear Lord,
As we recognize your greatness,
let us not keep it to ourselves.
Guide us to proclaim your majesty to all those we
meet today and every day.
We ask this through Jesus Christ.
Amen.

Mothering Sunday

God our Father,
Your Son, Jesus Christ,
lived in a family at Nazareth.
As we meet together now
help us to learn more about what it is
to love our families and friends as you love us.
Through Jesus Christ our Lord,
Amen.

A prayer of confession

Heavenly Father, parent of us all,
we know we don't always treat each other
as you want us to.
Lord God, forgive us;
and help us to be more loving.

There are times when we insist on getting our own
way despite what others feel.
Lord God, forgive us;
and help us to be more loving.

Sometimes we increase the tension when we ought
to seek peace, or say things that hurt one another.
Lord God, forgive us;
and help us to be more loving.

God has loved us, sending his Son Jesus to show us
the true meaning of forgiveness.
Lord God, forgive us;
and help us to be more loving.
Amen.

A prayer of praise

Lord, you are father and mother to us, an ever-loving
parent, more faithful than we can imagine.
Bless our family relationships.
Help us to reflect your love in the way we love our
parents, our children, our brothers and sisters and all
with whom we live.
Great God, father and mother, ever-loving parent,
we praise and honour you. We love and trust
you. Surround us and those we care for with your
everlasting love.
Amen.

A prayer for the sharing of the peace

May God, who watches the world with us,
grant peace in our hearts and hope in our lives,
that we may be at peace with one another.

A prayer of intercession

Loving God of the ages, like a mother you brought
the world to birth, and we rejoice that we are part
of that creation. Help us to care for your earth in all
its complex beauty, and to nurture our children's
generation in that sacred duty.
You offer us life in abundance.
Help us to live as your children.

We remember the mothers around us, and the
blessings they give to their families, and we pray for
those who find it hard to cope. We think of all who
offer care and nurture to others.
You offer us life in abundance.
Help us to live as your children.

We pray for all parents who, like Mary, have lost
their children before their time. Grant your blessing
of peace in times of grief, your comfort in places of
sorrow.
You offer us life in abundance.
Help us to live as your children.

God who is mother and father to us, receive the
prayers we offer in the name of Jesus, son of Mary,
who gave up his life for the sake of your love, and is
alive with you and the Holy Spirit, now and for ever.
Amen.

A prayer activity

*Show the children a sticking plaster and ask who
puts a plaster on them when they're hurt. Talk about
why we use plasters – to keep the wound clean
and to help it heal. Explain that when we put some
of God's love, gentleness, kindness, forgiveness
or thankfulness into a sad situation, God can start
making it better. Give each child at least one large
blank plaster. They could write a word connected to
God's love on their plaster and then decorate it using
felt tips. Invite them to hold their plasters and then
join in with the response to this prayer. They can take
the plasters home as a reminder of the healing love
of God.*
When we fall and need your love, Lord,
thank you for your care.
When we don't know who to turn to, Lord,
thank you for your care.
When we get into scrapes, Lord,
thank you for your care.
For your gifts that we can wear, Lord,
thank you for your care.
For our mothers and our carers, Lord,
thank you for your care.
For those who share your love, Lord,
thank you for your care.
Amen.

A prayer of blessing to say together

Father in heaven, bless all mothers
and those who look after us in our daily lives.
Make us grateful for their kindness and thankful
for their care.
Help us to respond to them in loving obedience,
following the example of Jesus, your Son,
our Lord.
Amen.

Holy Week

Call to worship for Good Friday

Insults, torture, mocking, whipping,
accusations, beatings,
shouts of 'Crucify! Crucify!'
A journey to a hill,
the carrying of a cross,
wood, nails and human flesh hammered together.
The most awful of days!
In the middle of it all, Jesus,
the one who was innocent,
but the one who died.

A prayer of confession

Lord Jesus Christ,
as your disciples we confess that we have failed both
you and those people who suffer innocently, as your
disciples also failed you from the first.
When we are tempted to betray you for the sake of
selfish gain,
Christ have mercy. **Lord, forgive us and help us.**
When we do not keep watch in prayer,
and seek to avoid sharing in your suffering,
Christ have mercy. **Lord, forgive us and help us.**
When we choose the way of the sword,
the way of violence in place of the path of peace,
Christ have mercy. **Lord, forgive us and help us.**
When we run away from difficult situations and desert
those who need us,
Christ have mercy. **Lord, forgive us and help us.**
When we do not admit to being your followers,
and are fearful of what others might say,
Christ have mercy. **Lord, forgive us and help us.**
When we spurn your sacrificial love
and will not offer you the sacrifice of our own lives,
Christ have mercy. **Lord, forgive us and help us.**
Cleanse us from our sins by your precious blood,
and graciously restore us to your service.
For your praise and glory alone.
Amen.

A prayer for all ages for a Maundy Thursday supper

Three different voices could lead this prayer:
1: Lord, we come as your people.
   We bring ourselves,
2: our stories,
3: our offerings.
1: May we listen to each other,
2: affirming each other
3: and enjoying each other's company.
1: As we share, we remember:
2: your passion,
3: your death,
2: praying with you in the garden,
3: standing with you at the cross.
1: As we share, we look forward:
2: to the joy of your resurrection,
3: to the celebration of your triumph,
2: to the challenges that lie ahead
3: and our life of shared joy.

1: Come now, Jesus our Saviour,
   bless this evening:
2: bless our food,
3: our groups,
   ourselves,
   our church.
Amen.

A prayer activity for Maundy Thursday

*Invite everyone to draw around their feet on a piece
of paper and to cut out the outlines. Stick the feet in a
circle shape onto a big piece of paper. In the middle
of the circle write, 'Jesus washed his disciples' feet'.
Say:*
Dear God, thank you that Jesus did kind, good things
for people.
Help me to help other people too.
Thank you that Jesus cleaned people's dirty feet to
show that he loved them.
Thank you for loving me. Help me to love others.
Amen.

A prayer of intercession

On this most solemn day we pray with Christians
throughout the world: that God will guide us,
strengthen us in faith, and give us courage to
proclaim the name of Jesus Christ.
Silence
Crucified Jesus,
hear our prayer.
For the ministers of the church,
for those who teach, those who pastor, those who
proclaim the word, those who lead worship, those
who counsel, those who provide vision.
Silence
Crucified Jesus,
hear our prayer.
For those preparing for baptism,
for those who are new to faith,
for all whose faith is tested.
Silence
Crucified Jesus,
hear our prayer.
For the unity of Christian people: that God may heal
our divisions and keep us from further break-up of our
communion with each other.
Silence
Crucified Jesus,
hear our prayer.
And let our cry come unto thee.
Amen.

A sending out prayer

Jesus Christ,
Saviour of the world,
you died to make us good:
continue within us your healing work
so that we may live as your servants
and children of your kingdom,
now and for ever.
Amen.

Harvest

God of abundance,
God of fruitfulness,
God of generosity,
God of love beyond measure.
God of extravagance,
God of celebration,
God of goodness,
God of love beyond imagining.
We gather bringing the best that we can offer
to give thanks for the good things you give us,
to share your generosity with others
and to celebrate by feasting at your table.

A prayer of confession

Lord, we are sorry for all the times we have done
things we should not have done. We are sorry for all
the times we have borne bad fruit.
Please forgive us in the name of your Son,
Jesus Christ.
We want to do good things.
Please help us to be like trees that bear good fruit.
When people see what we do, may they see that we
are rooted in you.
In the name of Jesus Christ our Lord,
Amen.

A prayer of praise

Grain swelling, swaying gently in the breeze,
the combine harvester working by floodlight,
the golden harvest brought safely in.
God of the abundant harvest,
we give you thanks.
Apples and plums ripening, the allotment swelling
with produce, a glut given out to family and friends.
God of the abundant harvest,
we give you thanks.
Market stalls groaning,
fruit and veg spilling onto the street.
God of the abundant harvest,
we give you thanks.
Amen.

A prayer for those whose livelihood is dependent on the harvest

God of the harvest, so much depends on timing:
when to gather in the crops, waiting for the best
time, but watching the weather anxiously, nervous of
everything being destroyed.
Often, we see none of this uncertainty in our food
supplies.
Be with everyone whose livelihood depends on the
harvest, and guide their decisions for the benefit of all
of us.
Through your Son, Jesus Christ.
Amen.

A prayer for all ages

Lord of the harvest,
the harvest of people,
you need workers.
What can I do?
I can try
at home,
at school,
and in my leisure time,
to see others as you see them;
to welcome them as you welcome them;
to love them as you love them.
Lord of the harvest,
the harvest of people,
you need workers.
Will I do?
Amen.

A prayer of intercession

When we hear the gentle sound of the rain watering
the earth,
help us to remember the thirst of those whose land
is dry.
When we feel the warmth of the sun on our faces,
help us to remember the plight of those locked away
in darkness.
When we buy the fruit of the world's harvest,
help us to remember the hunger of those whose
basket is empty.
When we enjoy the ease of communicating around
the world,
help us to remember those who are isolated from
their friends.
When we relax in times of holiday,
help us to remember those who have to work without
ceasing.
When we celebrate our blessings at harvest time,
help us to remember those who experience disaster.
May our remembering reactivate our conscience
and result in a renewed commitment to Christ in our
neighbour.
Amen.

A prayer activity

Invite everyone to join in, helping the very youngest.
The first person says, 'At harvest, we thank God
for...' and names something beginning with A, e.g.
apples. The second person says, 'At harvest, we
thank God for apples and bananas' (or anything else
beginning with B). Continue through the alphabet,
asking everyone to join in with the list each time.

A sending out prayer

May we find heaven in the wildness of creation;
may we seek justice in bread for the world;
may we know resurrection in the sunsets of autumn;
and may we find God in the sharing of it all.
Amen.

Bible Sunday

Come as God's chosen ones, holy and beloved,
to worship the Lord.
God of all peoples, nations and races,
we come to worship you.
God of Greek and Jew, slave and free,
we come to worship you.
God of men and women, young and old,
we come to worship you.
God of evangelical and liberal, the assured
and the seeker,
we come to worship you.
God of every church and denomination,
sect or fellowship,
we come to worship you.

A prayer of confession

We bring you our heartfelt thanks that you are a God
who forgives,
and who has shown us how that forgiveness is
effective in human life.
We recall how Jesus expressed forgiveness in
reassuring words and affirming actions, restoring
health and sanity and social acceptability.
We acknowledge that Jesus Christ is the same
yesterday, and today, and for ever.
Therefore we seek forgiveness for all in our lives that
is contrary to your will – no matter how seemingly
trivial or how immense the matter,
nor how longstanding the problem.
Allow a time of silent prayer
We pray too for forgiveness for those sins of a
corporate nature, to which we contribute by being
part of this society at the present time.
We bring to mind the consequences of our material
well-being in the midst of so much poverty,
and of the effect of our exports of arms to the trouble
spots in the world.
Allow a time of silent prayer
Lord, have mercy upon us.
Christ, have mercy upon us.
Amen.

A prayer of praise and thanksgiving for all ages

Dear Father God,
I am glad I can eat.
I am glad I can breathe, rest and play.
I am glad I have people who love me.
I am glad I can learn about you
in the Bible, and from other people.
But most of all,
I am glad I am alive
with everyone here, and with you today.
Amen.

A prayer of intercession

On this Bible Sunday we pray for all who enable us to
hear and understand the Bible.

We pray for biblical scholars, who produce
commentaries and give lectures, that our knowledge
of the ancient world and of the thought processes of
the time be deepened.
Guide them in their studies, that fresh insights may
be made available to the Church.

We pray for those who translate the Bible into the
many English versions we have today.
May each one bring the word of God alive to a
particular section of the population.

We pray for all preachers, ordained or lay, who feel
called to expound the scriptures in the public worship
of the Church. Grant that their study of the text might,
by the guidance of the Holy Spirit, be fused with their
own experience of life, and so come with creative
insight to those who hear them.

We pray for those who read the scriptures in public
worship, that their gift might make the meaning clear;
for those who interpret the text by banner-making,
calligraphy, sacred dance, drama, or by arranging
flowers, that their art might bring new insight.

We pray for those who set the words of scripture to
music, as hymns, anthems or musical productions,
that they might give the words new life in this different
medium.

We pray for those who produce Bible study notes,
or group discussion material. May their ability to
encapsulate the essence of a passage help your
people to understand better, and may their knowledge
of how we learn best enable us to ground the
readings more deeply in our lives.
Amen.

A prayer activity

*Take a copy of the Bible. The children may be thrilled
if it is a particularly special or old edition, and they will
handle it carefully. Hand it to each person, children
and adults alike, in turn and pray for them by name:*
Dear God, please help .... to learn more of your
good news in the Bible.
*At the end, read out Psalm 119.105. Then invite
everyone to say Amen.*

A sending out prayer

God of glory,
You speak to us through your written word,
and share our lives through your living Word.
Send us out so that our lives and words
speak of your glory
in all that we do and say this week.
Amen.

All Saints

Call to worship

We are the saints God has called.
We are the saints God has called.
God has called us to worship.
God has called us to worship.
We will worship in the light of Jesus.
We will worship in the light of Jesus.

A prayer of confession

Loving God,
We seek your forgiveness:
for failing to give account of the faith that is in us;
for falling silent when we should have spoken out;
for being too quick to condemn and criticize;
for being too slow to show compassion;
for not living as examples of your love;
for not behaving as the saints we were called to be.
Have mercy on us and forgive us.
Amen.

A prayer of praise

We come to worship with Christ in our midst.
With Christ's light we can see God and we are moved
to praise and adoration.
With Christ's light we can see ourselves as we really
are and we are moved to confession.
With Christ's light we can see others as our
neighbours and we are moved to compassion.
Christ is the world's light:
Glory to God on high.
Amen.

A prayer for all ages

Loving Lord Jesus, thank you for all your saints.
Thank you for those whose names and stories we
know.
As we try to follow in your way,
help us to be more like them.
Thank you for those whose names have been
forgotten, but who made your world a happier place.
As we try to trust you in everything we do,
help us to be more like them.
Thank you for the saints we hear about in the
news, and those we meet in our homes, in our
neighbourhood, at school and at work.
As we try to share your love and peace with others,
help us to be more like them.
Thank you for calling each one of us to be saints.
As we try to follow the example of saints past and
present,
help us to be more like you.

A prayer of intercession

Show us, Jesus, what it is to be poor in spirit,
and so to proclaim God's kingdom.
In the steps of the saints,
bless us, we pray.
Help us, Jesus, to mourn for our sin,
and the brokenness our neighbours suffer.
In the steps of the saints,
bless us, we pray.
Open our eyes to our weakness, good teacher,
that in humility we may serve your troubled world.
In the steps of the saints,
bless us, we pray.
Grant us the will to forgive and be merciful,
and so to receive your mercy.
In the steps of the saints,
bless us, we pray.
Teach us how to be the makers of peace,
worthy to be called the children of God.
In the steps of the saints,
bless us, we pray.
Strengthen us when we are persecuted in the name
of right, and for the sake of justice, that the kingdom
of heaven may be ours.
In the steps of the saints,
bless us, we pray.
Jesus, our teacher and our friend, give us the will to
be your servants, and to follow the example of the
saints of old, that the name of God may be glorified,
and the kingdom proclaimed on earth.
Amen.

A prayer activity

*Give each child a 'hoop' of yellow card (to look like a
halo) and a pencil. Explain that in traditional pictures
saints are shown with halos over their heads as a
sign of their goodness. Play a quiet worship song or
music in the background. Ask everyone to think about
one thing they could do or one thing about them they
could change to become more of a 'saint' for God,
and to write it on the 'halo'. Then say this prayer:*
Lord, help me to be more of a saint.
Help me
to listen to your words,
to pass on your message,
to show others your love.
Amen.

A sending out prayer

May the light of Jesus shine in us.
Amen.
May the light of Jesus shine through us to others.
Amen.
May we all be saints for Jesus.
Amen.

Remembrance

A gathering prayer

O God,
You are almighty and everlasting,
yet compassionate and ever-loving;
be with us as we gather before you today
to remember those we have loved,
those we admire,
those we have never known,
whose sacrifice ensured that we enjoy freedom
from tyranny and fear.
Amen.

A prayer of confession

Heavenly Father,
As we are reminded of the names on our war
memorials,
we realize how quickly and easily we forget.
We forget who people were and what they did,
we forget the contributions they made
and what they meant to their families.
We confess that sometimes we forget you
and what you have done for us.
Forgive us for those times,
and help us to see you in the lives of all we love,
those we remember,
and in the beauty of the world around us.
Forgive our past doings
so that we may praise you for all
you have done for us.
We ask this in Jesus' name.
Amen.

A prayer of thanksgiving for all ages

Lord, we are sad when we think of war,
of the soldiers who must fight and all the people who
are killed.
Today we remember their sacrifice with great
sadness.
We thank them for what they did for us.
We also remember that they won for us a victory,
that without their bravery our lives would have been
so very different, without the freedom we enjoy.
We thank them for what they did for us.
We are sad, too, at the thought of your suffering,
that you, too, had to be a great hero, and walk to
Jerusalem, be arrested, tried and killed on the cross.
We thank you for what you did for us.
But we remember that you won for us a victory,
that on Easter morning you rose again,
to help us overcome our human nature,
so that we might rise again with you.
We thank you for what you did for us.
Amen.

A prayer for those who haven't experienced the events of war

Lord, I have no memory of war.
Yet –
I remember what it's like to feel scared;
I remember what it's like to feel sad;
I remember what it's like to lose something precious
to me.
Help me to use my own memories in understanding
what this act of remembrance is all about so that I
can join my prayers with those who do remember.
Amen.

A prayer of intercession

Lord God, who has seen every war:
We recognize in your company that all battlefields are
tragedies,
where everyone loses and no one truly wins,
for we destroy our true selves in the process of
armed struggle.
This day we pray for those places across the globe
where nations, groups and individuals refuse to turn
swords into ploughshares:
turning on their brothers and sisters and upon you;
turning food and medicine into bombs and bullets.
We pray for legitimate armed forces,
for guerrilla forces and terrorist organizations
each caught in their own web of human conflict.
Silence
We pray for civilian people drawn into suffering,
regardless of age, gender or faith;
for places where homes are destroyed, citizens
become refugees, and casualties become statistics.
Silence
We pray for humanitarian organizations tending the
sick and injured, restoring relationships,
rebuilding communities, crossing political barriers.
Silence
And we pray for each other, as we recognize our
own conflict situations, in communities, churches and
homes, and the internal conflict of conscience and
personality.
Silence
To all of us you say:
'I come that all may have life in its fullness.'
'Peace be still.'
'Be still and know that I am God.'
Amen.

A sending out prayer

Go in peace.
We go in peace.
Work for peace.
We will work for peace.
May peace fill your lives,
your hearts and your homes.
Amen.

Christmas Day

A prayer of approach

This is the day we have been waiting for throughout Advent.
Glory to God!
This is the day: we anticipated that things would be different.
Glory to God!
This is the day: we have longed for and pinned our hopes on.
Glory to God!
This is the day: we have come to celebrate and sing and pray.
Glory to God!
This is the day: we have come, awestruck and struggling for words.
Glory to God!
This is the day: we have come, ourselves, to worship.
Glory to God!
Amen.

A prayer of confession *based on John*

Voice 1: Lord God, we have heard of your light, as your prophets bore witness.
Voice 2: We have confessed your Son, Jesus Christ, as the light of the world.
Voice 1: Yet, although we were made through him, we have sometimes failed to recognize him.
Voice 2: When he came to us, who belong to him, we have sometimes failed to receive him.
Voice 1: Although we are your children, we have sometimes behaved as if we were purely of natural descent, and not born of God.
For the sake of Jesus Christ,
who came to bring grace and truth, pardon
and forgive us, confirm and strengthen us in
goodness, and keep us in everlasting life.
Amen.

A prayer of thanksgiving

Give individual children, or pairs, a piece/pieces from a nativity set. The children build the scene up and as each part is put in place use the following responses:
Stable and animals
Thank you for our homes; please help us to remember those who have nowhere to live.
Let us rejoice and say,
Glory to God in the highest and peace to his
people on earth.
Joseph and Mary
Thank you for people who care for us; please show us how we can care for others too.
Let us rejoice and say,
Glory to God in the highest and peace to his
people on earth.
Shepherds
Thank you for people who tell others about Jesus; please help us to talk about you to our friends.
Let us rejoice and say,
Glory to God in the highest and peace to his
people on earth.
Sheep

Thank you that you care for us as a shepherd cares for his sheep.
Let us rejoice and say,
Glory to God in the highest and peace to his
people on earth.
Amen.

A prayer of intercession

This offers a chance to express the difficulties that people can experience around Christmas. Give each person two slips of paper. On one they write the best thing about Christmas; on the other the worst thing. These should remain anonymous. Collect the prayers in a large basket and put them on the communion table or another table in the worship space. Pray a blessing over the prayers, such as:
May the glory of the Lord shine upon us and scatter the darkness from before our path, that we may ever walk in his light. **Amen.**

A prayer of praise

Mary had a baby boy,
God is with us.
Born in a stable in Bethlehem,
God is with us.
Joseph gave him the name Jesus,
God is with us.
Angels appeared to the shepherds,
God is with us.
They ran to see Jesus in Bethlehem,
God is with us.
Thank you, God, for Jesus,
God is with us.
Jesus is with us every day,
God is with us.
Thank you, God, for Christmas Day,
God is with us.
Amen.

A prayer for all ages

Lord God, you made us through Jesus:
we are glad and rejoice.
Lord God, you enlightened us with Jesus:
we are glad and rejoice.
Lord God, you lived among us as Jesus:
we are glad and rejoice.
Lord God, you would live in us by Jesus:
we are glad and rejoice.
Lord God, no one has ever seen you,
but we are glad and rejoice,
because we can know you in Jesus.
Amen.

A sending out prayer

Light has dawned for the righteous.
Go with the love of the Christ child in your hearts and proclaim the joy of his coming to all.
Amen.

A ROOTS resource PRAYER & PRAYER ACTIVITIES © ROOTS for Churches Limited

Gospel Reading Index